Robert Vaupel

High Availability and Scalability of Mainframe Environments using System z and z/OS as example

High Availability and Scalability of Mainframe Environments using System z and z/OS as example

by
Robert Vaupel

Impressum

Karlsruher Institut für Technologie (KIT)
KIT Scientific Publishing
Straße am Forum 2
D-76131 Karlsruhe
www.ksp.kit.edu

KIT – Universität des Landes Baden-Württemberg und
nationales Forschungszentrum in der Helmholtz-Gemeinschaft

KIT Scientific Publishing 2013
Print on Demand

ISBN 978-3-7315-0022-3

Contents

Contents

5. Workload Management

Contents

List of Figures

List of Figures

List of Figures

List of Tables

Preface

Asking people whether they ever used mainframe computers? The usual answer is No. People are often not aware what a mainframe computer is and what role it plays in the real world. Good examples are ATM, which book on mainframe computer. Everybody who uses its money card is accessing mainframe computer technology. Generally mainframe computing is everywhere where critical data processing is required. The dominating mainframe computing platform is IBM System z and its main operating system z/OS.

While mainframe computing is the backbone of industrial and commercial computing, the answer of many students about the acquaintance with mainframe computing would not be different to those of usual people. In order to emphasize the importance of mainframe computing, the KIT together with the FZI formed an alliance with IBM R&D Germany the Informatics Innovation Center (IIC). The IIC is a platform for cooperation between research, academic education and industry exchanging knowledge, experience and providing a higher degree of industry experience for bachelor and master students. Part of the IIC are lectures about mainframe computing with emphasis on System and z/OS underlining the strength and special capabilities of mainframe technology.

The present book analyzes why mainframe technology is highly scalable and how it provides high availability enabling the technology as base for critical business operations. It gives examples on how scalability must be build throughout the complete hardware and software stack providing elasticity of the business. High availability solutions ensure that the business can operate with any interruptions surviving any kind of possible disaster. The book is the result of the fruitful cooperation between academy and industry and helps to strengthen the knowledge of students and everybody involved with computers about mainframe technology.

I am very happy, that Robert Vaupel, Senior Technical Staff Member of IBM and Manager of the IIC, contributes to the goal of the IIC so well with this book. I hope the readers are like me amazed about the remarkable technical solutions of mainframe computers which are often far looking into the future, in strong contrast to the reputation of mainframe computing which is often called legacy technology.

Prof. Dr. Ralf Reussner Director of IIC

Acknowledgments

Many thanks to the following people for their contribution to the project:

Dieter Wellerdiek IBM Systems & Technology Group, zOS WLM/SRM Development, IBM R & D Böblingen, Germany

Joachim von Buttlar IBM Systems & Technology Group, System z Firmware Development and Simulation, IBM R & D Böblingen, Germany

Robert R. Rogers IBM Systems & Technology Group, Power & z Systems, Distinguished Engineer - z/OS Designer/Philosopher, Software Architect: System z - Core Technologies, IBM Poughkeepsie, USA

1. Introduction

A mainframe computer is what businesses use to host their commercial databases, transaction servers, and applications that require a greater degree of security and availability than is commonly found on smaller scale machines. Such computers typically execute hundreds of applications, they connect to thousands of I/O devices, and serve thousands of users simultaneously. Mainframes can be best defined by their characteristics:

- To ensure a reliable and predictable execution of transactions
- To store business critical data

1.1. Motivation

The characterization and definition of mainframes also define their most important features: RAS. RAS is an abbreviation which stands for reliability, availability, and serviceability, or optionally scalability, or security. These features lead to the subject of this course which shows the requirements and efforts to provide and support computing environments which are highly available at best without any interruption of the operation and which are highly scalable to support the requirements of large customer installations. We will use System z® and its main operating system z/OS® as example to describe these features.

The requirements of highly resilient business environments become obvious if we take a look at cost of unexpected interruptions of business operations caused by computing failures (see table 1.1). Today's business operations are highly dependent on non interruptible operations and even short downtimes can't be afforded anymore. Over the last 40 years IBM® developed the System /360 architecture into a highly resilient and non interruptible computer environment. As a result 95% of the world's biggest companies use System z. The highest usage can be found in the financial industry. Around 97% of all retail banks, insurance companies and brokerage firms use System z as their main back-end server environment. 65 to 70% of all relevant data for companies is stored on databases on System z. High Availability is one of the most important aspects for business operations and it goes hand in hand with scalability which defines the ability of an environment to adapt to changing business needs. System z and its main operating system z/OS are a perfect example how high availability and scalability is implemented and which hurdles must be taken to get to an operational environment which meets the requirement of nearly no downtime and which is flexible enough to meet capacity requirements for world wide operating businesses.

Industry Sector	Loss per Hour
Financial	$8,213,470
Telecommunications	$4,611,604
Information Technology	$3,316,058
Insurance	$2,582,382
Pharmaceuticals	$2,058,710
Energy	$1,468,798
Transportation	$1,463,128
Banking	$1,145,129
Chemicals	$1,071,404
Consumer Products	$989,795
Source: Robert Francis Group 2006: "Picking the Value of PKI: Leveraging z/OS for Improving Manageability, Reliability, and Total Cost of Ownership of PKI and Digital Certificates."	

Table 1.1.: Cost of Downtime by Industry

System z and z/OS are also the best examples to show how High Availability and Scalability requirements are implemented from hardware, firmware layers, operating system, to the application layers. They need to be covered at all layers and also require interaction across the whole operating stack. This course consists of five segments:

1. Introduces System z hardware and firmware and shows which efforts are undergone to support scalability for high frequency processors and how to support dozens of processors in parallel. High availability features are discussed which enable the System z environment to continue to operate even if processors, parts of the main memory or complete parts of the system fail.

2. This segment introduces z/OS which is the main operating system used to run large transaction environments of System z. The roots of z/OS go

40 years back into the past and it is a very good example how legacy computing technology meets the requirements of the modern business world.

3. At this point we will focus on the dispatching processes of the System z Hypervisor as well as the z/OS operating system. The main focus is on how the different dispatching processes meet the requirements of their environments, at which points they work together and at which points they become problematic for system scaling. The second part of this segment highlights a feature named Hiperdispatch which has been introduced to overcome the scalability limitations of large n-way systems such as System z.

4. One important aspect of system operation is the supervision and controlling of the work which flows through the system. A well tuned environment is crucial for running business applications efficiently and furthermore it is a guarantee to maintain high availability at the application level. z/OS includes a component named Workload Manager (WLM) which controls and manages the workload of the system. WLM is the main component for autonomic performance management and it also includes capabilities to maintain application availability.

5. The last segment goes beyond the single system. z/OS systems can form a cluster environment named a Parallel Sysplex®. The Parallel Sysplex was originally introduced to overcome limitations of computing speed. While this is no longer the biggest issue with today's technology the Parallel Sysplex is nowadays the base for a continuously operating environment on a global scale.

1.2. High Availability

In this section we want to take a look at the terminology around High Availability. High Availability means a resilient IT infrastructure which allows to mask individual component failures and which also allows to recover from errors. High Availability is based on an infrastructure which is created of reliable components. Reliability is the probability of a single component or device to perform its intended function during a specified period of time under stated conditions. Mathematically reliability can be expressed as a probability density function:

$$
\begin{aligned}
R(t) \;&=\; Pr[no\ failure\ in(0,t]] \\
&=\; Pr\{T > t\} \\
&=\; \int_{t}^{\infty} f(x)\ \mathrm{d}x \\
&=\; \begin{cases} e^{-\lambda t} & \text{for random failures,} \\[4pt] \frac{1}{\sigma\sqrt{2\pi}} \int e^{\frac{1}{2}(\frac{T-\mu}{\sigma})^2} & \text{for wear-out failures.} \end{cases}
\end{aligned}
$$

A failure is usually regarded a random phenomenon. For random failures the exponential function $e^{-\lambda t}$ describes the probability of the failure occurrence. Another set of failures are wear out problems which typically occur towards the end of the life-cycle of a device. These failures typically follow a normal distribution. At the beginning of the life cycle failures may occur which are based on insufficient tests, design flaws or oversights. Such errors are named infant mortality failures and they should be avoided by following design, implementation and testing guidelines. In any case reliability is concerned with the fact that failures should be avoided and for cases where they can't be avoided that the system should be designed to survive them.

For our discussions we are also primarily interested in reliability during the "useful life period" of a device. The reliability measure is the Mean-Time-Between-Failures (MTBF):

$$
MTBF = \Theta = \frac{1}{\lambda} = \frac{T}{r}
$$

with λ = failure rate, T = total time, r = number of failures. This is sometimes also defined as Mean-Time-To-Failures (MTTF) in case the system is replaced after the failure. The time after the failure occurrence until the system is operational again is defined as Mean-Time-To-Repair (MTTR). Availability is now defined as the probability function of the total time the system is up and running divided by the time the system should be operational, (see also table 1.1):

$$
PA(t) = \frac{MTTF}{MTTF + MTTR}
$$

Our discussion of System z will start with the components of the system and techniques to support the claim of the system to provide extraordinary high reliability. System z is currently known to provide a reliability of 99.999 % which

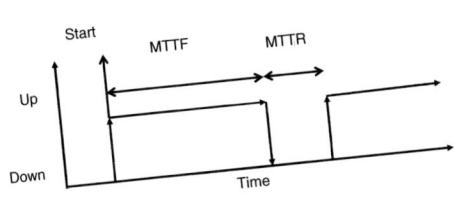

Figure 1.1.: Definition of Availability

means that the probability for the system to be non operational is less that 31.5 seconds per year. Nevertheless high reliable components are not sufficient to support the customer demand for a continuously operating environment. We will also discuss Disaster Recovery techniques and system and environment layouts which are necessary to achieve a maximum resilient business environment.

1.3. Scalability

The second feature of a modern business environment which we will discuss in this course is scalability. Scalability in our context means how the environment is able to adjust to different business needs and we will also discuss techniques and functions which enable the system to provide a stated capacity and performance. We will encounter that increasing the processor frequency is not sufficient anymore to provide higher system capacity and we will discuss the difficulties which occur when an existing environment grows bigger. Scalability will also cover the ability of the system to incremental grow based on required demand. System and business growth on an application scale can be achieved in two ways:

1. Horizontally, that means if more application instances are needed more systems need to be deployed.

2. Vertically, which means that an existing system can grow to support more instances of the same application as well as to support multiple different applications.

System z is the best example for an environment which support vertical growth if needed. We will see that System z and especially z/OS allow to host multiple applications at the same time and we will discuss the functions which are required to ensure a meaningful operation under such conditions. System z can be upgraded in very small incremental steps. Figure 1.2 shows the capacity range of high-end z196 systems. The possible system configuration of the z196 7xx systems encompass a range from 150 to 6140 Million of Service Units (MSU) which is a measure of system capacity (see [21]). The important factor is that the high end z196 mainframe can cover a capacity range which allows to scale 40 times from the smallest to the largest system.

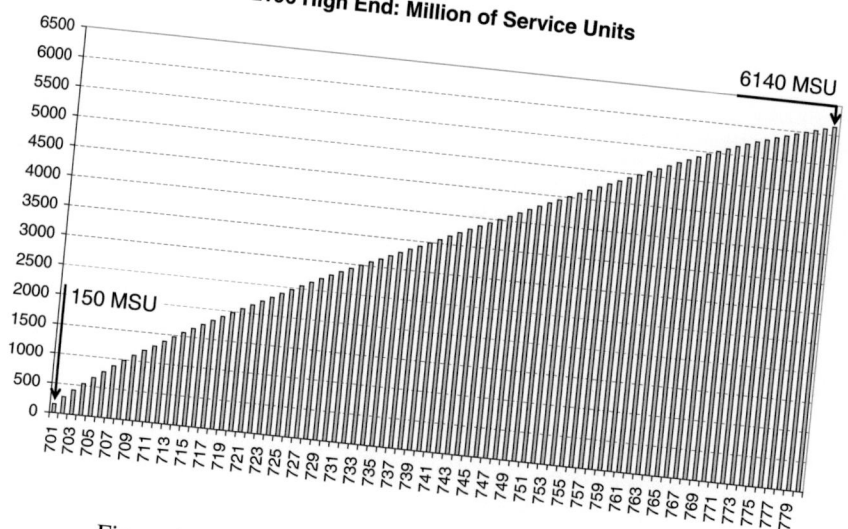

Figure 1.2.: Capacity Range of a High-End System z196

In addition low end z196 systems exist which provide further upgrade capability in the range from 30 to 1000 MSU. The low end systems are available in 3 configurations: 401 to 415, 501 to 515, and 601 to 615. The first letter determines the single engine speed and the two following letters the numbers of available physical processors. This allows installations with smaller capacity requirements to adjust their systems to their needs. If this is not sufficient another set of smaller systems named z114 are available which cover the capacity range from 3 to 388 MSU. These systems are available with 26 different single engine speeds and up to 5 physical engines. The newer zEC12 mainframe which became available in September 2012 provides the same choice of models like the earlier versions z10™ and z9® did.

1.3 Scalability

The possibility to grow the systems incrementally and to cover a very wide capacity range requires that the software from the virtualization layer up to the middleware which process the end user applications provide the elasticity to deal with such high differences. Also upgrades and downgrades can be applied instantaneously and the software layer must react accordingly to them. We will discuss these functions in detail and we will give examples for the different layers how it is possible to provide the elasticity so that the capacity can be used by the end users.

2. z/Architecture

In the segment we will discuss the design of System z and which functions and techniques are used to support the claims of high availability and scalability.

2.1. A Little History

Since when does System z exist and what where the design decisions to create such an environment? The roots of System z and z/Architecture are now nearly 50 years back in history to System /360 which has been introduced on April 7th, 1964. System /360 was the first computing architecture. The promise which was made at that time to the the customer was that all following systems of the same architecture were compatible to the first systems, meaning that programs which were created on the first systems will still run on all future environments.

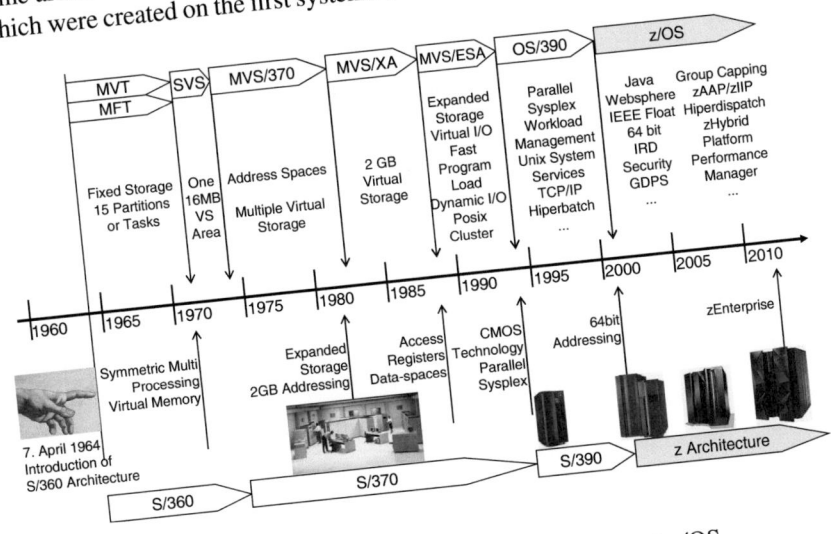

Figure 2.1.: History of System z Architecture and z/OS

Why was this necessary? Prior to System /360 different system designs existed. More important, with every new system a new system design was introduced. That required the user to re-program nearly everything so that it could run on the new hardware. This was highly inefficient and therefore IBM introduced a system architecture with the promise of upward compatibility for all future environments.

Figure 2.1 shows the major development steps from System /360 to System z from 1964 to today. The graphic also covers the development of the main operating system of System, z/OS. The name System /360 was created from 360 degree of a circle meaning that this architecture covers all computing aspects from hardware to operating systems for all IBM computers. System /360 was also introduced for commercial and technical processing. Aside of compatibility the focus was also on easy extending the environment by adding additional processors and I/O units. Thus scalability was a major design point of the system architecture.

While System /360 was nearly unchanged during its first years the first major enhancement was the introduction of virtual storage and multi processing in the 1970s. The increasing capacity demand and the necessity of exploiting the enhanced architecture lead to the development of a common operating system: Multiple Virtual Storage (MVS^{TM}). MVS is still the base for z/OS today's operating system for System z and was introduced in 1974. With the introduction of MVS, virtual storage and symmetric multi processing an architectural change from System /360 to /370 was carried out. System/370 still maintained the compatibility to System /360 but marked a major milestone of advanced computer technology.

The following years and developments were marked by the hunger for more system memory. The initial System /360 architecture used 24 bit for addressing which just allowed to address 16 MB of virtual and physical memory. This became too small and in the early 1980s the addressing was increased to 2 GB or 31 bit addresses. The 32nd bit of the address was used to distinguish a 31 bit from a 24 bit address and we will also later see that both the architecture and the operating system underwent every effort to maintain compatibility to 24 bit addressing and programs written on older technology.

Storage was still the main concern during these days. On the one hand main memory was very expensive on the other hand storage was the limiting factor of computer technology while processor technology advanced much faster. Many attempts were made to overcome the limiting factor main memory and one of such developments were the introduction of expanded storage. Expanded stor-

2.1 A Little History

age was a 4KB addressable storage which extended the main memory. While it was not byte addressable it was not so easy to access the storage by programs. Thus it was first primarily used as a fast paging device and only later techniques, like data spaces and Hiperspaces™ allowed to use the storage more directly. Nevertheless in 2001 with the introduction of the System z architecture and the z/OS operating system the addressability was extended to 64 bits and the limitations of only 2 GB addressable storage were finally removed. At that time the cost for storage was relative small compared to other elements of the system and nowadays environments can afford hundredths of GB of main memory.

But before the change from 31 bit to 64 bit addressing was made another important development must be noticed. System /360 and its successor /370 was based on bipolar chip technology. Bipolar chip technology was in the 1980s the fastest existing chip technology but its manufacturing costs and further more the cooling problem of the thermal effects of the chip caused a high problem to future development of the architecture. As a matter of fact System /370 based on bipolar technology reached a scalability limitation at the end of the 1980s which could not be overcome within this technology. In 1994 IBM introduced a completely re-newed generation based on CMOS (complementary metal-oxide-semiconductor) chip technology. The new generation was named System/390® and the first notice to be made was that the single processor speed of the new system reached only 28% of the speed of the last bipolar system of System /370 while the available system capacity even was shrinking to only 16%. This was a significant scalability issue and in order to overcome this limitation a cluster technology the Parallel Sysplex was introduced which allows to couple multiple OS/390® and later on z/OS systems via a fast storage device the coupling facility.

The fourth generation of new System /390 hardware based on CMOS technology finally reached the capacity and performance of the previous bipolar System /370 hardware. Nowadays the CMOS technology advanced to performance and capacity ratings which are higher than ever before. System z196 with 5.2 GHz frequency is the fastest commercial processor in the industry. System z is also a wonderful example of a technology which scales since 50 years and which were able to overcome a technological limitation by changing the base of its chip technology. The first S/360 systems provided a capacity of roughly 0.005 Million Instructions per Second (MIPS) and a 2817-701 which is a one way z196 offers a capacity of 1200 MIPS. With the very high increased in system capacity the focus for scalability changes from providing the minimum capacity as it was in the early 90s to exploiting the available capacity.

We will also see that the introduction of very high clock frequency does not alone provide a high system capacity and that advanced techniques are necessary to exploit the this technology. On the other hand the focus of the Parallel Sysplex technology is no longer scalability but high availability and continuous operations of the environment. The Parallel Sysplex technology has been enhanced to support a Geographically Dispersed Parallel Sysplex™ (GDPS®) environment and thus providing a resilient business environment on a global scale.

2.2. System z CMOS Heritage

System z196 is the latest system of the CMOS mainframe heritage started in 1994 which replaced the bipolar technology of the 1980s. Figure 2.2 shows the development of the processor frequency starting with the fourth generation of CMOS mainframe processors. We remember that the fourth generation was the first processor which provided the same capacity and speed than the earlier bipolar technology. Generation 5 (G5) and 6 introduced IEEE standard binary floating point and copper technology. System z900 was the first system of the System z architecture and it introduced full 64 bit architecture.

System z990 also where a milestone in processor technology. It was the first multi book system and it introduced super-scalar processor pipeline. A significant advance was made with the change from System z9 to z10. System z10 increased the clock frequency by 2.5 times. This now required significant improvements of the System z microprocessor. Enhancements of the super-scalar pipeline became necessary as well as for the cache topology between the microprocessor and main memory. Another significant advance in this direction was made with the System z196 microprocessor which also introduced a new out-of-order pipeline on System z. It should be noted that this was by far not the introduction of out of order processing. The last generations of bipolar technology also already used out of order processing. But the high clock frequency and using the existing microprocessor technology efficiently now require again more sophisticated processor design. Until now the advantage of the newest generation was mostly given by incremental technology advances. In addition System z196 completes the cache topology which was introduced with System z10. System zEC12 has been released in September 2012 and it is the newest member of the System z family. The processor frequency increased to 5.5 GHz and the processor has been enhanced for its out-of-order processing. The following chapters will discuss the System z microprocessor technology with examples shown for System z10, z196 and zEC12. The discussion will focus on the necessary functionality to exploit high processor frequency and to provide scalability and elasticity on large systems.

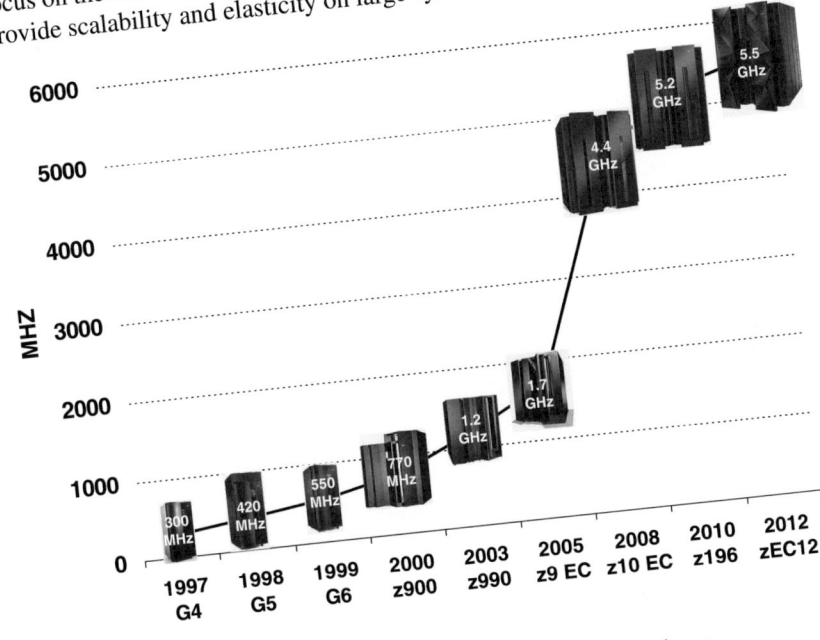

Figure 2.2.: System z: CMOS Mainframe Heritage

At this point we also need to introduce a common terminology for a System z mainframe environment. Such a computing system is named a Central Electronic Complex (CEC) or Central Processing Complex (CPC).

2.3. System zEC12 Central Electronic Complex

The term Central Electronic Complex becomes much more clear when we take a look at the possible expansions for a System zEC12 compared to a classical mainframe environment. Figure 2.3 shows how a zEC12 may look like. The classical mainframe consists of two frames, the A and Z frame which will be discussed later in more detail. In addition Blade Center Extensions named zBX and enumerated as B, C, D, or E frame can be added to the classical mainframe.

In the first stage this provides a closer integration of application servers running on Linux and Windows environments to the transaction and database servers running on the classical mainframe environment. Using zBX extensions also integrates many manageability aspects on a single console which make complex environments more suitable for large installations. the zBX extensions were introduced with System z196. The z196 was the first System z which provided the structure of a classical mainframe and up to 5 zBX extensions.

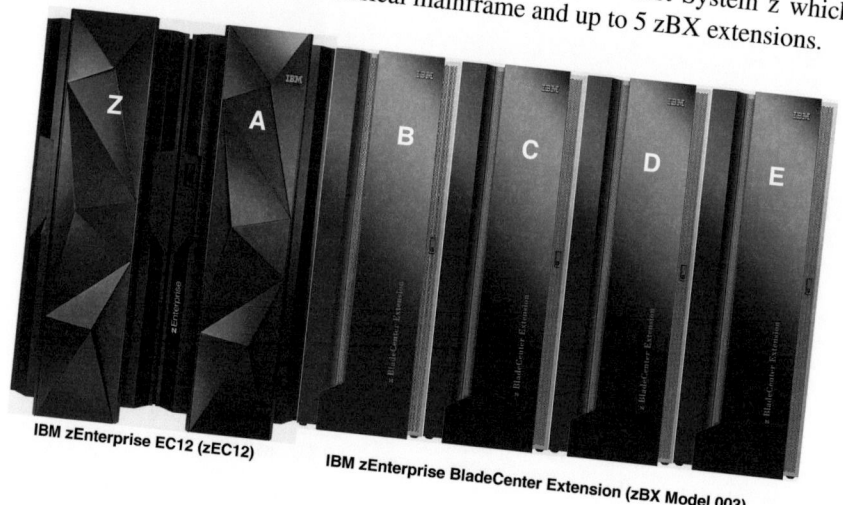

IBM zEnterprise EC12 (zEC12)

IBM zEnterprise BladeCenter Extension (zBX Model 003)

Figure 2.3.: System zEC12 Frames and Blade Extensions

In our excursion on High Availability and Scalability we will concentrate on the classical mainframe environment which is the Z and A frame of the CEC.

2.4. System zEC12 Components

Figure 2.4 shows how the high end System zEC12 looks when the covers are removed. The depicted system is a water cooled model which is only available for the largest extension of the largest models H89 and HA1. Water cooling is optionally, the standard cooling method uses a refrigerator liquid in a closed circuit cycle. The water cooling models allow the installation to provide additional cooling which is especially advisable in warmer region.

The A frame of the CEC contains the system processors, I/O cages, optional battery backup systems and the cooling environment. The HA1 model contains

2.4 System zEC12 Components

120 processors of which 101 can be used for customer workloads. The processors are contained on 4 books. The HA1 as well as the H89 are always made of 4 books. Smaller models like the H66 consist of 3 books, the H43 of 2 and the H20 of 1 book. The number denotes the maximum number of processors which can be used for workloads. The additional processors are utilized for internal processing or as spares. One book can keep up to 30 processors. The books also contain the memory cards of the system.

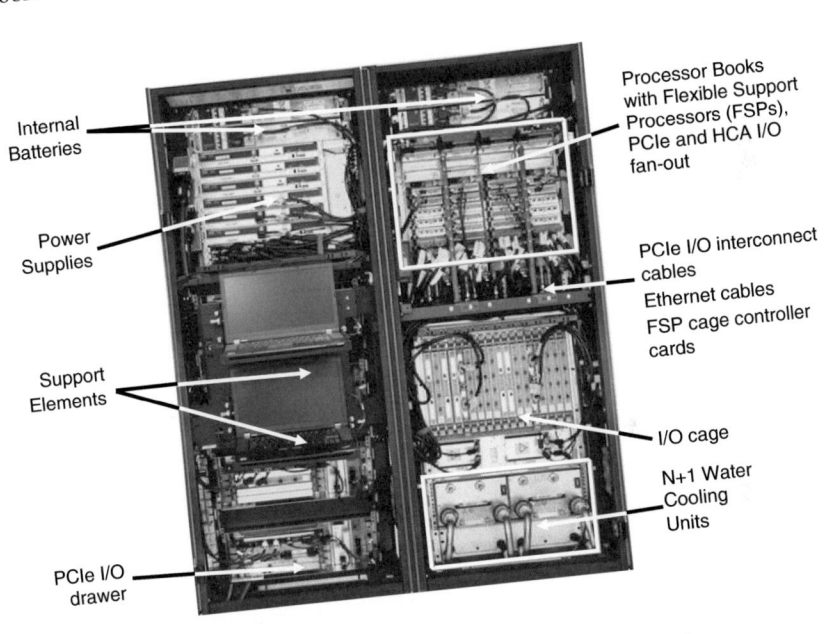

Internal
Batteries

Power
Supplies

Support
Elements

PCIe I/O
drawer

Processor Books
with Flexible Support
Processors (FSPs),
PCIe and HCA I/O
fan-out

PCIe I/O interconnect
cables
Ethernet cables
FSP cage controller
cards

I/O cage

N+1 Water
Cooling
Units

Figure 2.4.: Under the Hood of System zEC12

The Z frame contains the Support Elements (SE) which are used for maintenance. Usually only a system technician has a need to use a support element for example when the replacement of a part becomes necessary. The management of the system is usually done from a Hardware Management Console (HMC) which is connected remotely to the CEC. The Z frame also contains power supplies and additional I/O drawers. It should be noted that the general structure of the z196 is the same just with a smaller number of total processors. The biggest z196 has 96 processors of which are 80 can be used for workloads.

2.5. System z Multi Chip Module

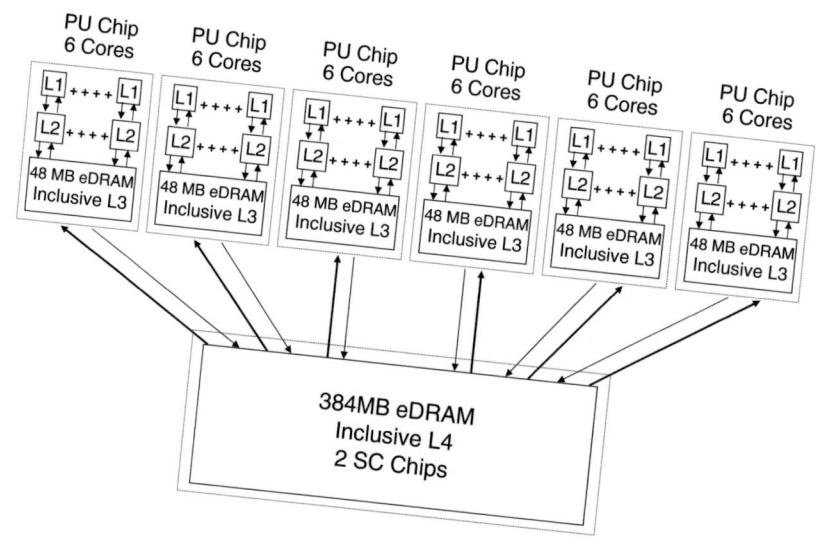

Figure 2.5.: System zEC12 Cache Level Structure

The heart of all System z systems is the Multi Chip Module (MCM). The MCM contains the processor and storage controller chips. The MCM for z196 and zEC12 always consist of 6 processor chips with up to 6 physical processor units for a zEC12 system and 3 or 4 active processor cores for z196. The processor cores are complemented with a Level 1 cache and an additional Level 2. The cores of the same processor chip then share a common Level 3 cache and all processor chips a common Level 4 cache on the same book. Figure 2.5 depicts the cache hierarchy on one book for the zEC12 system.

The structure for the z196 is the same but the cache sizes have changed. Table 2.1 shows the differences in cache sizes for z196 compared to zEC12. It can be observed that the L1 cache structure for zEC12 is smaller because of the higher clock frequency. On the other hand the shared cache structures on the processor chip and the book have doubled in size. When a processor changes a data item it is stored through Level 1 and 2 caches into the Level 3 cache. Data from the Level 3 cache is cast out to the Level 4 cache based on a Last Recently Used (LRU) algorithm.

The 4 level cache hierarchy becomes necessary to reduce the access of data from main memory. On System z10 a 3 level cache hierarchy was already implemented while earlier systems only contained a 2 level cache hierarchy. Introducing this hierarchy and making efficient use of it is a significant factor of system performance which we will discuss in much more detail when we take a look at work dispatching across the firmware and operating system layers of a System z.

Cache	z196	zEC12
L1	64KB 128KB (1) 128KB (2)	64KB (1) 96 KB (2)
L2	1.5 MB	1MB (1) and 1 MB (2)
L3	24 MB	48 MB
L4	192 MB	384 MB
Notes:	(1) Instruction Cache (2) Data Cache	

Table 2.1.: Comparison of Cache Size for System z196 and zEC12

The processors on each chip are complemented by a Cryptographic Co-processor (CoP). The interface to the Storage Control (SC) chip supports a data transfer rate of 41.6 GB/sec for z196 and 44 GB/sec for zEC12 between memory and Level 4 cache. Finally the chip has an interface to the to the Host Channel Adapter (GX) and the memory controllers (MC). The chip area for z196 is $512.3mm^2$, consists of 13 layers of metal and 3.5 km of wire. The chip has 1.4 billion transistors and is made of 45nm of Silicon on Insulator (SOI) technology.

For a zEC12 the chip area is bigger and has a size of $597mm^2$ and consists of 15 layers of metal and 7.68 km of wire. The zEC12 chip has 2.75 billion transistors and is made of 32nm of Silicon on Insulator (SOI) technology. A more detailed description of the processor structure, used processor technology and MCM layout can be found in [17].

2.5.1. Memory

Maximum physical memory size is directly related to the number of books in the system. Each book may contain up to 960 GB of physical memory, for a total of 3840 GB (3.75 TB) of installed memory per system.

A System z CEC has more memory installed than ordered. Part of the physical installed memory is used to implement the redundant array of independent memory (RAIM) design, resulting on up to 768 GB of available memory per book and up to 3072 GB (3 TB) per system.

The minimum installed memory is 40 GB per book and the minimum amount of memory that can be ordered is 32 GB for small machines with up to 256 GB installed memory and up to 256 GB for large systems with 1776 to 3056 GB installed memory.

2.5.2. Book

The MCM, DIMMs, together with power supplies, cooling interconnects and fanout cards are placed in a book. A z196 can have up to 4 books and up to 96 processors and the zEC12 4 books with 120 processors.

2.5.3. Processor Characterization

In each MCM, some PUs may be characterized for customer use. The characterized PUs may be used for general purpose to run supported operating systems (as z/OS, z/VM®, Linux on System z), or specialized to run specific workloads (as Java, XML services, IPSec, some DB2 workloads) or functions (as Coupling Facility Control Code).

The maximum number of characterized PUs depends on the System z model. Some PUs are characterized by the system as standard system assist processors (SAPs), to run the I/O processing. Also as standard, there are at least two spare PUs per system, which are used to assume the function of a failed PU. The remaining installed PUs can be characterized for customer use. The System z model nomenclature includes a number which represents this maximum number of PUs that can be characterized for customer use, as shown in table 2.2 for the zEC12.

System assist processors and spare PUs are required to run the system and to provide the redundancy against PUs errors. General purpose PUs as well as special processors are used to run customer workloads. The differentiation is made for licensing reasons and to provide an environment on System z which maintains the high investment in technology for legacy workloads as well as

Model	Books	PUs	CPs	IFLs ICFs	zAAPs zIIPs	SAPs	Spares
H20	1	27	0 to 20	0 to 20	0 to 10	4	2
H43	2	54	0 to 43	0 to 43	0 to 21	8	2
H66	3	81	0 to 66	0 to 66	0 to 33	12	2
H89	4	108	0 to 89	0 to 89	0 to 44	16	2
HA1	4	120	0 to 101	0 to 101	0 to 50	16	2
Notes:	Number of processors for IFLs, ICFs, zIIPs, and zAAPs is for each type						

Table 2.2.: Number of Processing Units per zEC12 Model

to provide the possibility to run specialized functions on System z. Special purpose processors are:

IFL Integrated Facility for Linux allows to run Linux operating system as well as z/VM on System z to a lower price point than on regular purpose processors.

zAAP System z Application Assist Processors can be exploited by the z/OS operating system to run Java code and XML services aside from general purpose processors.

zIIP System z Integrated Information Processors are also exploited by z/OS to execute DB2 and IPsec services. In addition they also allow to execute the same workloads than zAAPs thus requiring installation to use only one type of assist processors if needed.

ICF The Integrated Coupling Facility is an assist processor to run the coupling facility control code which is the operating system for common data connection in a Parallel Sysplex.

2.6. System z High Availability Design

The following section will discuss two methods for achieving high reliability and availability of System z hardware. The two components used as example are the System z processor and memory design.

2.6.1. Transparent CPU Sparing

Transparent CPU Sparing is an error detection and correction mechanism which allows error detection during instruction execution and transparent error correction if spare processors have been configured to the system. The process is also called transient error recovery. It was introduced with 5th generation of CMOS processors and the original design uses two physical execution units on each core or physical PU (see figure 2.6)

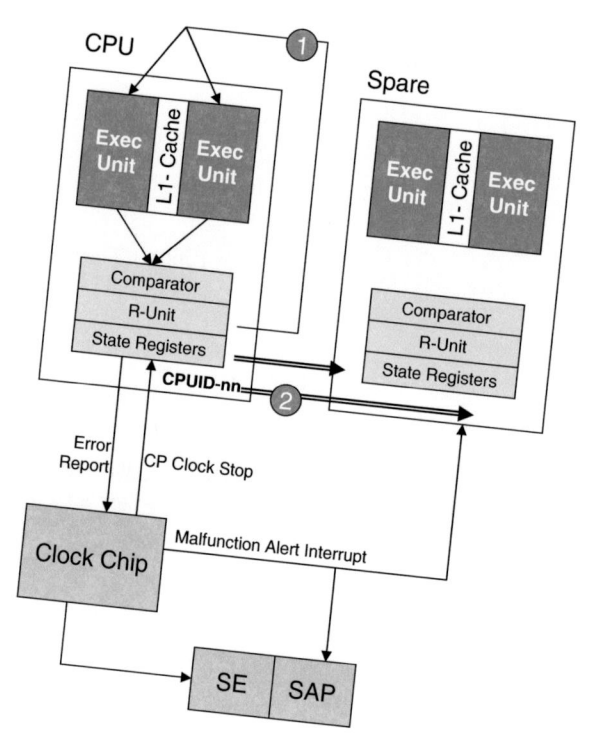

Figure 2.6.: Transparent CPU Sparing on System z9

Every Physical Processing Unit (actual Core on a PU chip) contains two execution units. Each instruction is fetched concurrently from the L1 cache by both execution units and processed. The result is compared and if it is equal processing is resumed with the next instruction. If the result is not equal the instruction is executed again to find out whether a temporary error existed. If it is still not the same an error mark is set. The R-Unit now signals the higher cache structures that the processing unit is running an error recovery process. The error recovery process resets all data store activities of the failing instruction. The CPU is now ready to get out of the configuration. The CPU is stopped and the CPU clock is stopped too. The error is signaled to the service assist processor and the service element. One possibility is now that the CPU is just configured out of the system. In this case the effect for the operating systems depend on their error recovery. A linux system for example may crash because a CPU fails. z/OS can mask the CPU and continue to process with the remaining CPUs in case more than 1 CPU is configured for the system. PR/SM™ can also mask the error by dispatching the logical CPs to fewer physical CPs.

Another possibility is to use a spare CPU. This requires that a spare CPU is configured to the system. The Service Assist Processor activates the spare processor and moves all register and cache contents to the new CPU. In addition the CPU id from the failing CPU is also moved to the spare CPU so that the new CPU looks identical to the failing CPU. The newly configured CPU can now immediately start to process the failing instruction again and can seamlessly and transparently replace the failing CPU.

2.6.2. CPU Error Detection for newer System z machines

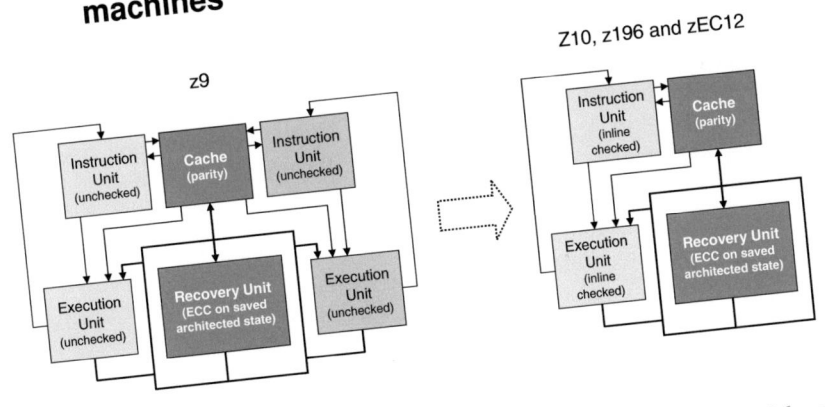

Figure 2.7.: CPU Error Detection and Recovery on System z10, z196 and zEC12

For System z9 each CPU chip includes two cores. System z10, z196 and zEC12 the CPU chip does not contain the execution units two times. Instead an error-correcting code (ECC) protected processor state is used inside the recovery unit (RU) to employ the same reliability features than its predecessors. Thousands of error checkers (parity, residue, illegal state, hardware redundancy compares, and so on) are embedded within the microprocessors and system cache hierarchy. Every instruction that executes successfully, and without error, updates the check-pointed state. Any error associated with the execution of an instruction blocks completion, and its associated state is not check-pointed.

Upon detection of an error within the microprocessor, execution is stopped, and the core enters a sophisticated recovery sequence. All the core's non-architectural facilities are reset, and the hardened architectural facilities are corrected as needed. Next, the core retries execution, starting at the check-pointed state. In this way, the microprocessor can recover after any soft failure. However, if instruction execution continues to fail, a sparing event is initiated on a spare core, whereby millicode copies the architectural state from the failing to the spare core. Then, the failing core is removed from and the spare core is added to the system configuration, and task execution restarts on the spare core[1].

2.6.3. Redundant Array of Independent Memory

The z196 RAIM memory subsystem is a revolutionary, next-generation memory design that tolerates complete failure of any single DIMM. This design yields the highest level of memory availability of any System z generation[2].

In order to implement RAIM, 'extra' memory is installed on each book. Each z196 book can contain up to 960 GB of physical memory, for a total of 3840 GB (3.75 TB) of installed memory per system (with four books). 20% of the physical installed memory is used to implement the RAIM design, resulting in up to 768 GB of available memory per book and up to 3072 GB (3 TB) per system. RAIM, and this additional memory, is provided as a standard feature of the z196 and zEC12.

Each book has from 10 to 30 DIMMs (depending on how much memory is installed). The DIMMs are connected through three memory control units (MCUs), each located on a processor unit on the book. Each MCU uses five channels, one of them for RAIM implementation, on a 4 +1 (parity) design. Each channel has one or two chained DIMMs, so a single MCU can have five

---

[1] More detailed descriptions can be found in [18] and [20] for z196 and [19] for z10
[2] The content of this section is based on [23]

or ten DIMMs. The parity of the four data DIMMs is stored and attached to the fifth memory channel. This data, along with CRC bus protection in each of the five channels allows for failures in a memory component to be detected and corrected dynamically.

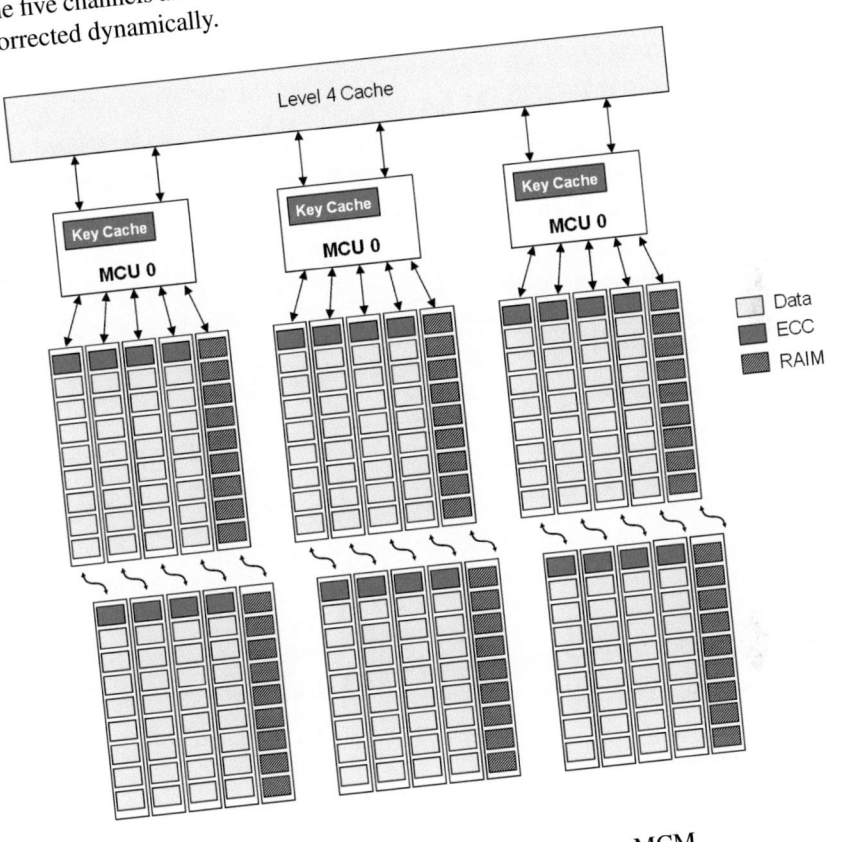

Figure 2.8.: z196 Memory within an MCM

Figure 2.8 illustrates the memory layout of a fully-configured book. The RAIM design detects and recovers from DRAM, socket, memory channel, or DIMM failures. It is loosely similar to a RAID level 3 design. Five memory channels are involved in any read or write request. (A memory channel is either one DIMM, or two DIMMs chained together.) Cyclic Redundancy Check (CRC) data is used on each channel bus to detect and isolate channel errors. On top of that, RAIM ECC is used to cover the entire end-to-end path from original store to the DIMMs to the final fetch. During reads, this CRC data is verified again, allowing for proactive error detection and correction. This allows the recovery from multiple chip failures that RAIM provides.

DRAM[3] and channel marking techniques are employed in the RAIM design, eliminating the need for DRAM sparing. DRAM marking eliminates the complexity of copying over chip data from one chip to another. Once a chip is known bad, it is marked as bad to the ECC code and the code automatically ignores all content from that DRAM. Likewise, a channel mark can be applied to one failing channel that is deemed to be unreliable. Once a channel mark is applied to a channel, all data from that channel is effectively ignored, even if there is another failure in another channel. For DRAM-only failures, data is corrected using in-line ECC correction. In the event of the detection of a memory control error with accompanying CRC violations, a 3 tiered recovery sequence is started; this can result in actions ranging from the dynamic correction of soft errors, bus data lane sparing, bus clock lane sparing, up to marking an entire channel bad and causing a service request to be issued.

New Errors	Marks			
	None	Single chip	Two chips	Third chip and channel mark
None	Good			
1 chip	Good			
2 chips, same channel	Correctable Error			Uncorrectable Error Service Request Part Replacement required
Full channel, CRC errors	Correctable Error			Uncorrectable Error Service Request Part Replacement required

Table 2.3.: RAS Capabilities for RAIM Memory

Table 2.3 shows the type of errors which can be corrected based on RAIM design. RAS features in detail are:

RAIM ECC

Five-channel ECC which can detect and correct new DRAM failures as well as most varieties of single channel failures in the memory subsystem.

DRAM chip marking

Up to two DRAM chip marks can be applied per rank in order to ignore errors from known defective DRAM chips. Unlike DRAM chip sparing, these marks can be applied without having to replicate any chip data.

---

[3]Direct Random Access memory

Channel marking

Channel marking is the ability to designate one of five RAIM channels as defective. The channel mark provides 100%correction of the data in the ignored channel. There are four levels of channel marking: dynamic, tier3, temporary, and permanent.

CRC Bus Detection

Upstream and Downstream channels are checked using CRC.

Tire 1 reset

Tier 1 recovery quiesces the channels, resets memory channel resources, and then resends stores that may have been dropped.

Tier 2 data calibration

Tier 2 recovery re-calibrates memory data buses and spares out bad data lanes.

Tier 3 clock calibration

Tier3 recovery re-calibrates memory clocks and spares out bad clock lanes. Firmware performs fast scrub to clean-up stale data.

Scrubbing

Scrubbing is the process of periodically reading, correcting, and writing back memory to correct soft errors. Scrubbing provides chip error counts which are used to apply DRAM chip and channel marks.

Service Request

A service request is an event which requests a part replacement. Some examples of memory-related service requests include:

- Permanent, full channel RAIM degrade.
- Overflow of the DRAM mark capabilities within a rank.
- Overflow of bus spare lanes within a channel or cascade.

2.7. System z Software and Firmware Layers

Firmware or Licensed Internal Code (LIC) is the layer between hardware and software on System z. This layer also includes the virtualization layer, the Logical Partition (LPAR) Hypervisor . This dates back to 1985 when logical partitioning was introduced on S/370. All future architectures implement logical partitioning as part of the firmware layer. On today's systems logical partitioning is always present and activate.

Figure 2.9 shows the software and hardware layers on System z. The firmware includes two special type of instruction code, the millicode and the i390 code which both implement certain function of the z/Architecture.

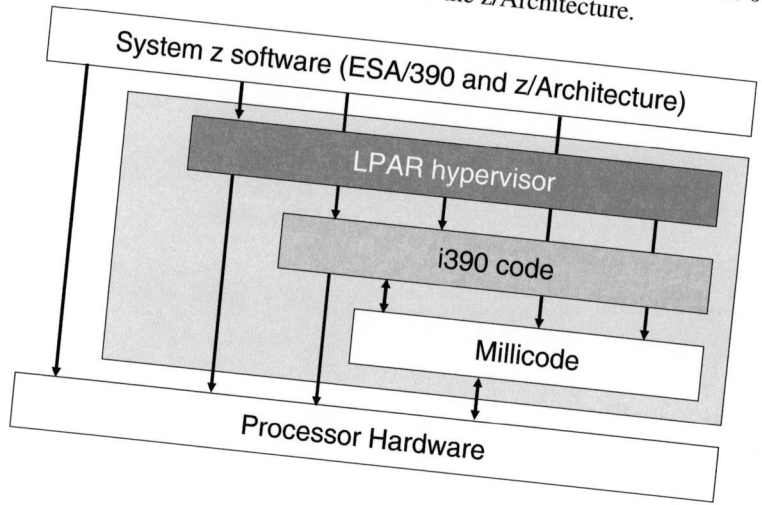

Figure 2.9.: System z Software and Firmware Layers

Millicode performs the more complex instructions in the System z architecture. The hardware typically executes many of the logical less complex and high performance instructions while the more complex instructions are implemented in millicode. Millicode is written and assembled in a manner very similar to System z Assembler language code. Functions implemented in millicode are:

- Interrupt handling (program, external, I/O, machine check)
- Virtualization: interpretive execution
- Special RAS (reliability, availability, serviceability) and debug functions
- Reset functions

i390 code runs mostly[4] on the System Assist Processor (SAP). Most of its functions are I/O related involving the channel subsystem. The code performs complex functions such as

- System initialization and reset
- I/O subsystem

---

[4]i390 code can run on all processors but it is mostly executed on the SAP

- Concurrent maintenance
- Communication with the Support Element (SE)
- A few instructions

System z firmware resides in the Hardware Storage Area (HSA) of the System z memory. This storage area has a fixed size of 16 GB. The "True HSA" is 12.5 GB, the LPAR Hypervisor requires 1.5 GB and the remaining 2GB are used for storage keys. The HSA also keeps the I/O configuration of the CEC. Altogether System z can have up to 3 TB of storage installed across the 4 books (768 GB per book). Aside from the HSA the installed memory is assigned to the logical partitions. Each partition has a certain amount of storage which is defined by the system administrator. The storage size can also be manually increased or decreased during runtime.

2.8. Instruction Execution

In this section we will discuss instruction execution on System z. As we already saw in the previous chapters System z processor architecture has been enhanced by additional cache levels since System z9. The additional cache levels became necessary to overcome the speed difference between the System z micro-processors which increased from 1.7 GHz on System z9 to 5.2 GHz on System z196. But this is not enough. We will see that instruction execution becomes more expensive and additional strategies must be used to exploit the high processor frequency. In addition we will discuss activities to optimize code execution on System z by enhancing the System z instruction set with instructions tailored for special purposes.

The base documentation for this chapter was taken from literature in [31], [26], [19], [18], and [20].

2.8.1. CISC versus RISC Architecture

System z is a Complex Instruction Set Computing (CISC) architecture. This means that certain instructions perform complex tasks similar to small programs. The opposite is a Reduced Instruction Set Computing (RISC) architecture which basically only contains of data fetch and store operations plus register to register arithmetic operations. Today's computing architecture in reality do not implement a pure RISC or CISC architecture anymore. For System z196 we will see that the micro-processors contain RISC execution units and the many existing CISC instructions are broken down to micro operations for execution.

Nevertheless System z also contains very basic instructions like RISC instructions. These are LOAD, STORE, and register to register operations like an Add Register operation (AR). More interesting is the question how a modern application on System z is composed, more of RISC like instructions or more of complex instructions. In the same context the question appears what influence on execution time the RISC-like instructions compared to the complex instructions have.

Figure 2.10 shows the percent of instructions for a Websphere transaction relative to the cycle time of an Add Register (AR) instruction. This analysis was performed on a System z990 in 2002 and does no longer depict the instruction decomposition of today's Websphere transactions but the general notion remains the same.

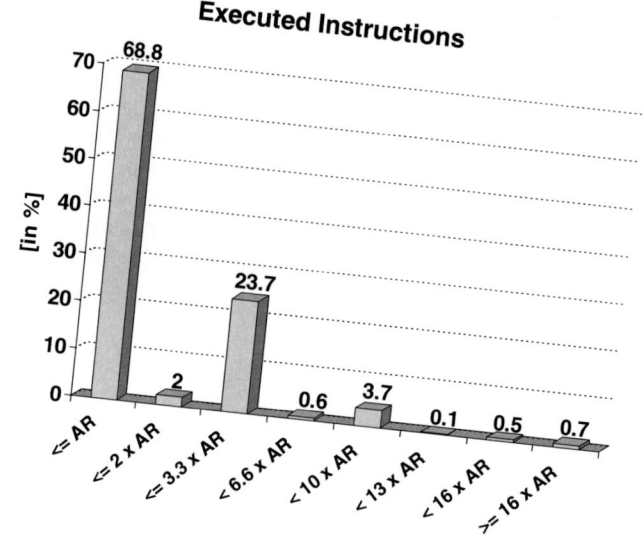

Figure 2.10.: Percent of executed Instructions relative to ADD REGISTER

The Websphere transaction was a very rudimentary transaction which updates a data base table and uses a set of system services during its execution. The transaction consisted of 135704 instructions. The instructions are counted by

2.8 Instruction Execution

their cycle times and then they are placed in relation to the AR instruction which is a very basic RISC like instruction on System z. We can observe that nearly 70% of the instructions are very similar to the AR instruction and do not require more than 1 cycle for execution. Only about 1.3% of the instructions require 10 times or more cycles for execution than the very simple instructions.

When we take a look at the time consumption and which instructions contribute most to the execution time of the Websphere transaction we can observe a different picture. Figure 2.11 shows the percent of execution time of all the instructions which we counted similar to the AR instruction or as multiple of the AR instruction. Now we can observe that the 0.7% of the instructions which require 16 times the cycle length of the AR instruction contribute for around 19% of the transaction execution time while the AR like instructions which account for the majority of the instructions contribute only for 33% of the transaction execution.

Time consumption of executed Instructions

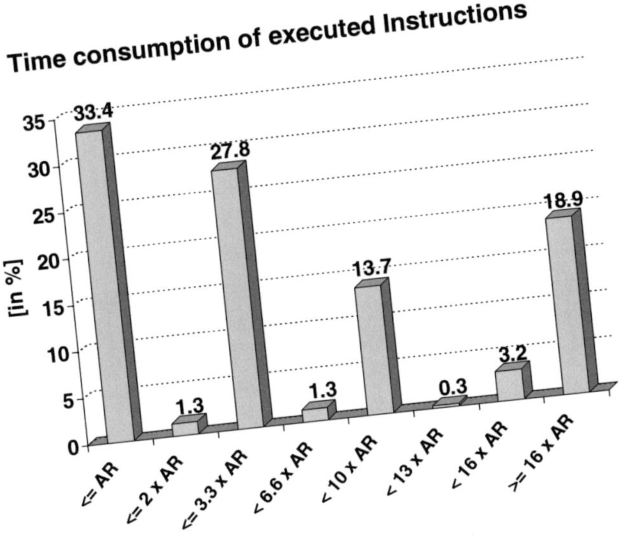

Figure 2.11.: Transaction Execution Time relative to the amount of Instructions

The question what is good and bad can't be simply answered just from this study. Such studies are performed to understand the mix of instructions used to perform a certain application or operating system function. Based on the de-composition it is than possible to either try to reduce very complex instructions if their use seems unnecessary or to do the opposite to introduce complex instructions and to reduce the number of very simple instructions which perform the same functionality. In the end a RISC instruction set attempts to reduce the cycle time while a CISC instruction set reduces the number N of executed instructions in the following equation:

$$ExecutionTime = \sum_{k=1}^{N} \frac{Cycles}{Instructions}(k) \bullet CycleTime \qquad (2.1)$$

2.8.2. Register Sets

System z Architecture has several sets of registers for different purposes:

- General purpose registers are used for address generation, address calculation as well as for integer arithmetic (signed and unsigned). Each register has 64 bits and is numbered from 0 to 63. System z also supports ESA/390 mode which is 31 bit addressing mode. In this case only the low order 32 bits are addressable.
- Program Access registers are used to define the addressing target for the general purpose register. When the program runs in access register mode the address contained in the corresponding general purpose register refers to a different virtual storage area (address space) than the one the program is located in.
- Control registers are used by the operating systems to control interrupt handling, virtual storage, tracing facilities and access to address spaces. The registers have 64 bits in z architecture mode and for ESA/390 mode only 32 the low order bits are addressable.
- Floating point registers are used for binary, decimal and hexadecimal floating point operations. Again these registers also have 64 bits. If extended precision is required (128bits) register pairs are being used.
- One floating point control register contains IEEE exception masks and flags and they define the rounding mode. This register has 32 bits.
- Millicode registers are used within the processors to hold intermediate results and to address data in customer storage and the Hardware System Area (HSA). These registers can't be accessed the programs. Millicode registers are different from general purpose registers and can only be used by millicode.

2.8 Instruction Execution

- The prefix register is used to define the absolute addresses of assigned storage locations for a CPU. It is again a 32 bit register and only used by the operating systems.

2.8.3. Program Status Word

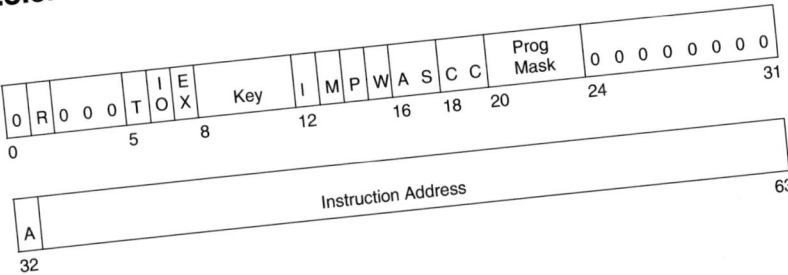

Figure 2.12.: Program Status Word in 31-bit Addressing Modes

The Program Status Word (PSW) contains information required for the execution of the current program, like the instruction address, the addressing mode, the condition code, interrupt masks, and an indicator of the execution mode.

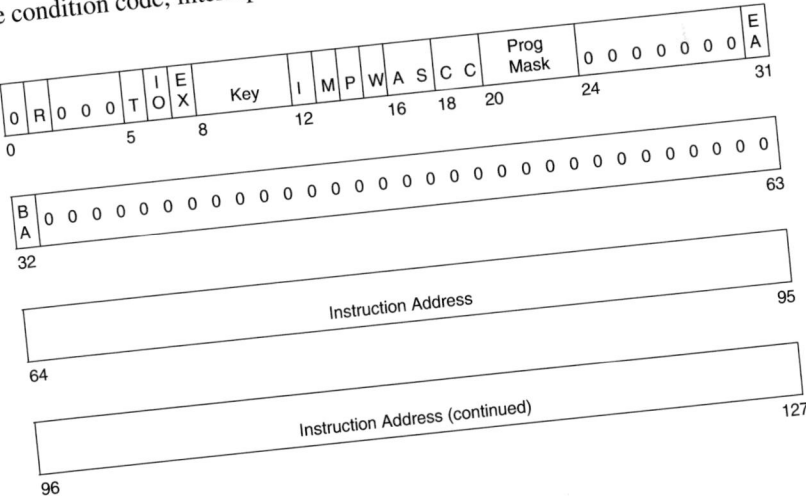

Figure 2.13.: Program Status Word in 64-bit Addressing Modes

Figure 2.12 shows the PSW format for 31-bit addressing mode and figure 2.13 for 64-bit addressing mode on System z. If the program is running in 24 or 31 bit addressing named ESA/390 architecture mode only 64 bits are used to maintain the program status. In z architecture mode 24, 31, and 64 bit addressing is possible. The addressing mode can change for each new program dispatch and different processors can run with different addressing modes at the same time. Also services exist to switch within one program between the addressing modes.

The meaning of the individual fields are:

- **R** enable program event recording (PER)
- **T** enable dynamic address translation (virtual storage)
- **IO** enable I/O interrupts
- **EX** enable external interrupts
- **Key** define storage protection key
- **M** enable machine checks
- **W** wait state
- **P** problem state (0 = supervisor state)
- **AS** address space

  00 = primary space mode

  01 = access register mode

  10 = secondary space mode

  11 = home space mode
- **CC** condition code

  00 = equal

  01 = first operand low

  02 = first operand high
- **Program Mask** which interrupts are enabled
  - Bit 20: Enable fixed-point overflow exception
  - Bit 21: Enable decimal overflow exception
  - Bit 22: Enable hex floating-point exponent underflow exception
  - Bit 23: Enable hex floating-point significance exception

2.8 Instruction Execution

- **EA** extended addressing (64-bit addressing mode, BA must also be 1)
- **BA** basic addressing (31-bit addressing mode, 0 = 24-bit addressing mode)
- **Instruction Address** is stepped by the length of the current instruction

The significant difference of bit settings between 31 and 64 bit addressing is bit 31 in 64 bit addressing mode which defines whether 64 bit addressing is used. For 31 bit addressing bit 32 is the first bit of the instruction address thus reducing the available address range to 2 GB instead of possible 4 GB. For 64 bit addressing this limitation does not exist.

2.8.4. System z Instructions

The current System z model the z196 contains 1079 instructions. The first System /360 had only 143 instructions but primarily over the last generations the number of available instructions grew very fast. We will discuss some reasons for this later on. The following list describes the general instruction types of System z:

- Load and store instructions which load data to a register and store data from a register to storage. These instructions support 8, 16, 32, and 64 bit operand lengths.
- Binary arithmetic operations. Instructions like ADD, MULTIPLY, SUBTRACT, and DIVIDE. These instructions can be register-to-register instructions, and register-storage instructions. The supported operand length are 16, 32, and 64 bits.
- Shift operations which shift bits from left or right, logically or maintaining signed arithmetic, and rotate bits. These instructions support 32 and 64 bit operand lengths.
- Bitwise logical operations, like AND, OR, EXCLUSIVE OR. Operand lengths of 8, 16, 32, and 64 bits are supported as well as operands with 1 to 256 bytes. These instructions also support combinations of ROTATE AND "bitwise" operations.
- Comparison instructions support 16, 32, and 64 bits and signed and unsigned (logical) arithmetic.
- Branch instructions which support absolute and relative offsets.

- Subroutine linkage which consists of BRANCH instructions, SAVE, and optionally SET MODE functions.
- Bit testing and counting to test masks and identify special bits.
- Storage-to-storage copy and compare instructions. These instructions can support short (8 bytes), long, and extended operands which allow the move and compare of very large data areas. The long and extended formats are interruptible.
- Conversion from and to packed decimal format
- String processing like string translations and search capabilities
- Conversion between little and big Endian
- Checksum generation
- Sorting, like COMPARE AND FORM CODEWORD, or UPDATE TREE
- Data encryption
- Atomic updates and locking like COMPARE AND SWAP, or LOAD AND ADD ON CONDITION

We will discuss some of these instructions later. As the list shows different instruction formats exist, like register-to-register instructions where both operands are registers (RR), or register-storage instructions where one operand is a register and the other a storage location (RX) or storage-to-storage instructions where both operands are storage locations (SS) or storage-to-storage instructions where both operands are storage locations. Altogether 45 different instruction formats exist from which RR, RX, and SS instruction formats are the most commonly used formats. In the following we will give two simple examples for a RR and a SS instruction and the notation which is used.

Register-to-Register Format

The first instruction which we will take a look at is the ADD REGISTER instruction. It adds the content of two registers. We will use an "at sign" in front of a two digit number throughout this document to denote a register, for example @01, means register 1. This notation is used by some compilers. Other notions are R1, R01, or just a number to denote a register.

Figure 2.14 shows the simple example where the contents of register 6 and 7 is added together and the result is saved in register 6 which is the first operand of the operation. This is also common for most instructions that the result is placed in the first operand or at the location to which the first operand points

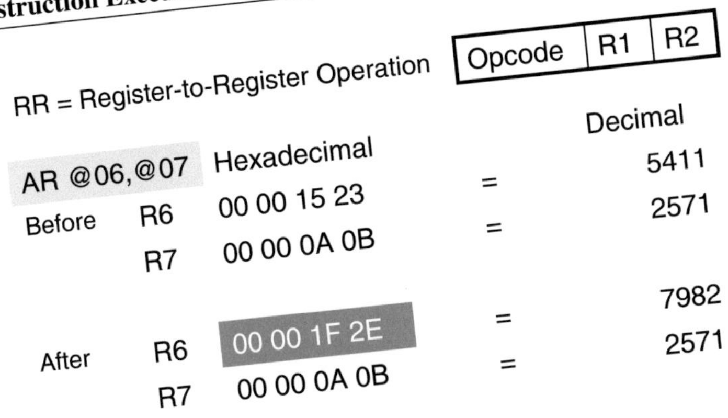

2.8 Instruction Execution

RR = Register-to-Register Operation

Opcode	R1	R2

AR @06,@07   Hexadecimal   Decimal

Before   R6   00 00 15 23   =   5411
         R7   00 00 0A 0B   =   2571

After   R6   00 00 1F 2E   =   7982
         R7   00 00 0A 0B   =   2571

Figure 2.14.: ADD REGISTER Example

to.

Storage-to-Storage Format

Our second example is a MOVE CHARACTER between two storage locations, see figure 2.15. The storage locations are described by base registers
which contain the base address of the storage location. In our example the first
operands base register is register 5 and the address contained in register 5 is
0x1000. The address of the storage locations is then found by adding a displacement to the content of the registers. The location of the first operand is
then found at storage location 0x1018.

The first operand is the target of the operation. Together with the address a
length field is defined which describes how many bytes should be overwritten
with data from the source location which is defined by base register 6 and
a displacement of 5. In our example we use a length of 6 that means that 6
characters are consecutively read from the first storage location and placed at
the target location.

2.8.5. Decimal Arithmetic

One of the most important formats on System z is decimal arithmetic and instructions. Decimal arithmetic is used to represent decimal numbers in com-

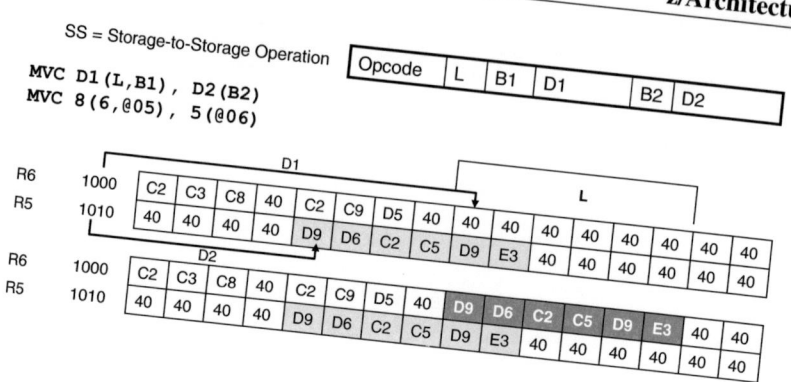

Figure 2.15.: MOVE CHARACTER Example

mercial applications. As we will see later decimal arithmetic is preferred and even required to avoid rounding problems.

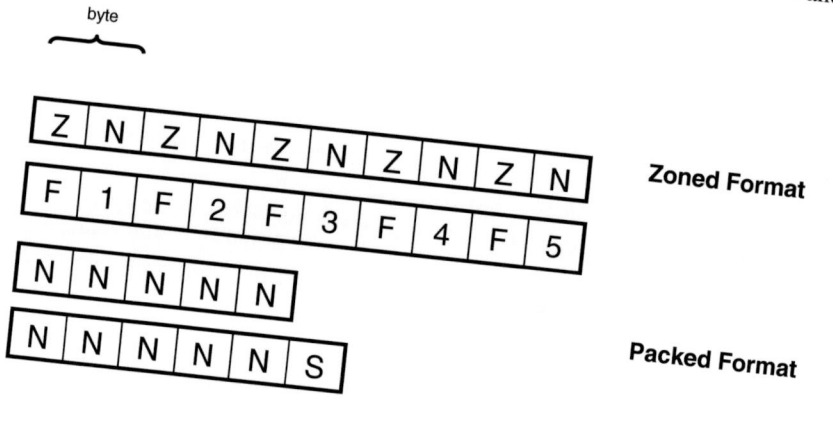

Figure 2.16.: Decimal Arithmetic Data Format

Two flavors of decimal instruction formats exist: Zoned and Packed decimal formats (see on figure 2.16). In both formats a decimal digit is encoded by 4 bits of which the bit combinations from 1010 to 1111 are no valid number. In zoned format the second half word is the zone character. The zoned format has advantages for printing decimal numbers. Within the system most decimal numbers are stored in packed decimal format. It requires N times four bits to encode the digits plus an additional half word to encode the sign. Table 2.4 shows the encoding of digits and signs. The rightmost hex value is the sign, A, C, E, and F mean plus and B, and D minus, for example 0x123C is decimal +123, and 0x456D is decimal -456.

System z and all of its predecessors support integer arithmetic (+, -, *, /), comparison operations, data validation, and conversion to EBCDIC. It is also possible to implicitly support a decimal digit but this is then interpreted by the software.

Code (Binary)	Recognized As	
	Digit	Sign
0000	0	Invalid
0001	1	Invalid
0010	2	Invalid
0011	3	Invalid
0100	4	Invalid
0101	5	Invalid
0110	6	Invalid
0111	7	Invalid
1000	8	Invalid
1001	9	Invalid
1010	Invalid	Plus
1011	Invalid	Minus
1100	Invalid	Plus (preferred)
1101	Invalid	Minus (preferred)
1110	Invalid	Plus
1111	Invalid	Plus (zone)

Table 2.4.: Halfword Codes for Decimal Format

2.8.6. Floating Point Arithmetic

System /360 already supported a hexadecimal floating point format (HFP). The radix of the exponent was 16 with a bias of 64 to support numbers bigger and smaller than 1. With the fifth generation of System /390 introduced in 1998 binary floating point (BFP) is supported. Decimal floating point (DFP) is supported by the firmware on z systems in 2007 and from 2010 on directly by the hardware. The decimal floating point is implemented corresponding to the IEEE standards 754.

Floating Point Format	Number Range Precision	Supports	
		Infinity	NaN
Hexadecimal (HFP)	$\sim 5.4x10^{-79} \leq M \leq \sim 7.2x10^{75}$	No	No
Binary (BFP)	$\sim 4.9x10^{-324} \leq M \leq \sim 1.8x10^{308}$	Yes	Yes
Decimal (DFP)	$1x10^{-398} \leq M \leq (10^{16} - 1)x10^{369}$	Yes	Yes

Table 2.5.: Floating Point Formats on System z

Table 2.5 shows the number ranges of the three floating point formats supported on System z. As an example figure 2.17 depicts the representation of the number PI with a decimal precision of 3.1415927 is shown for binary floating point (0x40490FDB) and hexadecimal floating point (0x413243F6) on Systemz.

Decimal Floating Point Arithmetic

The example in figure 2.17 shows the problem with binary and hexadecimal floating point arithmetic. While it is the natural way to depict data in a computer in binary or hexadecimal formats it is not natural to use this format in most human based calculations.

Binary Floating Point:
```
S exponent mantissa
0 10000000 10010010000111111011011
4     0    4   9  0   F   D   B
```

Hexadecimal Floating Point:
```
S exponent mantissa
0 1000001 001100100100001111110110
4    1    3   2   4   3   F   6
```

Figure 2.17.: Representation of PI = $\sim$3.1415927 in Binary and Hexadecimal Floating Point Format

As a matter of fact the conversion of decimal based numbers to both binary and hexadecimal floating point may result in an incorrect value when the data is converted back to decimal numbers. If we convert the number 0x40490FDB which is the representation of 3.1415927 back to a real number we obtain 3.1415927410125732 which returns a much higher precision which unfortunately is not correct. The correct precision would be 3.1415926535897932.

Now while this doesn't seem to be a big problem at a first glance we will use a much simpler example which may be the result of a real transaction: Assuming

2.8 Instruction Execution

a telephone company wants to add a sales tax of 5% to all telephone calls which were made from hotels which are supported by this telephone company. A telephone call costs 0.70. The result should be rounded to the nearest cent. In decimal arithmetic the calculation is simple: 1.05 x 0.70 = 0.735 and rounding results to 0.74.

When binary double arithmetic is used the situation gets more complicated. Converting 0.70 to binary double multiplying it with 1.05 and reconverting it to decimal arithmetic will result to 0.734999999999999986677323704498121 5-14916419982910 15625. Now rounding to the nearest cent results to 0.73 instead of 0.74.

The summary of this example shows that binary floating point cannot meet legal and financial requirement. Results are too imprecise and rounding does not help. Also errors can easily add up especially if more complex operations are involved. Thus a big need exists to support decimal floating point arithmetic on commercial computer systems.

It must also be noticed that 55% of all numerical data in databases are in decimal format and 43% of the remaining numerical data are represented as integers. This also shows that binary data doesn't play a high relevance for commercial computing.

Principles of Operations

The external part of the System z architecture is described in Principles of Operations [31]. There are additional instructions for special purposes which are not described there. these are for example

- Coupling technology instructions which handle special parts of the data exchange within a parallel sysplex environment
- Queued-direct I/O which allow direct memory data exchange between partitions
- Dynamic I/O Configuration related instructions which allow to update the I/O configuration in the HSA
- Service Call instructions (SCLP) to configure CPUs and memory
- Some instructions for logical partitioning and virtualization
- Instructions related to the CPU measurement facility

2.8.7. View of Instruction Execution

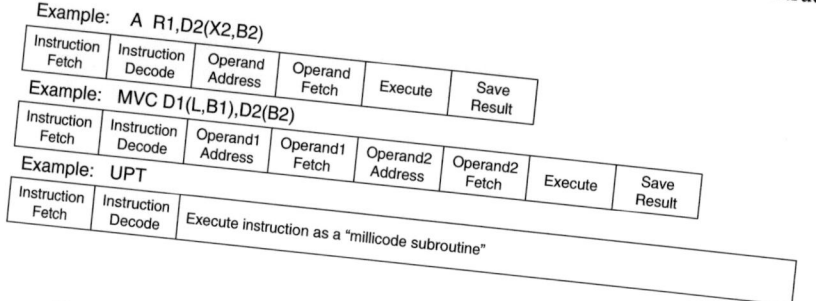

Figure 2.18.: Conceptual View of Instruction Execution

Programmers think of the execution of their program in the sequence they wrote them(see figure 2.18). This conceptual view of program execution is not true in todays computers anymore. The computer decomposes the instruction into micro parts and the assembly of the parts results in executing the instruction (see figure 2.19).

Example: A R1,D2(X2,B2)

Instruction Fetch	Instruction Decode	Operand Address	Operand Fetch	Execute	Save Result

Example: MVC D1(L,B1),D2(B2)

Instruction Fetch	Instruction Decode	Operand1 Address	Operand1 Fetch	Operand2 Address	Operand2 Fetch	Execute	Save Result

Example: UPT

Instruction Fetch	Instruction Decode	Execute instruction as a "millicode subroutine"

Figure 2.19.: Decomposition of Instructions (System z Examples)

A simple instruction like adding a storage location to a register consists already of 6 steps:

1. Fetching the instruction
2. Decoding the instruction
3. Generation of the Operand Address
4. Fetching the Operand
5. Executing the instruction
6. Saving the result

For more complex instructions, more steps are possible. This technique is named pipelining and by closer looking at it it allows to execute multiple stages

2.8 Instruction Execution

of the instructions simultaneously as long there are no dependencies between these stages.

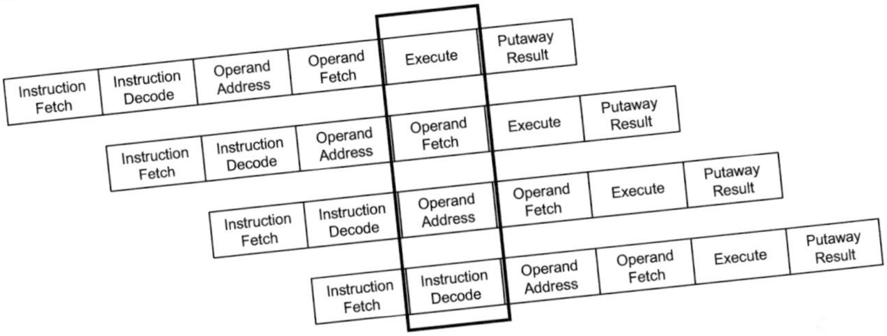

Figure 2.20.: Pipeline View of Instruction Execution

Figure 2.20 shows a simplified picture of executing 4 different instructions in parallel. Such an instruction pipeline is similar to an older instruction pipeline of a System z900 system. The real pipelines for z10 or z196 systems are too complicated to fully depict. This picture assumes 4 instructions of a length of 6 machine cycles. Ideally all instructions can be processed simultaneously with the result that the machine can complete every machine cycle one instruction. But in reality that will not happen because it assumes that there are no delays in the pipeline. Most common reasons for the pipeline to stall and to reject the execution are:

- Address Generation Interlock (AGI): This results in waiting for a previous instruction to compute an operand address. On z10 and z196 AGI bypasses exist which allow the results of Load Address to become available before saving the result. Also a group of instructions on z10 and single instructions on z196 can be stalled in the decode/issue unit until the interlock is resolvable in order to avoid that the pipeline is rejected later on.

- Operand Store Compare (OSC) requires to wait for a re-fetch of a recently modified operand. The data is unavailable while the store queue waiting to be updated in L1 cache.

- Instruction Fetch Interlock (IFI) reloads instructions as a result of stores into the instruction stream. This causes a pipeline flush, clearing the decoded instructions and re-fetching of instruction cache line which is very costly.

- Branch mis-prediction occurs if a branch takes place in another way than the processor has guessed. Branch prediction logic is very complex on z10 and z196.

The success of an in-order pipeline depends on its ability to minimize the performance penalties across instruction processing dependencies.

2.8.8. Super-Scalar Instruction Execution

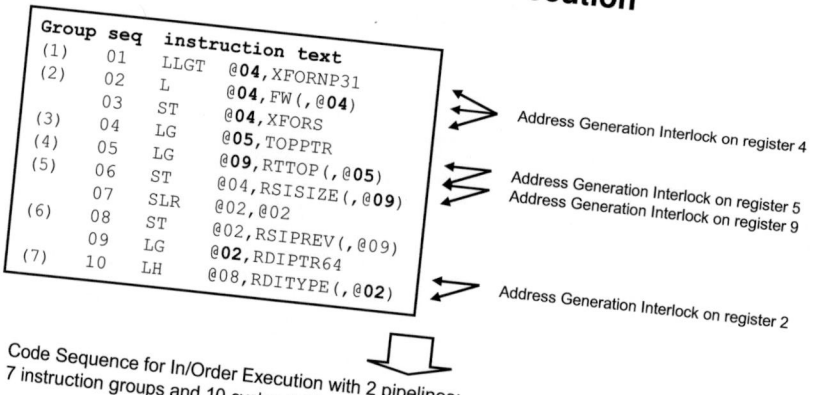

Figure 2.21.: Example of Super-Scalar Processing

The next step for speeding up instruction execution is to have multiple pipelines so that groups of instructions can flow through the pipelines. This was done the first time on System z with the z990 by introducing super-scalar processing. System z10 has two execution pipelines and the z196 has five of them.

Figure 2.21 shows an excerpt of a program consisting of 10 assembler instructions. The example shows how the code sequence can be executed with two instruction pipelines. By analyzing the code sequence it is necessary to maintain the sequence of the results. An address generating instruction must be performed before the following instructions which use its results. For example instruction 01 loads an address into register 4 and the two following instructions depend on the result of register 4. As a result instruction 01 must be executed before instructions 02 and 03 while instructions 02 and 03 can be executed in parallel. As a result instruction 01 is an instruction group (1) as well as instructions 02 and 03 which form instruction group (2). By analyzing the sequence of the program we can observe that 7 instruction groups can be created and that 10 cycles of address generation interlock delays occur.

The bottom of part of figure 2.21 shows that instruction pipelines are unequally filled. We can see that this example can still be improved and we will discuss improvements later. Also the instruction sequence is still maintained and it is a very good example for in order execution by using two instruction pipelines.

2.8.9. System z10 Microprocessor Pipeline

System z10 is a very good example to describe the techniques which we have discussed to so far. System z10 is a superscalar processor with up to two instructions which can be sent through at a given time. System z10 also has a much higher frequency than all previous processors. A z9 had a frequency of 1.7 GHz while z10 has 4.4 GHz. As a result the z10 has an instruction pipeline of 14 stages for fixed point instructions (z9 only had 6 stages). Even if the instruction set is complex most instructions are RISC like instructions. Restrictions on instructions which can be pipelined are for example:

- Either of the two instructions can be a branch instruction but not both
- Instructions which depend on each other can also not executed simultaneously as we saw in the previous example.

The second dependency can be mitigated by a technique called operand forwarding which typically works in cases when an arithmetic instruction depends on a load or a store on the result on an arithmetic instruction.

Figure 2.22 shows the microprocessor pipeline of a z10 processor. The pipeline is separated into instruction fetching, instruction decoding and issuing, storage access through data cache, execution including fixed point and floating point operations, and results check pointing. The instruction fetch unit (IFU) is designed to deliver instructions far ahead of processor execution along either the sequential or predicted branch path. The IFU also redirects the instruction fetch addresses during pipeline flushes, millicode execution entries and exits, and interrupts. The unit incorporates a 64 KB instruction cache and a 2-way 128-entry Translation Look-aside Buffer (TLB). The IFU incorporates the branch prediction tables which evaluate and keep track of the taken and not taken paths. Once valid instructions pass from the IFU to the instruction decode unit (IDU) they enter into the two-wide super-scalar pipeline. Two pipeline cycles D1 and D2 are used to decode the instruction set needed for instruction grouping and steering. This and other control information, such as storage access controls and branch handling, are then fed into an eight deep instruction queue and address queue. Two instructions are then brought into the grouping logic (D3) and three grouping stages G1 to G3 are needed to schedule up to two instructions into an execution group and to create a pipeline that handles hazard. This scheme assumes instruction execution to be done with a fixed number of number of cycles after issue and then involves rejecting and re-issuing instructions upon the detection of any pipeline hazard or reject condition. All stall conditions like AGI are evaluated in the two first stages G1 and G2 of the grouping and stage G3 issues the instructions or holds them back.

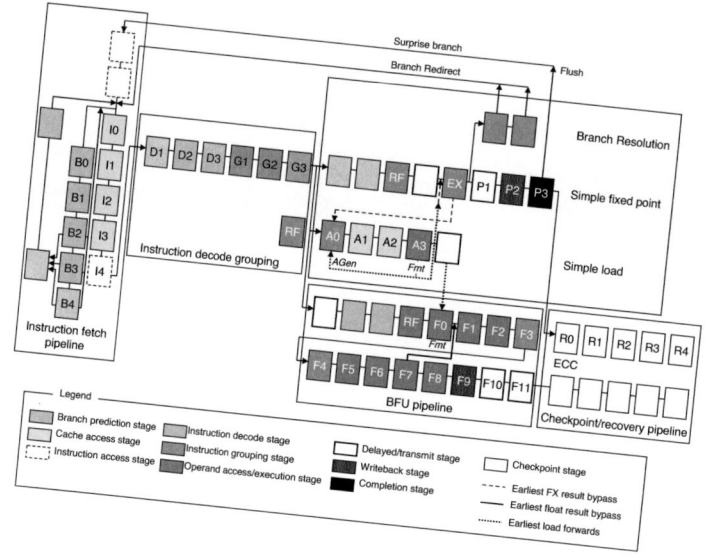

Figure 2.22.: System z10 Microprocessor Pipeline

2.8 Instruction Execution

Any issued instruction that requires storage access is processed through one of the two super-scalar pipes where the D-cache is first accessed (A0 to A2) and is then followed immediately by fixed point execution. Every pass through the pipeline can include both load and execute functions. The load/store unit (LSU) includes a 128 KB D-cache and a 2-way 512 entry TLB. The points where operand forwarding is possible in the pipeline is from step A3 to A0 and also from A3 to EX. Also the result from EX can be fed back to the address generation step A0. The two examples shown in figure 2.23 describe these result forwarding bypasses:

Example 1 shows that the result of the load instruction (R1) is used in the execute of the AR instruction

Example 2 shows that the result of the Add instruction (R1) is directly put away in the write back stage of the Store instruction.

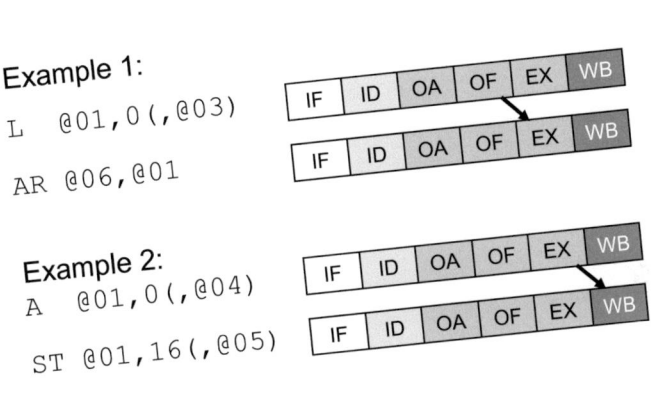

Figure 2.23.: Examples of Result Forwarding

Most instructions can be executed in the two FXU execution pipes in a single cycle; some less frequently used instructions, such as control operations, can be done only in the first pipe. Results are staged through two put-away cycles P1 and P2 before they are written into the general purpose registers (GPR) file or the LSU store buffer. The put away delays are added to allow time to suppress any premature GPR update from the second pipe in case of a branch miss-prediction in the first pipe. If there are no reject conditions, interruptions, or branch miss-prediction, the instruction is considered to be complete once all the results are available (P3).

Instructions executed in the binary floating-point unit (BFU) can be operated in pipeline mode, while instructions executed in the decimal floating-point unit (DFU) are non pipelined. During BFU and DFU operations, instruction information and operand data (from either the GPR or cache) is staged through the FXU. The resulting condition code or arithmetic exceptions are also sent back to the FXU for consolidation (F9/P1 and F10/P2) before instruction completion (F11/P3).

2.8.10. Instruction Re-Ordering

Figure 2.21 already showed an example how two processor pipelines can be filled with instructions. We also noticed that the two pipelines were not filled optimally. By going back to this example we can demonstrate how instruction re-ordering can improve the program execution.

There are some other effects which need to be noticed too. System z10 increased the clock frequency by 2.5 times compared to System z9. High frequency is great but may also have some negative effects:

- Some instructions can no longer be done in the shorter cycle time and now take more than one cycle to execute, for example instructions that involve sign propagation.

- Keeping the pipeline fed with instructions and data is very challenging.

- Some pipeline hazards are more costly. Longer cycles causes more cycles lost on reject/recycle and branch mis-predict.

On System z196 these challenges are addressed by out-of-order execution. The first step to fill the pipeline more efficiently and to try to reduce address generation interlocks by re-ordering code sequences. The re-ordering mechanism still maintains the logically order of dependent instructions but it is now possible to execute some independent instructions earlier to fill the two pipelines better. Figure 2.24 uses the same example as in 2.21 but now re-orders the code sequence. The bottom part shows the re-ordered sequence which consists of only 5 instruction groups and only 6 cycles of address generation interlock delays. This re-ordering attempts to execute instructions in parallel which do not have any dependency on each other. As a result the two instruction pipelines are much better filled and the execution delays are also significantly decreased.

This re-ordering example conceptually shows how code fragments can be optimized and it is not from a System z196 processor. System z196 uses instruction re-ordering but the example does not imply that the re-ordering would be close to what System z196 microprocessors would do.

2.8 Instruction Execution

Original Code Sequence: 7 instruction groups and 10 cycles AGI delay

AGI	seq	instruction text		seq	instruction text
	01	LLGT	@04,XFORNP31	03	ST @04,XFORS
<4>	02	L	@04,FW(,@04)		
	04	LG	@05,TOPPTR		
<2>	05	LG	@09,RTTOP(,@05)	07	SLR @02,@02
<2>	06	ST	@04,RSISIZE(,@09)	09	LG @02,RDIPTR64
	08	ST	@02,RSIPREV(,@09)		
<2>	10	LH	@08,RDITYPE(,@02)		

Reordered Code Sequence: 5 instruction groups and 6 cycles AGI delay

AGI	seq	instruction text		seq	instruction text
	01	LLGT	@04,XFORNP31	04	LG @05,TOPPTR
<2>	05	LG	@09,RTTOP(,@05)	07	SLR @02,@02
<2>	02	L	@04,FW(,@04)	06	ST @04,RSISIZE(,@09)
	08	ST	@02,RSIPREV(,@09)	09	LG @02,RDIPTR64
<2>	03	ST	@04,XFORS	10	LH @08,RDITYPE(,@02)

Figure 2.24.: Example of Instruction Re-Ordering

2.8.11. Register Renaming

The next possible improvement can be achieved by using a larger set of internal registers than external registers which are available for the programs. For example the code sequence shown in figure 2.25 does not allow that the LOAD operation in instruction (3) could be executed at the same time or before the AR instruction from (2) because both use Register 1. With additional internal registers and mapping of instructions to internal registers it is possible to keep the value from LOAD operation prior to the AR operation in one register P1 and the result from the second LOAD operation in another internal register P2. By re-assigning or re-naming the registers it is now possible to either execute the second LOAD instruction at the same time of any of the other instructions or potentially even before them.

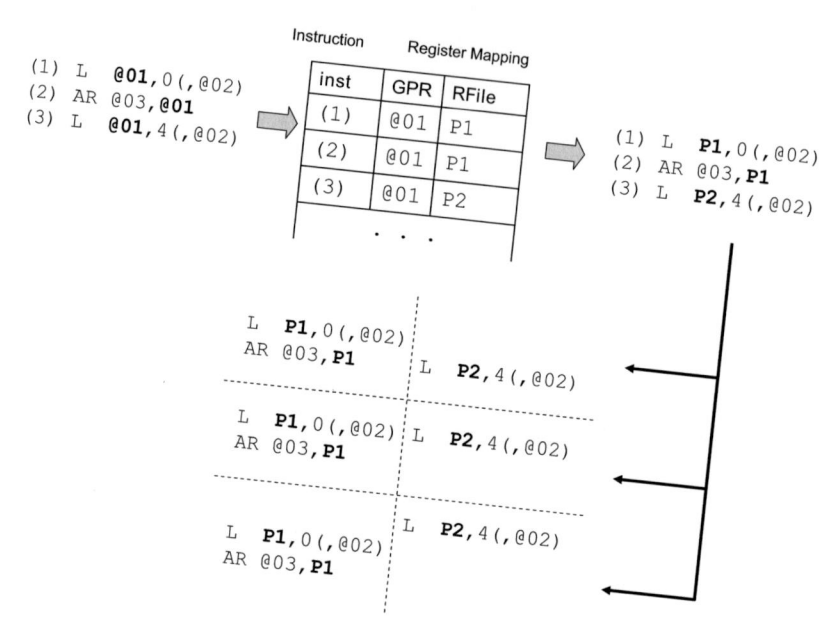

Figure 2.25.: Example for Register Renaming

Instruction Format	Example	Corresponding RISC Micro Operations
Register-Storage (RX)	A R1,D2(X2,B2)	LOAD REG <- D2(X2,B2) ADD R1,REG
Storage-Storage (RS)	MVC D1(L,B1),D2(B2) Condition: L ≤ 8 bytes	LOAD REG <- D2(B2) STORE REG -> D1(B1)
Reg-Reg-Storage (RS)	CS R1,R3,D2(B2) Function: IF R1 == D2(B2) THEN STORE R3 -> D2(B2) ELSE LOAD R1 <- D2(B2)	LOAD REG <- D2(B2) STORE PRETEST COMPARE R1,REG ----- scartch CC STORE R3 -> D2(B2)

Table 2.6.: Examples for Decomposing CISC Instructions into RISC Micro-Operations

2.8.12. Instruction Cracking

System z196 is more RISC-like than its predecessors. The technique which contributes to it is named cracking and it breaks up complex instructions into its atomic micro operations which can be executed in one processor cycle. Table 2.6 shows 3 examples of typical System z instructions:

- System z has many register-to-storage operations (RX format). Such an operation can be broken up into two micro operations. The ADD operation for example into a LOAD data from storage into an internal register, named REG and then followed by an ADD operation which adds the content of REG to R1.

- Another example exists for the move character (MVC) operation which copies data from one storage location to another. If the length value is less or equal 8 bytes the operation can be executed by a LOAD followed by a STORE operation.

- More complex is the last example in table 2.6. The operation is named compare and swap (CS) which is an atomic instruction used to implement access to locks[5]. The function of the operation is that the content of the storage location is compared with the content of R1 and based on the result either the content of R3 is saved to the storage location or the content of the location is saved in R1. If the storage location described by D2(B2) is a lock the instruction allows to set a use indicator into the lock to prevent other programs from using the protected resource. The instruction can be cracked into two groups of micro operations: A LOAD of the content from storage to an internal register and a test whether it is possible to store anything at the designated location followed by a compare of the content of the internal register with R1. The second set of micro operation is a STORE of R3 to the storage location depending on how the condition code is set from the STORE PRETEST[6] or COMPARE.

2.8.13. Out-Of-Order Execution

Figure 2.26 shows a simplistic example of how cracking, renaming, superscalar and out-of-order processing work together. The short program segment adds to number pairs, stores the sum and then copies a short string. A, B, C,

---

[5]We will discuss this instruction later again
[6]STORE PRETEST tests whether storing R3 to the storage location described by D2(B2) is possible at all. If not the operation is canceled and an exception is generated.

D, E, F, G, and H symbolize storage locations in this example. The RX type ADD and the SS type MVC instruction are cracked into two micro operations as shown in the previous example. The next step is to rename R1 dependent on the instruction where it is used. For the MVC instruction one internal register is used to keep the content of storage location H. After renaming 5 internal registers are being used. All inter instruction dependencies between the two number add pairs are removed. Finally execution groups are created. This depends very much on how much of the data is already in L1 cache. The upper example assumes that all data is already in L1 cache and the 10 micro operations can be executed in 4 execution groups. However, if one or more storage operands are not in L1 data cache, then there are delays in the pipe and the real-time execution grouping will be different. The lower alternative grouping would result if none of the operands are in L1 data cache.

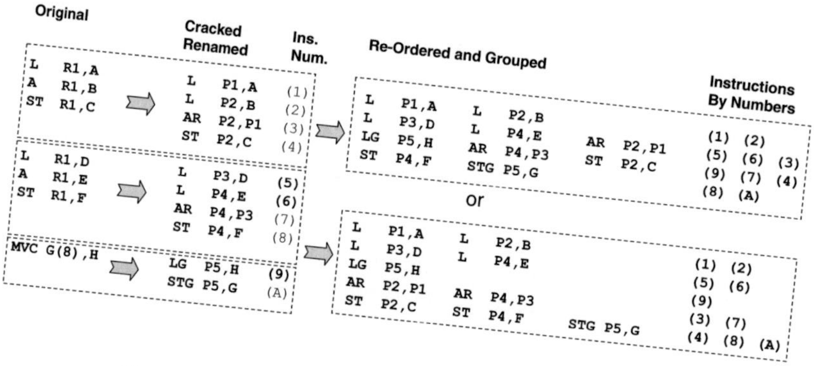

Figure 2.26.: Example for Out-Of-Order Execution

This exposes another advantage of super-scalar and out-of-order execution. The processor can detect earlier that data items need to be loaded into cache and can launch multiple fetch requests simultaneously. If the instructions were executed single file and in-order, the program would sequentially experience a cache delay on each instruction. But with super-scalar and out-of-order processing, using the lower grouping, five of the required fetches would be launched in the first three cycles, and accesses would be substantially overlapped providing a significant speed-iup of the program.

2.8.14. System z196 Microprocessor Core

Figure 2.27 shows the components of a z196 microprocessor. The processing flow can be roughly divided into two phases: the front-end processing with branch predicting, instruction fetching and decoding and the instruction or better out of order micro operation execution.

The branch prediction runs asynchronously ahead of instruction fetching and pre-fetches instructions from L2 or higher level caches into the 64KB L1 instruction cache. The z196 microprocessor fetches up to 3 CISC instructions per cycle from the I-Cache for decoding.

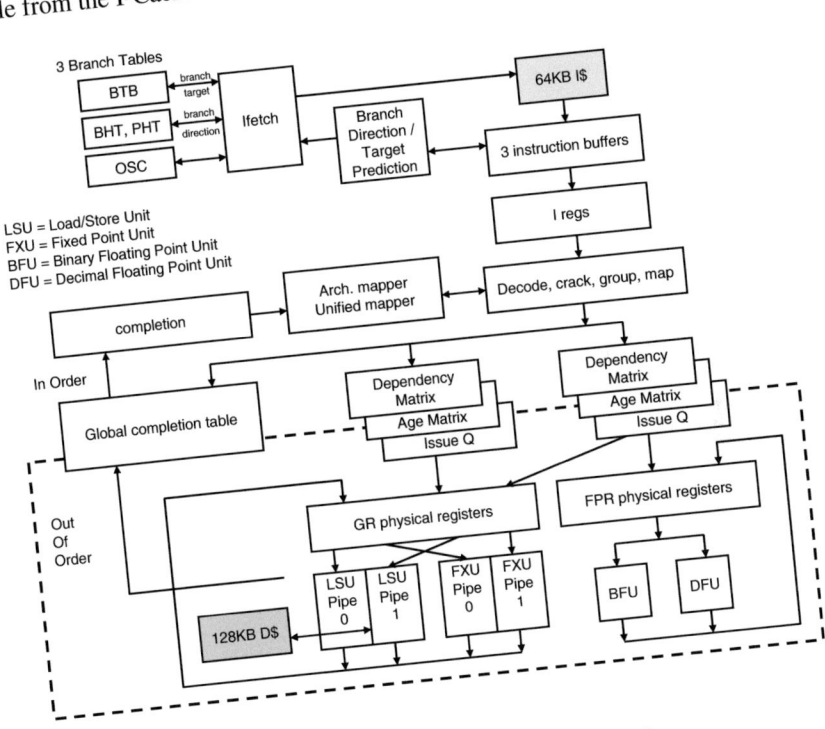

Figure 2.27.: System z196 Microprocessor Core

The decoding process also encompasses the cracking, grouping and register renaming of the instructions. In the next step the dependencies between the micro operation and instructions are book kept in a dependency matrix. Based on the age of the micro operations in the pipeline they are being issued for execution. The issue queue can keep up to 72 micro operations and instructions in flight. The z196 microprocessor contains 2 fixed point arithmetic instruction units (FXU), 2 load and store units (LSU) and a binary (BFU) and a decimal (DFU) floating point execution unit. The issue queue consists of two halves. One half drives one LSU, one FXU and either the BFU or DFU execution units. The other half drives the other LSU and FXU. As a result up to 5 micro operations can be executed per cycle.

The z196 tracks instructions as groups of up to three micro operations. A group is completed when the previous group has completed and all micro operations of the next-to-complete group have finished without errors. Up to 1 group can be completed per cycle. Completion can be stalled for multiple cycles so that all error checking information can be propagated to the centralized completion logic. The global completion table keeps track of the groups of instruction to be completed.

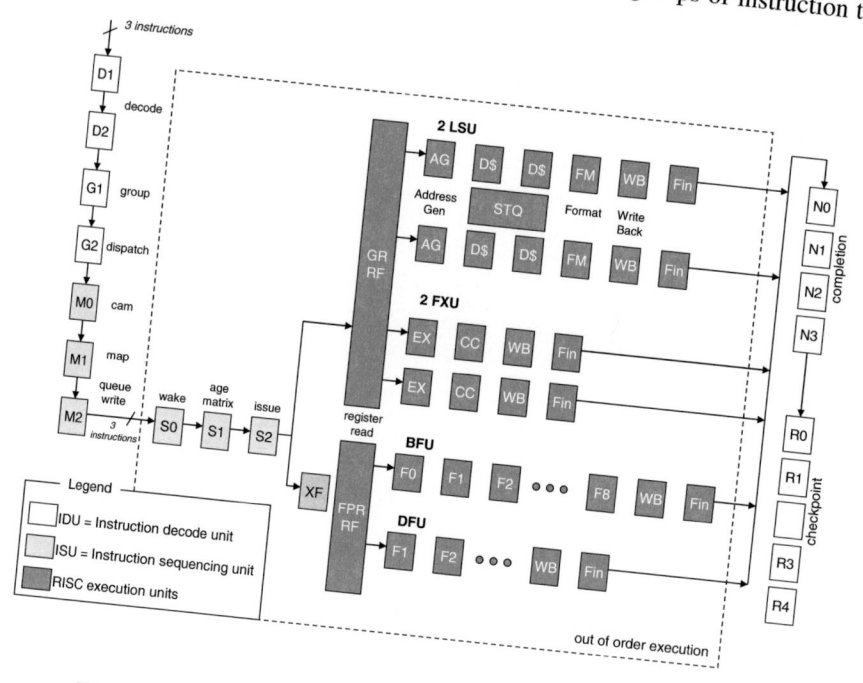

Figure 2.28.: System z196 Microprocessor Execution Pipeline

Figure 2.28 shows the execution pipeline of a z196 microprocessor. Compared to the System z10 pipeline (see figure 2.22) the pipeline for fixed point arith-

2.8 Instruction Execution

metic instructions grows from 14 to 15 to 17 stages. Similar to the z10 microprocessor results of previous completed instructions can be forwarded. The dependencies are kept in the dependency matrix.

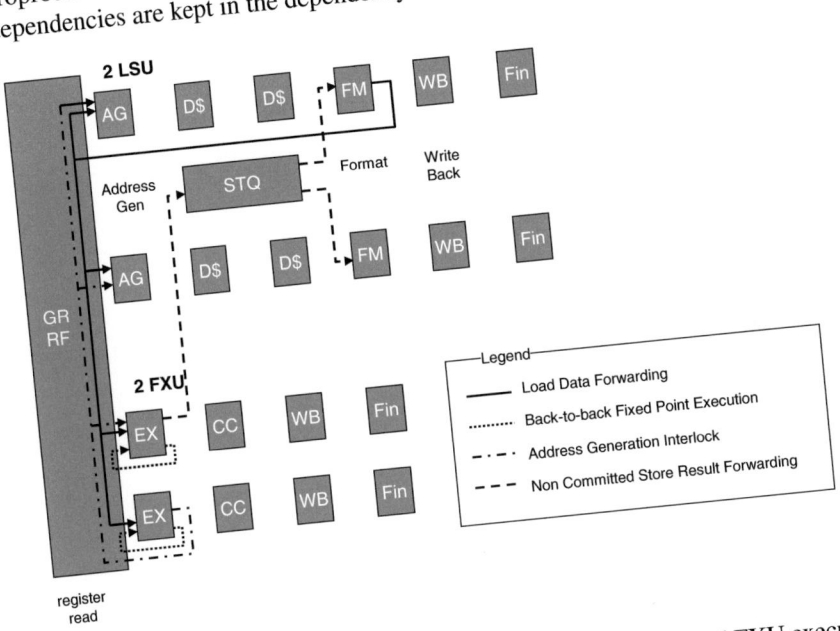

Figure 2.29.: Result Forwarding within the System z196 LSU and FXU execution units

Figure 2.29 shows only the LSU and FXU parts of the pipeline and the possible result forwards. After a LOAD instruction the result can be forwarded to be loaded in the next micro operation. Arithmetic operations can forward their result to follow-on arithmetic instructions, or to resolve address generation interlocks. In cases where the execution of instructions is not predictable the results of an instruction can be kept in a Store Queue (STQ). This helps LOAD operations which need logically be executed after STORE operations. If the STORE operation has completed and has placed its result in the STQ the LOAD operation can use the result directly. If the store data is not in the store queue the LOAD instruction is rejected and re-issued until the store data is either in the STQ or L1 data cache. A similar Store/Load hazard exists for STORE operations which depend on the execution of a LOAD instruction (Load data forwarding). The data from the previous executed instruction is kept in the register file (also referred to as load data queue) for the not yet completed micro operation.

2.8.15. System z196 Instruction Handling

System z196 consists of out-of-order execution units which process RISC like micro-operations but the System z instruction set is a CISC instruction set. When we take a look at the 1079 instructions which are currently supported on System z196 we can characterize them in the following categories:

- 340 instructions are RISC like instructions and can be mapped to a single micro operation

- 269 instructions can be cracked at issue and decomposed in a LOAD or STORE and register-to-register operation or LOAD and STORE operations like the AR and MVC instruction shown in table 2.6.

- 211 additional medium complex instructions are cracked in micro-operations when they are decoded.

- 219 instructions are more complex and they are executed by millicode programs.

- 24 instructions are conditionally millicoded and 16 instructions are storage sequencer.

2.8.16. System z196 Instruction Optimization

Compared with System 360 (143 instructions) from 1970 the instruction set has grown by a large extent. Even System p only supports 700 instructions from which nearly half are vector related operations. At the end of the excursion to instructions and how they are optimized on z10 and z196 processors we will take a look at new instructions which have been introduced for z196 processors to improve program execution. Considering the C++ code line and its translation to assembler code by the gnu compiler as shown in figure 2.30 we can observe that it results in an AGI delay and a possible branch miss prediction, both reasons to hold up the execution speed in processors with long instruction pipelines.

Every new System z generation introduces a set of new instructions for optimization reasons. This is one reason for the growth of the instruction set from 143 to 1079 instructions. For this specific example we will take a look at an instruction which has been introduced for z196. The instruction can be used by

2.8 Instruction Execution

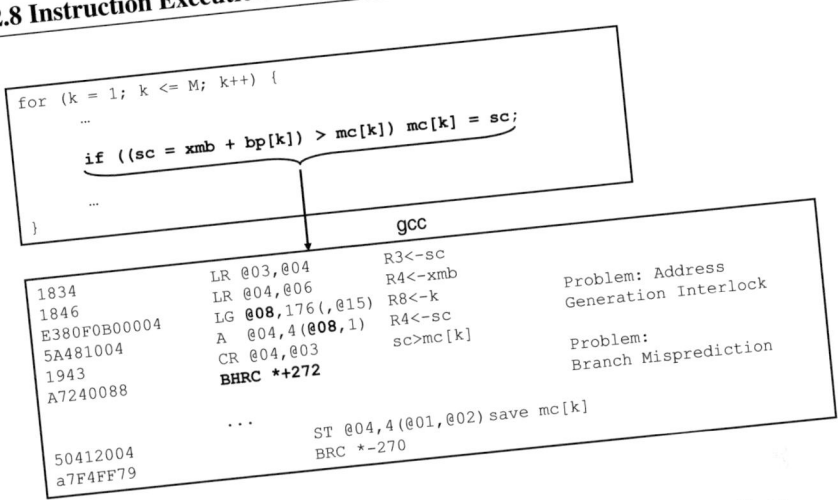

Figure 2.30.: Instruction Execution on older System z generations

a compiler to optimize code segments such the one which we are discussing. This conditional code sequence is often used in programs that the value of a table entry is modified depending on whether a new computed value is larger or not. In order to avoid the possible branch miss prediction it is helpful to load the result for the new table entry only if the previous compare operation has set a certain condition code. The LOAD ON CONDITION (LOCR) (see figure 2.31) instruction has been introduced to satisfy this requirement. The instruction loads the second operand to the location of the first operand if the Condition Code (CC) meets the condition specified by M3. Otherwise the first operand is not changed.

LOCR R1,R2,M3   **RRF-c**

B9F2	M3	/ / / /	R1	R2
0	16	20	24	28 31

Figure 2.31.: LOAD ON CONDITION (LOCR) Instruction

With the new instruction the assembler code sequence becomes significantly shorter. The advantage of the new LOCR instruction is that the pipeline is no longer flushed on a branch miss prediction thus reducing the execution steps significantly. In the present example it also resolves an AGI delay and further reduces the path length (see figure 2.32).

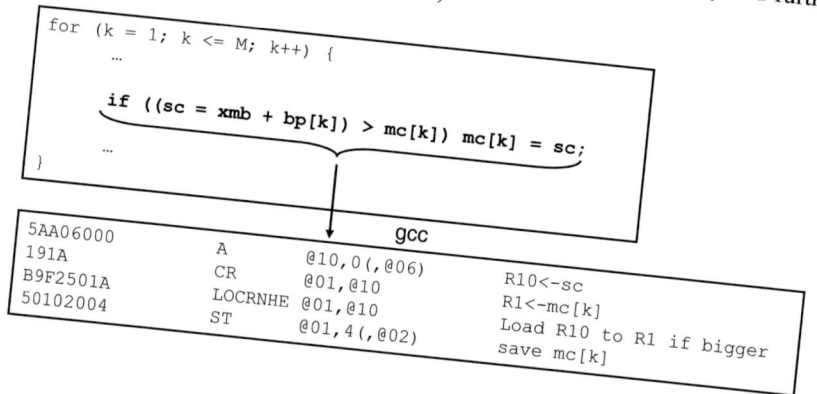

Figure 2.32.: Optimized instruction sequence by using LOCR

In figure 2.32 LOCRNHE is used which is an extended mnemonic created by the High Level Assembler (HLASM) for the LOCR instruction and M3 bit settings of 1100 (not high). HLASM supports extended mnemonics for all instructions depending on condition flags. It must also be noted that LOCR is just one example to demonstrate that hardware scalability also depends on optimizing the instruction set in order to allow compilers to generate more efficient code sequences.

For z196 new instructions were introduced which address three major areas of performance improvements:

1. New load, store and arithmetic operations to operate directly on the high word of a general purpose register. Also new branch and compare instructions that operate directly on high words have been added[7].

2. A set of new non destructive integer arithmetic instructions which include shift, add, subtract and logical operations. The traditional instruction architecture usually consists of two operands of which one keeps the result after execution. The original value has been destroyed. If software still requires both operands it must first copy the operand being overwritten to another register. The new operations eliminate this additional copy operation which is beneficial for some compilers.

---

[7]For details see [24]

3. Finally the LOAD ON COMPARE instructions as discussed in the previous example.

2.8.17. System z196 Microprocessor Summary

At the end of this section we should summarize what we learned from instruction execution on System z. With the high improvement on frequency of the z10 and even more the z196 microprocessor to previous generations a more sophisticated microprocessor design became necessary to really exploit the much higher clock speed. One aspect was the introduction of additional cache levels on z10 and z196 compared to z9 and older generations. In addition z196 introduces out-of-order processing to further improve the execution of instruction execution and we also have to mention comprehensive branch prediction methods which we didn't discuss in detail.

But that is not all. Each generation of System z also attempts to improve the instruction set compared to older generations. The LOCR instruction is an example to introduce an instruction which is very beneficial for program execution and which is primarily used by compilers. The LOCR instruction is also a very good example of a CISC instruction which provides significant benefit even if it seems to be rather complex at a first glance. In later segments we will see that the microprocessor design is not the only denominating factor to use the high processor frequency efficiently. This already shows that scalability of one processor generation to the next is not a simple enhancement of hardware but it also requires significant advances of the exploiting technologies.

2.9. Interrupts

Interrupts permit the CPU to change state as a result of an external event which typically comes from outside the system. Interrupts are also the cause how new program execution is started in the system as a result of the interrupt processing. To permit fast response to conditions of high priority and immediate recognition of the type of condition, interruption conditions are grouped into six classes: external, input/output, machine check, program, restart, and supervisor call.

Supervisor calls or SVC interrupts
These interrupts occur when the program issues an SVC to request a particular system service. An SVC interrupts the program being exe-

cuted and passes control to the supervisor so that it can perform the service. Programs request these services through macros such as OPEN (open a file), GETMAIN (obtain storage), or WTO (write a message to the system operator).

I/O interrupts

These interrupts occur when the channel subsystem signals a change of status, such as an input/output (I/O) operation completing, an error occurring, or an I/O device such as a printer has become ready for work.

External interrupts

These interrupts can indicate any of several events, such as a time interval expiring, the operator pressing the interrupt key on the console, or the processor receiving a signal from another processor.

Restart interrupts

These interrupts occur when the operator selects the restart function at the console or when a restart SIGP (signal processor) instruction is received from another processor.

Program interrupts

These interrupts are caused by program errors (for example, the program attempts to perform an invalid operation), page faults (the program references a page that is not in central storage), or requests to monitor an event.

Machine check interrupts

These interrupts are caused by machine malfunctions. When an interrupt occurs, the hardware saves pertinent information about the program that was interrupted and, if possible, disables the processor for further interrupts of the same type. The hardware then routes control to the appropriate interrupt handler routine. The program status word or PSW is a key resource in this process.

When an interrupt occurs the running program is interrupted and the PSW is stored and a new PSW which starts the interrupt processing is loaded. No registers are saved. This is done by software typically the interrupt handler of the operating systems, see Chapter 3. The six classes of interrupts are distinguished by the storage location at which the old PSW is stored and the from which the new PSW is fetched, see figure 2.7. For most classes, the causes are further identified by an interruption code and, for some classes, by additional information placed in permanently assigned real storage locations during the interruption. For external, program, and supervisor-call interruptions, the interruption

2.9 Interrupts

Real Address	Content
0x120 - 0x12F	Restart old PSW
0x130 - 0x13F	External old PSW
0x140 - 0x14F	Supervisor-call old PSW
0x150 - 0x15F	Program old PSW
0x160 - 0x16F	Machine-check old PSW
0x170 - 0x17F	IO old PSW
0x1A0 - 0x1AF	Restart new PSW
0x1B0 - 0x1BF	External new PSW
0x1C0 - 0x1CF	Supervisor-call new PSW
0x1D0 - 0x1DF	Program new PSW
0x1E0 - 0x1EF	Machine-check new PSW
0x1F0 - 0x1FF	IO new PSW

Table 2.7.: Interrupt Locations

code consists of 16 bits. For I/O interruptions the interruption code consists of 32 bits, and for machine-check interruptions of 64 bits. The interruption codes are stored at real address locations.

2.9.1. Enabling and Disabling

By means of mask bits in the current PSW, floating-point-control (FPC) register, and control registers, the CPU may be enabled or disabled for all external, I/O, and machine-check interruptions and for some program interruptions. When a mask bit is one, the CPU is enabled for the corresponding class of interruptions, and those interruptions can occur. When a mask bit is zero, the CPU is disabled for the corresponding interruptions. The conditions that cause I/O interruptions remain pending. External interruption conditions either remain pending or persist until the cause is removed. Machine-check-interruption conditions, depending on the type, are ignored, remain pending, or cause the CPU to enter the check-stop state. When a program interrupt is disabled, it is ignored and not left pending for later. The result of the operation is indicated in the cc. Finally IEEE exceptions set flags in the FPC register.

60

z/Architecture

Detailed description for interrupt processing can be found in [31] especially in chapter 5 and 6.

2.10. Timing Facilities

The timing facilities include three facilities for measuring time: the Time-of-Day (TOD) clock, the clock comparator, and the CPU timer. A TOD programmable register is associated with the TOD clock. The TOD clock is shared by all CPUs. Each CPU has its own clock comparator, CPU timer, and TOD programmable register.

2.10.1. Time-of-Day Clock

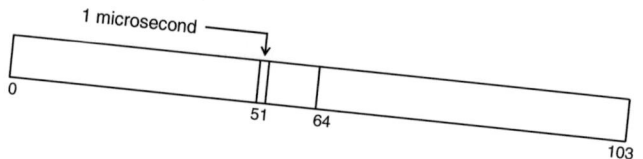

Figure 2.33.: Time of Day Clock

The TOD clock is a 104 bit register. It is a binary counter with the format shown in figure 2.33. The clock is nominally incremented by adding a one in bit position 51 which corresponds to one microsecond. In models having a higher or lower resolution, a different bit position is incremented at a frequency that the rate of advancing the clock is the same as if a one were added in bit position 51.

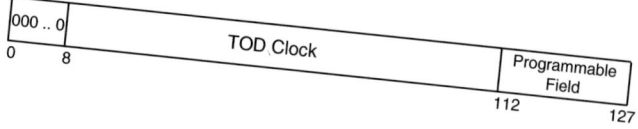

Figure 2.34.: Time of Day Clock Extended Format

A value of zero in the TOD clock is defined as January 1st, 1900, 00:00:00 UTC. The clock roughly overflows after 143 years so that the last possible date before an overflow is September 17th, 2042, 23:53:47 UTC.

2.10 Timing Facilities

The instruction STORE CLOCK (STCK) returns the first 64 bits of the Time-of-day clock and saves them into a 64 bit register. The instruction STORE CLOCK EXTENDED (STCKE) returns 128 bits for higher resolution.

The extended Time of Day Clock contains a leading byte which is currently 0 and which will be used after September 17th, 2042 to use the TOD clock for an extended period. The additional 8 bits are good until the year 38400 A.D. (see figure 2.34). For the extended format the microsecond is represented in bit position 59 and bit 111 equals a precision of 222×10^{-24}. The programmable field is used to generate a unique value and can be set by the instruction SET CLOCK PROGRAMMABLE FIELD (SCKPF).

TOD Clock Steering

TOD-clock steering provides a means to change the apparent stepping rate of the TOD clock without changing the physical hardware oscillator which steps the physical clock. This is accomplished by means of a TOD-offset register which is added to the physical clock to produce a logical-TOD-clock value.

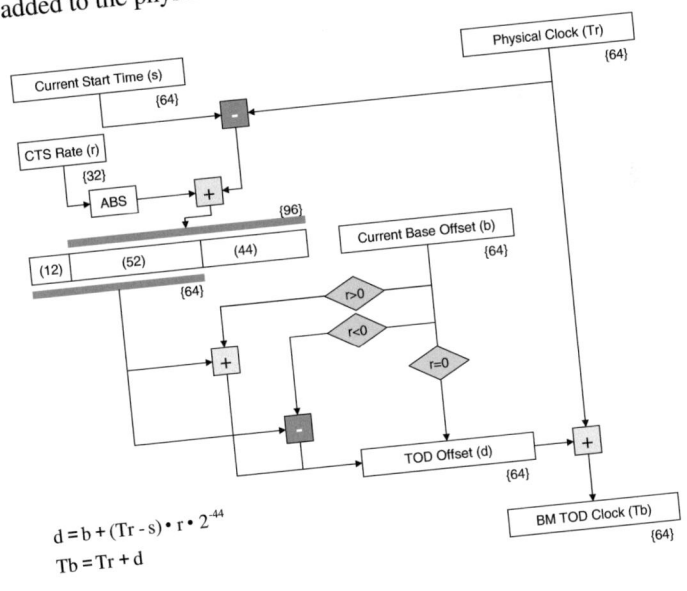

$$d = b + (Tr - s) \cdot r \cdot 2^{-44}$$
$$Tb = Tr + d$$

Figure 2.35.: TOD Clock Steering

Figure 2.35 shows how the Base Machine (BM) TOD Clock is derived from the Physical Clock (Tr) by adding the TOD Offset (d). The TOD Offset is calculated from a Base Offset (b) to which the first 64 bits of the result from the multiplication of the current start time (s) with the steering rate (r). By using the first 64 bits from the 96 bit result the value is automatically shifted by 44 bit positions and therefore multiplied with 2^{-44}. The steering is added if the steering rate is positive and deducted from the base offset if it is negative. If the steering rate is zero the base offset is directly used as TOD Offset.

The steering rate is calculated from a fine- and gross- steering rate:

Fine-steering rate is used to correct the inaccuracy in the local oscillator, which is stable over a relatively long period of time. The value normally is less than the specified tolerance of the local oscillator. The change occurs infrequently (on the order of once a day to once a week) and is small.

Gross-steering rate is used as a dynamic correction for all other effects, the most predominant being to synchronize time with an external time source or with other clocks in the timing network. The value normally changes frequently (on the order of once per second to once per minute).

2.10.2. Clock Comparator

Each CPU has a clock comparator which has the same format than the TOD clock. It is used to set a time value which is compared to the TOD clock. When the clock comparator is set and the value is less than the value of the TOD clock an external interrupt is generated.

2.10.3. CPU Timer

Each CPU also has a CPU timer. The CPU timer format is the same as the format of the TOD clock. Typically a value is set and the CPU timer is stepped backwards. When the timer expires, meaning it reaches a negative value, the timer requests an external interrupt. The CPU Timer stops when the CPU is in check stop state. Some instructions allow to set the CPU timer (SPT) and read it (STPT, and ECTG).

The CPU timer might step at a different speed that the TOD clock because it is only decremented when the CPU executes a unit of work. For a virtual system the logical CPU timer is stepped when the logical CPU is dispatched on a physical CPU. So it is not possible to tell in advance which timer expires first if the clock comparator is set to TOD clock plus 5 seconds and the CPU timer is set to 2 seconds.

2.11. Storage Addressing

2.11.1. Address Types

PSW Bits					Handling of Addresses	
5	16	17	DAT	Mode	Instruction Adresses	Logical Addresses
0	0	0	Off	Real mode	Real	Real
0	0	1	Off	Real mode	Real	Real
0	1	0	Off	Real mode	Real	Real
0	1	1	Off	Real mode	Real	Real
1	0	0	On	Primary-space mode	Primary virtual	Primary virtual
1	0	1	On	Access-register mode	Primary virtual	AR-specified virtual
1	1	0	On	Secondary-space mode	Primary virtual	Secondary virtual
1	1	1	On	Home-space mode	Home virtual	Home virtual

Table 2.8.: Handling of Virtual Addresses

Three basic types of addresses are recognized: absolute, real, and virtual. The addresses are distinguished on the basis of the transformations that are applied to the address during storage access. Address translation converts virtual to real and prefixing converts real to absolute. In addition to the three basic types, additional types are defined which are treated as one or another of the three basic types, depending on the instruction and the current mode, see table 2.8:

Absolute Address is the address assigned to a main-storage location.

Real Address identifies a location in real storage. A real address is converted to an absolute address by means of prefixing.

Virtual Address identifies a location in virtual storage. It is translated by using dynamic address translation to a real address or directly to an absolute address.

Logical Address specifies the storage-operand addresses for most instructions. Whether a logical address is treated as a real address or a virtual address is specified by PSW bits.

Instruction Address is the address used to fetch instructions from storage. In the same way as for logical addresses it is interpreted as a real or virtual address depending on the mode setting in the PSW.

Virtual Address Sub-classification is used to determine to which address space control element the actual instruction or logical addresses refer to. The address space control element points to an address space which doesn't have to be the address space where the program is located in. System z architecture distinguishes between primary, secondary, home, and AR specified address spaces. Depending on the mode the address space control element of CR1 is used for primary address space, CR7 for secondary address space, CR13 for home address space, or the ASCE specified by an Access Register. In Chapter 3 we will discuss addressing modes in more detail when we take a look at data exchange between address spaces.

2.11.2. Dynamic Address Translation

All operating systems on System z use virtual storage which allows to provide a much bigger storage to the applications than the storage which is actually installed. For this purpose the concept of an address space is used which maps the virtual storage for executable programs. We will discuss later how the address space mapping looks for z/OS.

The virtual storage is created by multi level lookup tables in storage that describe the the virtual-to-real address translation. This process is called dynamic address translation and depicted in figure 2.36.

The 64 bit virtual address consists of 6 parts:

BX The Base index (12 bits) addresses 4096 bytes which make up 1 page

PX The Page Table index (8 bits) address 256 pages (1,048,576 bytes or 1 MB) which make up 1 segment

SX The Segment Table index (11 bits) address 2048 segments (2,147,483,648 bytes or 2 GB)

RSX The Region Second Table index (11 bits) address additional 2048 segments or regions (4 TB)

2.11 Storage Addressing

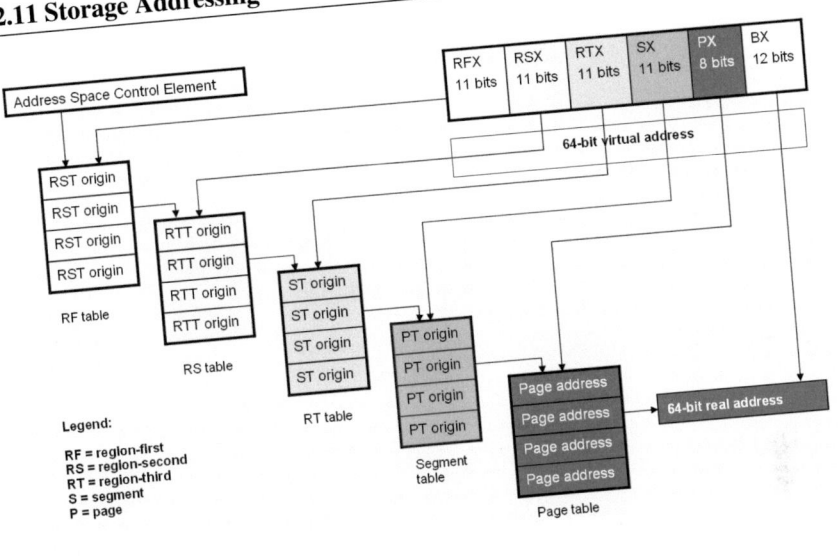

Figure 2.36.: System z Dynamic Address Translation

RTX The Region Third Table index (11 bits) and now 8 PB[8]

RFX The Region First Table index (11 bits) up to 16 EB[9]

The base of the address space is described by the address space control element which is contained in control registers 1, 7, 13, or are described by access registers. The address space control element provides the pointer to the first region or segment table. It is obvious by this enumeration that the process of dynamic address translation is not for free. Therefore it is possible to use only parts of the region control tables. If only 4 TB are installed on a system which is still the case for most environments only one region control index is required for addressing the storage. Another way to speed up the addressing is by Transaction Look-aside Buffers (TLB) which are contained in L1 storage of the CPUs.

Each CPU has its own TLB. The TLB is filled by hardware automatically as the program executes. When the DAT tables are changed, the TLB entries are purged too.

---

[8] 8 Peta Byte
[9] 16 Exa Byte

2.11.3. Large Page Support

With the growing size of storage - especially virtual storage -, page tables become huge. One page table entry covers 4KB of data and requires 8 bytes of storage. This means that the page tables to map 4GB of storage already require 8MB storage. This is a limitation which is addressed by large storage pages. A large storage page is a 1 MB area and eliminates the need for 256 page table entries. The segment table entry now references directly to a large page instead of a page table in this mode (see figure 2.37).

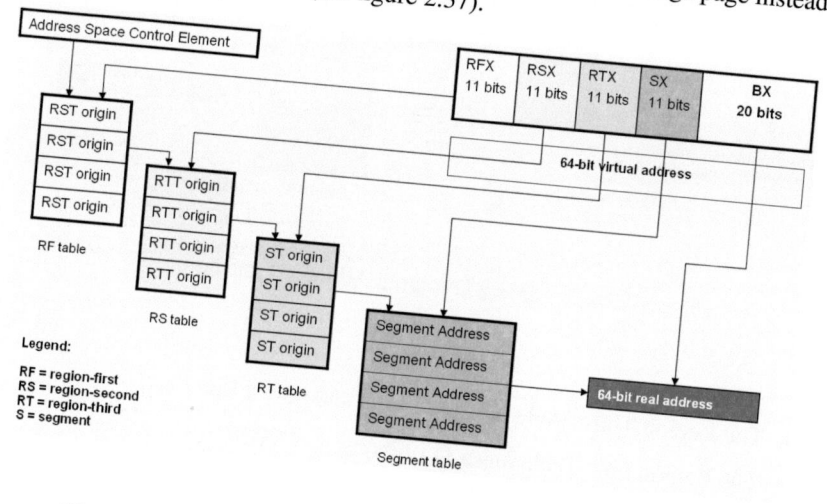

Figure 2.37.: Dynamic Address Translation for Large Pages

2.11.4. Storage Protection

Figure 2.38 depicts the key storage protection mechanism. A storage key is associated with each 4K-byte block of real storage. The storage key consists of 7 bits: 4 access control bits, a fetch protection bit, a reference bit and a change bit. The access control bits correspond to the storage key. The meaning of the storage keys is interpreted by the operating systems. For example in z/OS key 0 to 7 is for privileged users and key 8 to 15 for non privileged users. the fetch protection bit prevents storage alteration if the Key relation does not exists and also prevents fetching storage if the PSW key is not 0. The exception is if the P bit (bit 15 of the PSW) is zero and indicates that the CPU executes in supervisor state.

2.11 Storage Addressing

The other form of storage protection is DAT or page protection. The P bit in the page table entry can be set to 1 thus indicating that the 4KB page cannot be altered. This is used, for instance, to implement the POSIX fork() function. The P bit is also present in the segment table entry to protect an entire segment from being altered and starting with System z10 also in all region table entries which prevent storage alteration for large sections of the entire memory.

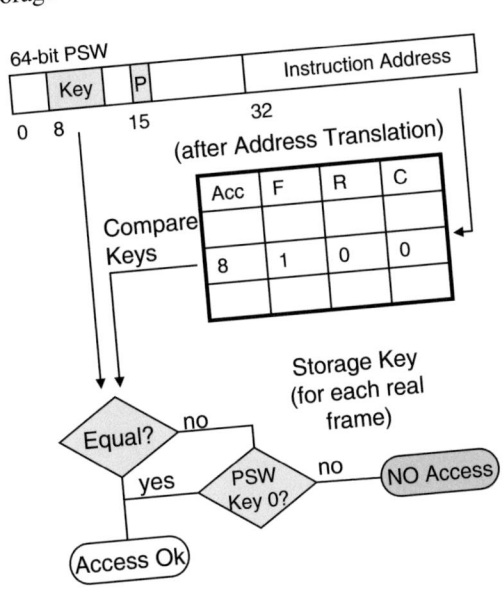

Figure 2.38.: Storage Protection

2.11.5. Prefixing

The low address range of main memory is used to exchange information between the system (hardware) and software (operating systems, Hypervisor). These storage locations are located in the address range 0 to 0x1FFF of real storage and named assigned storage locations or prefixed save area. Each CPU now must manage their own information therefore the storage location for each CPU must be mapped to a different place in absolute storage. This is accomplished by using a prefix register for each CPU which specifies this absolute address. The prefix registers for the CPUs are set by the operating systems.

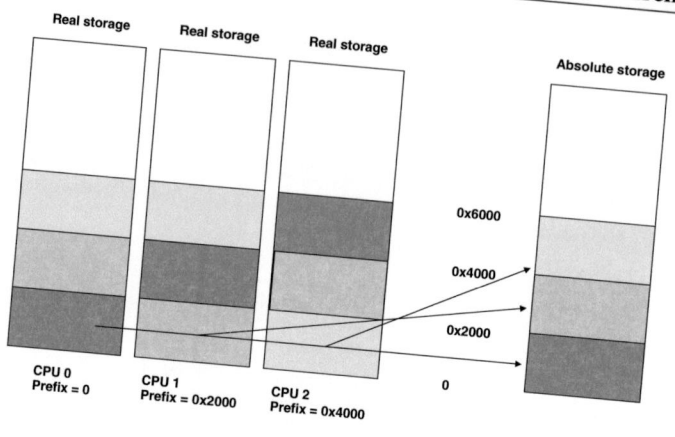

Figure 2.39.: Prefixing

The example shown figure 2.39 assumes that the Prefix Register for CPU 2 contains 0x4000. The assigned storage location for CPU2 which is located at real address 0 to 0x1FFF is now converted to absolute address 0x4000 to 0x5FFF. The prefix register always has the effect that the real storage range of 0 to 0x1FFF and the absolute storage range from the base value of the prefix register up to this value plus 0x1FFF are swapped. This also allows to go backward from absolute storage and find the real storage locations for the assigned storage of each CPU.

2.12. Multiprocessing

The multiprocessing facility provides the interconnection of CPUs, including shared main storage, CPU-to-CPU interconnect, and TOD-clock synchronization. The CPU-to-CPU interconnect is done by Signal Processor (SIGP) and a CPU address which is a unique number in the configuration. SIGP allows a CPU to modify the state of other CPUs by Starting them when the CPU is stopped state, by accepting external interrupts and by reporting CPU errors.

2.12.1. Atomic Instructions

The second part of multiprocessing is to provide a set of atomic instructions which are not interruptible and which allow to update atomic variables:

TS TEST AND SET is an old instruction which is primarily used for compatibility with System/360. The instruction sets the condition code based on the value of a storage location and sets the storage location to all ones.

CS COMPARE AND SWAP tests a storage location against a reference value and modifies it if the location hasn't changed. the instruction and all of its companions can be used to implement locks. We already discussed this instruction from the point of Instruction Cracking in Section 2.8.12.

PLO PERFORM LOCKED OPERATION can be used for complex locking protocols of up to 8 operands. The instruction only locks against other PLO locks.

LAA LOAD AND ADD performs an ADD operation and modifies the content of a storage location. This instruction provides an atomic operation without using a CS instruction to lock the storage location against alterations. The instruction has been introduced to satisfy the needs of compilers for example the GCC compiler for the _sync_fetch_and_add() built-in operations similar to the optimization discussed for the LOCR instruction in section 2.8.15. LAA is the basic example for a complete set of instructions provided with z196, see [31] chapter 7.

```
              LHI    @01,-1           create lock (0xFFFFFFFF)
              LHI    @00,0            create expected lock (0)
LOOP          CS     @00,@01,LOCK     if LOCK = 0,
                                      store R1 into LOCK
*             BRNZ   LOOP             didnt get the lock, try again

                                      proceed
*
DONE          ...
              ...                     full word
LOCK          DS     F
```

Figure 2.40.: Compare And Swap Example

For using an instruction like CS in a multiprocessing environment it is necessary to take a closer look how the instruction operates and which problems may take place. Consider the example for the COMPARE AND SWAP instruction shown in figure 2.40. The CS instruction tests the value of LOCK which is a storage location against the value in register 0 and if both are equal it saves register 1 to the location of LOCK indicating that the LOCK has been obtained.

```
            LHI     @01,-1            create lock (0xFFFFFFFF)
      LOOP  LHI     @00,0             create expected lock (0)
      *     CS      @00,@01,LOCK      if LOCK = 0,
                                      store R1 into LOCK
      *     BRZ     DONE              we got the lock
      TEST  LT      @00,LOCK          else, load LOCK into R0
            BRNZ    TEST              try again (simple fetch)
            BRU     LOOP              still locked
      *                              no longer locked,
      *                              try CS again
      DONE  ...
            ...                       proceed
      LOCK  DS      F
                                      full word
```

Figure 2.41.: Better Implementation for Compare And Swap considering High Frequency Locks

The difficulty is that the CS instruction locks the cache line exclusively before the test. If the lock is now held by another CPU, the cache line will bounce back and forth between the CPU owning the lock and the CPU requesting the lock. A better solution is shown in figure 2.41 if there is a higher likelihood that the requesting CPU might not be able to acquire the lock immediately. In this case it is better to to do a trial fetch first after the first attempt of getting the lock failed. The additional instructions of the second implementation cause much less overhead than the cache flushes caused by the requesting CPU.

2.13. Input and Output

System z uses dedicated I/O processors (System Assist Processors and Channels) to perform Input and Output to peripheral devices. These processors execute their own instructions named Channel Command Words (CCW). System z does not use memory mapped I/O which in contrast to Channels maps memory across system and device memory.

By using dedicated I/O processors the standard CPUs are free to execute in parallel and do not have to communicate with the I/O devices. The whole attachment to the system handling the I/O is named the I/O or Channel subsystem.

2.13.1. z196 I/O Infrastructure

The z196 supports two different types of internal I/O infrastructure[10]:

- InfiniBand-based infrastructure for I/O cages and I/O drawers
- PCIe-based infrastructure for PCIe I/O drawers with new form factor drawer and I/O features.

Infiniband

The InfiniBand specification defines the raw bandwidth of one lane (referred to as 1x) connection at 2.5 Gbps. Two additional lane widths are specified, referred to as 4x and 12x, as multipliers of the base link width.

Similar to Fibre Channel, PCI Express, Serial ATA, and many other contemporary interconnects, InfiniBand is a point-to-point, bidirectional serial link intended for the connection of processors with high-speed peripherals, such as disks. InfiniBand supports various signaling rates and, as with PCI Express, links can be bonded together for additional bandwidth.

The serial connection's signalling rate is 2.5 Gbps on one lane in each direction, per physical connection. Currently, InfiniBand also supports 5 Gbps or 10 Gbps signaling rates, respectively.

PCIe

PCIe[11] is a serial bus with embedded clock and uses 8b/10b encoding, where every eight bits are encoded into a 10-bit symbol that is then decoded at the receiver. Thus, the bus needs to transfer 10 bits to send 8 bits of actual usable data. A PCIe bus generation 2 single lane can transfer 5 Gbps of raw data

---

[10] A detailed description can be found in [17] and for PCIe in [25]
[11] Peripheral Component Interconnect Express

(duplex connection), which is 10 Gbps of raw data. From these 10 Gbps, only 8 Gbps are actual data (payload). Therefore an x16 (16 lanes) PCIe gen2 bus transfers 160 Gbps encoded, which is 128 Gbps of uncoded data (payload). This is 20 GBps raw data and 16 GBps of encoded data.

The new measuring unit for transfer rates for PCIe is GT/s (Giga Transfers per second) which refers to the raw data (even though only 80% of this transfer is actual payload data). The translation between GT/s to GBps is: 5 GT/s equals 20 GBps or 1 GT/s equals 4 GBps. The 16 lanes of the PCIe bus are virtual lanes, always consisting of one transmit and one receive lane. Each of these lanes consist of two physical copper wires. The physical method used to transmit signals is a differential bus, which means that the signal is encoded into the different voltage levels between two wires (as opposed to one voltage level on one wire in comparison to the ground signal). Therefore, each of the 16 PCIe lanes uses actually four copper wires for the signal transmissions.

2.13.2. I/O System Overview

The I/O subsystem design is architectured to provide great flexibility, high availability, and excellent performance characteristics, such as:

High bandwidth

The z196 uses PCIe as new internal interconnect protocol to drive PCIe I/O drawers. The I/O bus infrastructure data rate increases up to 8GBps. The z196 uses InfiniBand as the internal interconnect protocol to drive I/O cages and I/O drawers and CPC to CPC connection. InfiniBand supports I/O bus infrastructure data rate up to 6 GBps.

Connectivity options

The z196 can be connected to an extensive range of interfaces such as ESCON, FICON/Fibre Channel Protocol for storage area network connectivity, 10 Gigabit Ethernet, Gigabit Ethernet, and 1000BASE-T Ethernet for local area network connectivity. For CPC to CPC connection z196 uses Parallel Sysplex InfiniBand (IFB) or ISC-3 coupling links.

Concurrent I/O upgrade

You can concurrently add I/O cards to the server if an unused I/O slot position is available.

Concurrent I/O drawer upgrade

Additional I/O and PCIe I/O drawers can be installed concurrently without pre-planning.

2.13 Input and Output

Dynamic I/O configuration

Dynamic I/O configuration supports the dynamic addition, removal, or modification of channel path, control units, and I/O devices without a planned outage.

Pluggable optics

The FICON Express8, FICON Express8S and FICON Express4 features have Small Form Factor Pluggable (SFP) optics to permit each channel to be individually serviced in the event of a fiber optic module failure. The traffic on the other channels on the same feature can continue to flow if a channel requires servicing.

Concurrent I/O card maintenance

Every I/O card plugged in an I/O cage, I/O drawer or PCIe I/O drawer supports concurrent card replacement in case of a repair action.

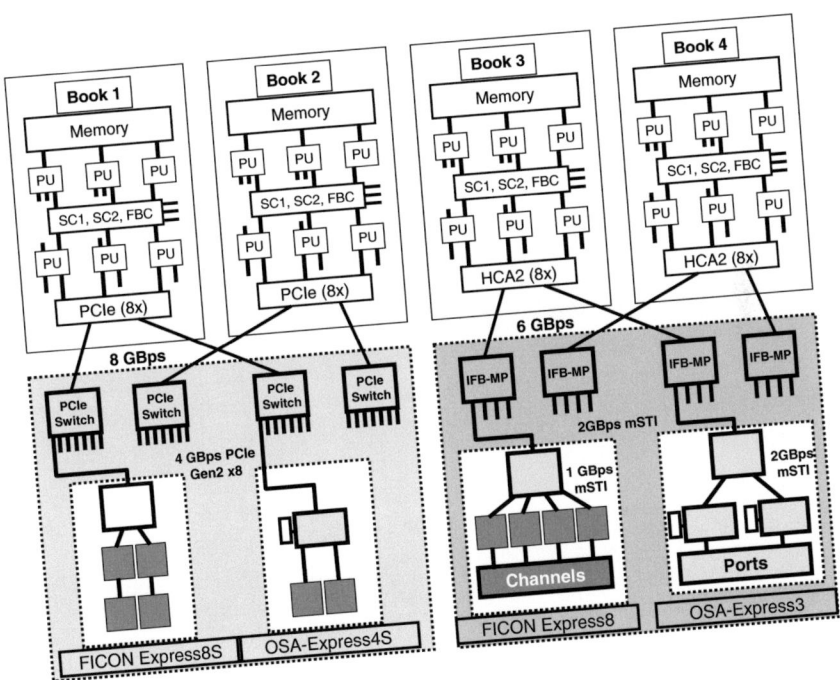

Figure 2.42.: z196 I/O Infrastructure

2.13.3. I/O Drawer

The I/O drawer is five EIA units[12] high and supports up to eight I/O feature cards. Each I/O drawer supports two I/O domains (A and B) for a total of eight I/O card slots. Each I/O domain uses an IFB-MP card in the I/O drawer and a copper cable to connect to a Host Channel Adapter (HCA) fanout in the CPC cage. The link between the HCA in the CPC and the IFB-MP in the I/O drawer supports a link rate of up to 6 GBps.

The PCIe I/O drawer attaches to the processor node via a PCIe bus and uses PCIe as the infrastructure bus within the drawer. The PCIe I/O bus infrastructure data rate is up to 8GBps. PCIe switch ASICs (Application-Specific Integrated Circuit) are used to fanout the host bus from the processor node to the individual I/O cards.

Figure 2.42 illustrates the IFB connection from the CPC cage to an I/O cage and an I/O drawer, and the PCIe connection from the CPC cage to an PCIe I/O drawer.

2.13.4. I/O Operation

The I/O subsystem consists of channels or channel paths which are independent processors that control the data transfer between main storage and device. The Channel Command Words specify the command code, for example Read, Write, Control, or Sense, the data address in absolute storage, a count field and several flag bits for example for command chaining. The data source in memory is pinned by the operating systems for the duration of the I/O operation. Also the operating system translates all virtual buffer addresses to absolute addresses.

The next component is the control unit. The control unit is the interface to the device. In older System /360, /370, or /390 environments the control unit controlled a number of real CKD or ECKD[13] Direct Access Storage Devices (DASD). Today the format of System z devices are emulated and the control unit is a like a separate processor complex with LBA devices attached to it on which the ECKD format is emulated.

A device is represented at least twice: By a device or Unit Control Structure in the operating system and by a sub-channel in the I/O subsystem.

---

[12]EIA stands for Electronic Industry Alliance and is the measurement unit for I/O and processor racks

[13](Extended)Count Key Data

2.13 Input and Output

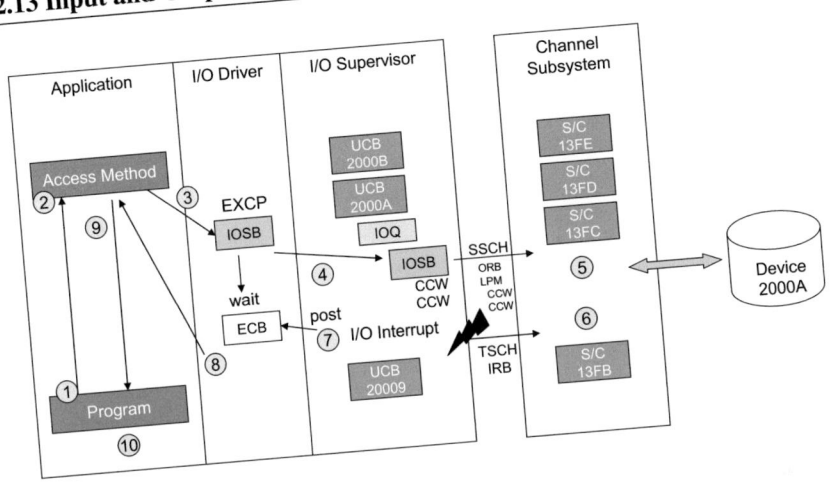

Figure 2.43.: System z I/O Flow

Figure 2.43 illustrates the I/O Flow from an operating system, z/OS in this case, to the device and the data transfer back to the memory of the operating system. The main I/O component in z/OS which interacts with the Channel Subsystem is the I/O Supervisor:

1. Application program issues Open macro and tells system which dataset it wants to access. OPEN tests access rights and locks dataset access. Now the application program can use PUT, GET, READ, or WRITE macros to access the dataset.

2. The access method create the channel program which contains of a sequence of channel command words. It also implements data buffering and synchronization and is able to re-initiate the I/O operation in case of an error.

3. The access method calls the I/O driver (usually EXCP) in order to move the data. The I/O driver translates the virtual addresses of the channel program into real addresses. For that reason the I/O driver enters supervisor state. Also the I/O driver can reserve pages in real storage to which the channel subsystem can copy data to or from.

4. The I/O Supervisor is called and the channel program is started. The channel program is queued to a Unit Control Block which represents the device in the system. If the UCB is already in use by another channel

program the current program is queued. Otherwise a start sub-channel command is issued to give the channel program to the Channel Subsystem. In any case the processor is given up now and the dispatcher can schedule a different program to execute.

5. A SAP (Service Assist Processor) executes the Start Subchannel and selects a channel to access the control unit and the device. The SAP and the channels use the control structures of the microcode which are the sub-channels and which are the device representation within the channel subsystem. For each device a sub-channel exists and resides in a hardware area designated for the hardware. The channels now executes the channel program and supervises the movement of data. The first channel initiates the data transfer to the I/O device. When data is transferred back to the system or a completion is send a different channel can execute it and controls the data transfer backwards.

6. The channel signals the SAP when the I/O Operation is completed. The SAP initiates the I/O Interrupt to the operating system.

7. A I/O supervisor routine executes the I/O interrupt and resumes the waiting task which initiated the I/O operation. Then the control is handed over to the dispatcher.

8. Eventually the dispatcher selects the originating task for execution which resumes the access method.

9. The access method checks the result of the I/O operation and provides its status back to the originating application program.

10. The application resumes its processing.

2.13.5. Logical Channel Subsystem

Channel paths are combined in logical channel subsystems. A logical channel subsystem can support up to 256 channels per Logical Partition and up to 65280 devices or sub channels[14]. Channels can be shared by logical partitions by using the Extended Multi Image Facility (EMIF). The introduction of EMIF was an important step to use channels more efficiently and also to allow to configure more channels to a logical partition for redundancy reasons.

System z currently supports 1 to 4 logical channel subsystems (LCSS). This Multiple Channel subsystems (MCSS) allow much larger configurations and

---

[14]256 out of 65536 sub-channels are reserved for internal use

2.13 Input and Output

can be efficiently used to consolidate multiple older systems on a new bigger CEC without changing the complete I/O configurations.

64512 sub-channels per LCSS are not much. Especially because the last physically build DASDs were only able to store 2.8 GB and 9.6 GB. Meanwhile the size restriction for devices has been resolved but the number of sub-channels was still a problem especially when Parallel Access Volumes (PAV) devices were introduced.

PAV devices make use of the fact that I/Os from different applications or logical partitions typically access different files or data sets on a device but for a single sub-channel only 1 I/O request can be executed at once. The solution is to introduce alias addresses for devices and allow to execute multiple I/Os to the same device in parallel. In seldom cases the I/Os might try to access the same extent in the same data set but even this is not a problem if the data set extent is in cache storage of the storage controller for read operations. As a result PAV devices speed up the I/O to the subsystem significantly.

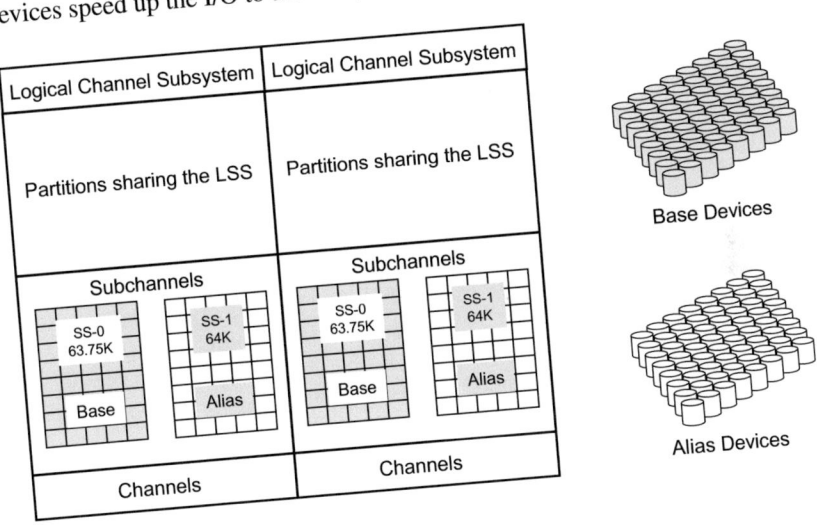

Figure 2.44.: Multiple Sub-Channel Sets for Base and Alias Device Addresses

PAV devices also underwent an evolution. The first implementation used static alias addresses which were fixed assigned to hot volumes. The second was to dynamically manage the alias addresses based on workload demand, importance and goal achievement. This was especially done for z/OS I/Os by introducing PAV management support for the z/OS Workload Manager. Finally the current implementation uses a dynamic assignment which just assigns an alias for an existing second or third I/O to the same volume and then release the alias back to an unused pool. The current implementation is the most dynamic evolution and allows the smallest number of alias addresses. Nevertheless all of these implementations use sub-channels which then can't be used for real device addresses anymore.

The solution are multiple sub-channel sets (MSS) per logical subsystem, see figure 2.44. At the moment 2 sub-cahhenl sets are supported with 65280 sub-channels in set 0 and 65535 sub-channels in set 1. These sub-channel sets are exploited by z/OS to access alias addresses of parallel access volumes and they are also exploited to assign sub-channels to mirror devices for techniques like Peer-to-Peer Remote Copy (PPRC) for building a fault tolerant z/OS cluster which is named Global Dispersed Parallel Sysplex (GDPS).

2.13.6. I/O Configuration

The I/O configuration for the hardware is defined in an I/O configuration data set (IOCDS). The I/O configuration encompasses the whole system, all their devices, cards, and connections. A component named Hardware Configuration Definition (HCD) is the software front-end to it. It allows to add, delete, and change I/O configurations dynamically by activating new I/O configurations. HCD keeps the software and hardware configuration in an I/O Definition File (IODF) from which the IOCDS for the hardware is derived. The I/O config-uration is also loaded in the HSA. With Dynamic I/O configuration the I/O definition in the HSA is dynamically changed. The second part of the IODF is operating system specific, for example the Unit Control Blocks (UCB) which correspond on z/OS to the hardware sub-channels are generated from it.

2.14. Logical Partitioning

Logical Partitioning and virtualization allows to run more than 1 operating sys-tem on the physical hardware at the same time. On System z two flavors exist:

1. Logical partitioning or LPAR which is part of the microcode (LIC = Licensed Internal Code)

2. z/VM is a multiple virtual machine manager which allows to execute a

nearly unlimited amount of virtual guests. z/VM needs to be installed in
a partition like any other operating system.

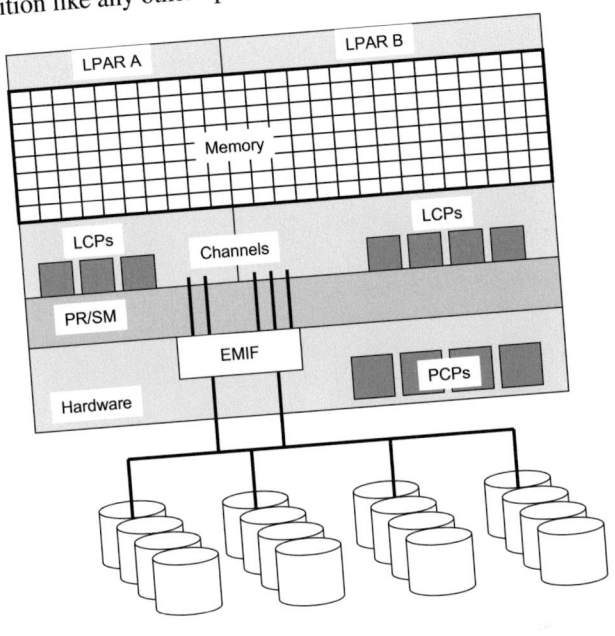

Figure 2.45.: Platform Virtualization on System z

Logical partitioning on System z separates the operating systems from the underlying hardware and is managed by the Processor Resource and System Management (PR/SM). The main resources: memory, I/O channels and processors
are made available to the logical partitions in the following way (see also figure
2.45):

- The system memory is partitioned between the logical partitions. That
  means each partition owns a separated part of the memory. It is possible to exchange data in speed but this is always isolated by the use of
  protocols. For example Queued Direct I/O allows to move data from one
  partition to the other but it uses a TCP/IP protocol.

- I/O channels and access to I/O devices can be dedicated or more efficiently be shared between partitions. Sharing of I/O channels is possible
  with a feature named Extended Multiple Image Facility (EMIF).

- Processors can be dedicated to a partition but then the processor is only available to one partition. More interesting is the case of sharing the processors between the partitions. This is especially of interest to discuss the necessary intersections between the operating system and virtualization layer especially with respect where it limits scalability on high end servers in chapter 4

2.14.1. z/VM

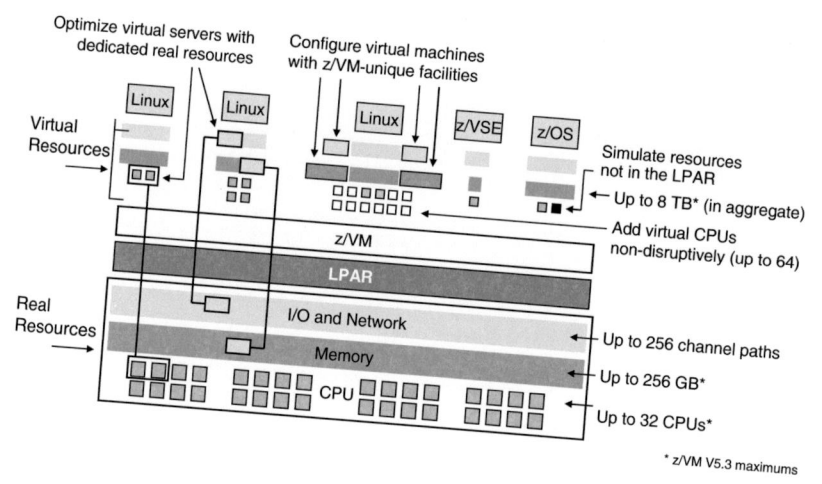

Figure 2.46.: Virtualization with z/VM 5.3

Virtual Machine (z/VM) is an operating system which provides an execution environment for other operating systems. The z/VM Control Program (CP) creates a virtual machine for each user. Each virtual machine has its own address space starting at address 0. This is virtual storage which is subject to paging. It is possible to define the architecture mode (ESA/390 or z/Architecture) for each virtual machine separately. CP can now virtualize or dedicate resources for the virtual guests:

Processors

can be simulated or dedicated. It is even possible to simulate more virtual processors than the hardware supports.

Storage

Virtual storage is controlled by the VM Resource Manager. It is also

possible to dedicate storage from the partition to a virtual machine guest
which might be required for performance critical guests.

I/ Configuration

is simulated for each virtual machine. The configuration may consist
of dedicated devices, for example consoles, and shared devices, for example mini-disks which are partitions on disks and assigned to virtual
machines or printers aka spooling devices.

Communication Paths

encompass channel-to-channel adapters which are shared between virtual machines, inter-user communication (IUCV) and virtual LANs.

2.14.2. Start Interpretive Execution

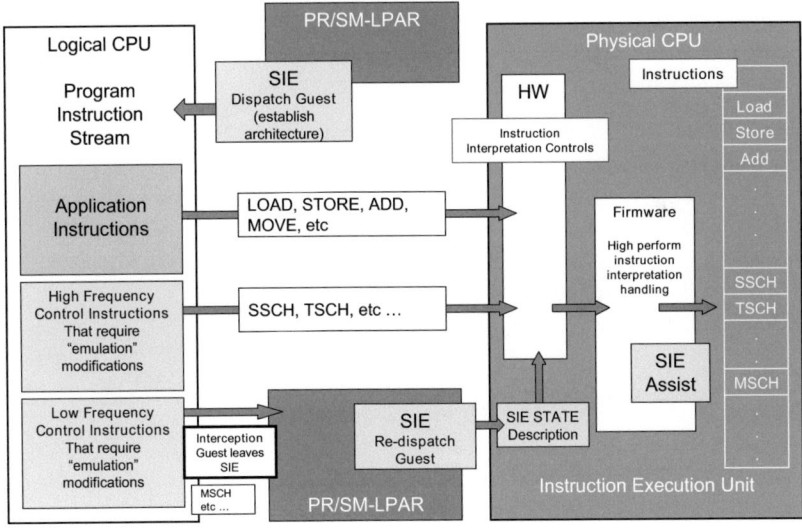

Figure 2.47.: SIE Instruction Flow

Both PR/SM and z/VM use the Start Interpretive Execution (SIE) instruction
to establish the architecture for the logical partitions. In the literature the virtualization layer is often called host (instance issuing the SIE instruction) and
the partitions which run the operating systems guests (programs running under SIE). With the SIE instruction on System z it is possible to provide each

guest its own architecture. The input to the SIE instruction is a state descriptor of the logical partition which encompasses for example the PSW, the registers and the CPU timers. On System z it is possible to run z/VM which is also a virtualization layer under PR/SM. With this configuration it is possible to have two levels of nesting for the SIE instruction (SIE under SIE).

When PR/SM issues the SIE instruction for a partition it loads the partition registers and state information. The guest then starts to execute instructions. Most of the instructions are interpreted directly by the hardware. Only few instructions require to end SIE and run a hardware emulation program. On SIE exit the host handles an interception or an interrupt:

- On an interception for example an instruction which requires emulation the host updates the state descriptor, sets an interception code in the state descriptor and resumes after the interception has been processed. Interceptions are guest interrupts which programmable.

- On a host interrupt for example an external, I/O interrupt, a translation exception, or the time slice ends (timer interrupt) the control is returned to the host and no interception code is stored

The SIE instruction[15] was introduced with System /370 Extended Architecture (XA) in the early 1980s. It was invented based on experiences with VM/370 on S/370 which completely used Trap and Emulate to virtualize other operating systems. The SIE instruction which is supported by the hardware now provides a much better performance. The SIE instruction is not documented in Principles of Operations (see [31]) and is partially documented in [6] and [7]. Since then many updates occurred.

2.14.3. Logical Processor Management

A partition can either have shared or dedicated processors. This the concept for the System z logical partition manager and this is not a must. We will see in chapter 4 that also on System z one exception exists where a special partition can use both dedicated and shared processors. Also it should be mentioned that prior to System z competitors also built hardware for S/370 and S/390 architecture. The concept of logical partitioning existed at that time already and both Hitachi and Amdahl the two main competitors supported so called L-shape partitions which could use dedicated and shared processors.

Partitions with dedicated processors own the physical processor to 100%. The

---

[15]On Intel based systems the VMX instruction provides a similar functionality

physical processor is not available to any other partition. Partitions with shared processors compete for the shared physical processors. By definition a partition cannot have more logical processors than physical processors which are active on the box. The only exception exists when a physical processor is malfunctioning and must be configured off-line and no spare processor can take over the function of the physical processor. In such cases partitions may have more logical than physical processors.

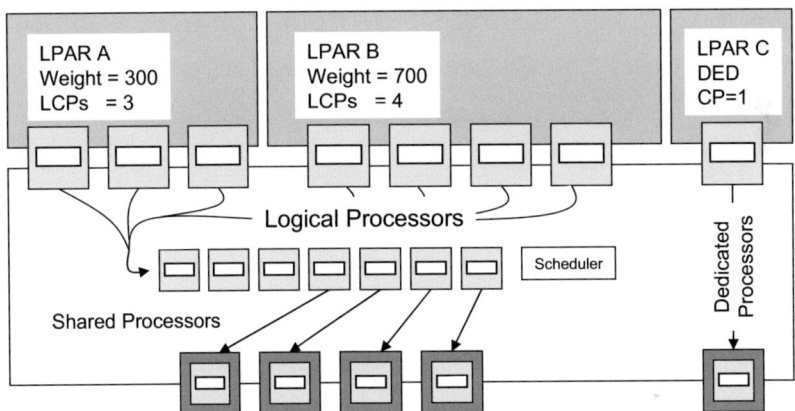

Figure 2.48.: Logical Processor Management

Each partition which uses shared processors also has a weight defined. The weight defines the share of the physical processor pool which is guaranteed to the partition assuming the number of logical processors is high enough to support this share. PR/SM now dispatches the logical processors on the shared physical processors. It uses a time slicing algorithms and determines the priority of logical processors based on the partition share and the time the logical processors have used their share. We will discuss this in more detail on the following pages.

When a logical processor is dispatched on a shared physical processor it is possible to complete the dispatch cycle in one of two modes:

Weight Completion = Yes
    A logical processor must complete its guaranteed share even if the wait

state PSW is loaded. This option is a CEC (Central Electronic Complex) wide control and effects all partitions. It guarantees that all partitions have always their share available to it but it doesnt allow partitions to use more than its share.

Weight Completion = No

(standard mode of operation) If the logical processor loads the WAIT State PSW the SIE is exited and the control is returned to PR/SM to dispatch another logical processor. Nearly all installations use this mode of operation because it allows to effectively use the available capacity of the CEC.

A detailed discussion about the dispatching for PR/SM and z/OS follows in chapter 4.

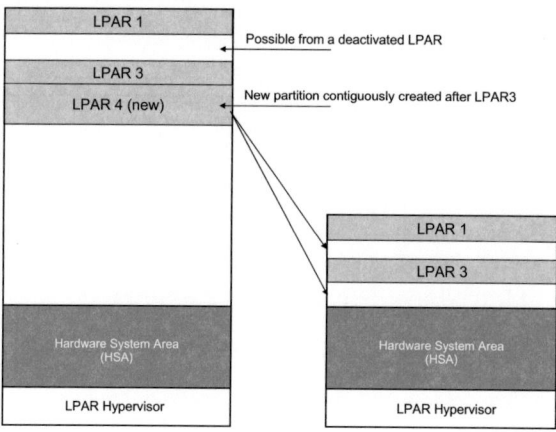

Figure 2.49.: Mapping of Absolute to Physical Storage

2.14.4. Storage of a Logical Partition

The storage assigned to a logical partition is called a zone. The zone origin is the host absolute address where the zone starts. This is zone address zero. The zone limit is the host absolute address where the zone ends. Origin and limit pairs are associated with a zone number (LPAR number).

The absolute storage of an LPAR must be contiguous. Activating and deactivating LPARs leads to fragmentation of storage. From both a scalability and avail-ability point of view the question comes up how unused storage can be assigned to a single LPAR? The result is another mapping of storage, see also section 2.11.1. For this purpose the absolute storage is mapped to physical storage and the absolute storage is defined larger than the available physical storage, for example twice as big, see figure 2.49. If a partition has been deactivated some parts of the absolute storage becomes de-fragmented. A new LPAR 4 is now created contiguously after LPAR 3 in absolute storage. With the mapping it is now possible to map it to unused areas in physical storage and therefore avoid that certain amounts of LPAR activations and de-activations make it impossible to run the CEC without restart.

2.14.5. Storage of a Virtual Machine under z/VM

z/VM provides a more sophisticated level of virtualization than LPAR which has its main focus on efficient platform virtualization. z/VM even supports SIE under SIE by interpreting of the SIE instruction by z/VM. This allows in theory an arbitrary number of nesting levels. It is useful for testing new z/VM versions on existing z/VM versions.

A more realistic scenario is a guest operating system under z/VM which runs in a logical partition. The primary address space created by z/VM describes the virtual machine's absolute storage. The ASCE is contained in CR1 of the host which is z/VM.

The virtual machine now may use its own virtual storage which requires two DAT translations. The translations are all done in hardware without shadow tables:

1. Guest-2 (the hosted OS) virtual to guest-2 absolute

2. Guest-1 (z/VM) virtual which is the guest-2 absolute address to guest-1 absolute

Scenario

We assume an application runs in the operating system hosted under z/VM. This operating system is named guest-2. z/VM is hosted under LPAR and z/VM is guest-1. The LPAR is managed by the LPAR hypervisor which is the host:

Step 1 The application uses a virtual address (guest-2 virtual) which is trans-lated to a guest-2 real address by using the operating system's DAT tables. Then the guest-2 real address is translated to guest-2 absolute address by using the operating system's prefix register, see section 2.11.1.

Step 2   The resulting guest-2 absolute address is taken to be guest-1 virtual address. It is translated to guest-1 real address using z/VM's DAT tables. Then by using the z/VM's prefix register the guest-1 absolute address is generated.

Step 3   The guest-1 absolute address is now translated to the host absolute address by adding the LPAR's zone origin. It is also checked against the LPAR's zone limit to ensure that it is in the valid addressing range.

Step 4   Finally the absolute storage address is translated to a physical address where the data item or instruction can actually be found.

2.15. Summary

At the end of our excursion to System z hardware we observed that System z currently provides the fastest commercial computer system. But this is not the denominating factor which of System z importance in the industry. The value of System z is defined by its RAS criteria from which we explicitly emphasize High Availability and Scalability.

From a "High Availability" point of view we learned that redundancy and error detection mechanisms are built in across all hardware components. Two good examples are CPU error detection and sparing as well as the introduction of RAIM to protect the storage against chip and channel errors. The principle is always to keep the system running and thus maintain the business operations.

For "Scalability" we have the same emphasis. The main example besides many others in this chapter is to use the high processor frequency as efficient as possible. The use of four cache levels grants this requirement as well as the exploitation of an out-of-order design for the z196 microprocessor shows that many functions have been introduced under this aspect. We will see that this is a good start but not everything and that additional techniques must be deployed before an application can really exploit the hardware efficiently.

3. z/OS

In this chapter we will discuss the main features of z/OS operating system which is the main operating system for transaction processing and to host database on System z. z/OS evolved from MVS which was introduced in 1974 (see figure 2.1). MVS provided virtual storage for all users and applications and thus allowed to fence applications against each other. By looking at the structure of the address spaces we will discuss the attempts which were made to scale the environment by preserving the compatibility of earlier architectural developments. Thus z/OS is a perfect example how a modern operating system maintains their roots and compatibility to its earliest days. We will further discuss in this chapter how program execution works on z/OS, how programs can be protected against errors, and how data can be exchanged between address spaces. We will take a look at the changes for controlling the operating system storage which is another good example to show the required changes for supporting scalability from a 2 GB to a 16 PB environment. Finally we will introduce the main subsystems and how the system is internally structured and how the system can be customized.

3.1. z/OS Structure

Figure 3.1 depicts the structure of z/OS and the z/OS stack.

z/OS basically is structured in three parts:

Basic Control Program
> (BCP) encompasses the major operating system functions like: Supervisor/Dispatcher, Console Services, Recovery, Storage Management, Unix System Services, IPL, Resource and Workload Management, and Sysplex Communication. These are mainly core services and on its own not sufficient to run user programs or applications.

Base elements
> encompass all functions which are required to establish a complete runtime environment. These encompass functions like system installation,

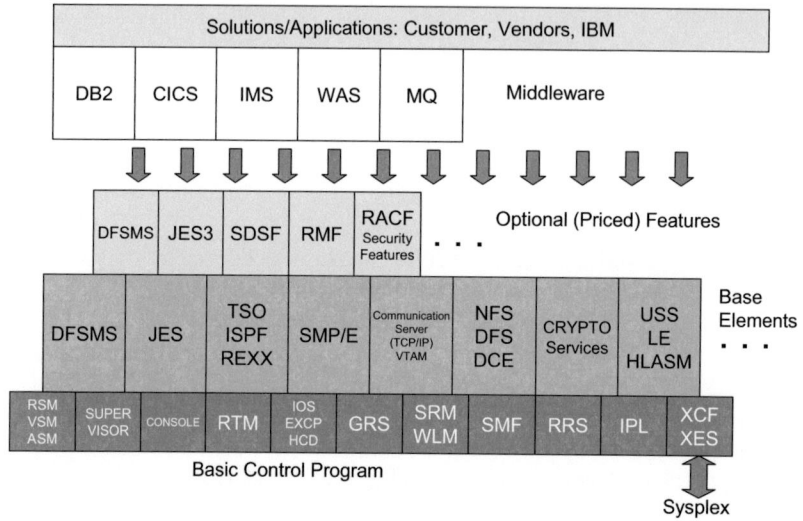

Figure 3.1.: z/OS Structure and Stack

I/O storage management (DFSMS), UNIX system shell services, the Job Entry System, Time Sharing Option (TSO), and the language environments. The job entry system for example is crucial to execute programs on z/OS. But an installation has a choice to select one of two job entry systems: JES2 or JES3. Therefore this function is not part of the BCP but a required add on to it.

Optional Features

cover functions which are recommended but either not required or which can be exchanged by vendor components. Resource Measurement Facility (as reporting and monitoring product), and Security features are examples for such functions.

The middleware and major subsystems complete the operating system stack on top of these functions. These are functions which provide runtime environments to execute huge numbers of customer transactions with the guaranteeing the qualities required for consistent database management aspects. On z/OS the main classical subsystems are Customer Information Control System (CICS®) and Information Management System (IMS™) which are two transaction monitors with integrated database capabilities. Currently the most important database is DB/2 which can be used by those transaction monitors and also by applications running on other platforms. Newer middleware developments encompass Message Queueing systems and Websphere® Application Server to enable Java applications on System z platform. Also vendor subsystems like SAP, Oracle, and SAS can be found on z/OS systems.

z/OS in Numbers

z/OS (BCP+Base Elements+Optional Features) is more than 100 Million Lines of Codes. In order to develop this code another 750 million lines of test code and tooling is required. Altogether more than 850 million lines of code need to be maintained for just the operating system without the middleware.

The Basic Control Program is more than 40% of the executable lines of codes as well as number of parts. The second biggest part are UNIX System Services (USS) which provide a full UNIX runtime environment based on ISO standard POSIX 1003.1. So it can be said that z/OS provides two faces: a classical runtime environment and a UNIX environment and combines the functionality of two operating systems.

3.2. Address Spaces

The address space is the basic concept of z/OS and MVS. The ability to provide each user with its own virtual storage map gave the first operating system its name: Multiple Virtual Storage (MVS). Address spaces provide a virtual storage map and provide the runtime environment for the user programs. The term user just means everybody or everything which wants to use z/OS or MVS system resources. This can be an external user, a batch program but also a complete transaction monitor which executes multiple tasks at the same time. So the address also provides all structures to execute programs and access data.

Figure 3.2 shows that the address space grew in size over time. Initially MVS was designed as a 24 bit operating system which allowed to address only 16MB of storage. When this became too small the architecture was extended to 32 bit of which the highest bit was used to identify 24 bit addresses from 31 bit addresses. Therefore it was then possible to address 2 GB of storage. z/OS finally introduced 64 bit addressing mode which now allows to address 18EB of storage at least theoretically.

Figure 3.2 also shows that the virtual storage is divided in private areas (gray) which are exclusively for the programs of the address space and common areas (white). The common areas are the same across all address spaces and describe shared virtual storage areas.

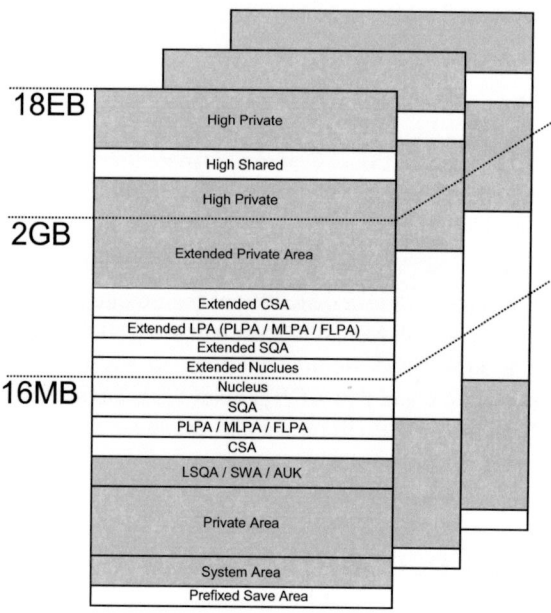

Figure 3.2.: Address Space Structure Structure

The meaning of the common area sections is:

Prefixed Save Area:
> This is a fixed storage area which also has a fixed real to virtual storage mapping. It contains the basic anchors of the data structures for the z/OS system and it is established and used by the IPL process.

Link Pack Areas:
> PLPA, FLPA and MLPA are common storage areas in which programs can be pre loaded which are often used in the system. Programs in such areas are similar to dynamic link libraries of other operating systems and they reside in storage to avoid too many reloads from disks. Such programs also need to be coded reentrant to that multiple users can use them at the same time.

CSA and SQA:
> Common System Area and System Queue Area contain system structures and can be used to share memory between applications and operating system components.

Nucleus:
> contains the operating system modules which also need to be in storage.

With the extension of the 24 bit addresses to 31 bit all of the common areas except the prefixed save area were extended to 31 bit too. Because the common areas were the highest addresses of the original architecture they were now mirrored and the extended common areas are the low 31 bit addresses. As a result the private storage areas consist of two areas above and below 16MB line.

With the introduction of 64 bit addresses another High Shared area is defined above the 2GB line. This area relates to the SQA and CSA areas and is used to keep common and shared storage elements. All other areas above the 2GB line are for local application data.

3.2.1. Address Space Types and Storage

Address Spaces provide all the control structures to execute programs and to access data. Figure 3.2 shows that address spaces evolved over time and that the addressing concept was finally extended to 64 bit addressing. But this wasnt a straight development. First the addressing range was extended from 24 bit addressing to 31 bit addressing. When it became obvious that 31 bit addressing was not sufficient efforts were made to provide more virtual storage to applications without extending the 31 bit addressing mode. This was done by introducing two additional space concepts which were just established to keep data (see figure 3.3):

Data Spaces: are spaces primarily for operating system and prioritized tasks and functions to keep additional amounts of storage.

Hiperspaces: are spaces which offer services to also allow middleware and applications to keep memory objects in storage.

Data Spaces and Hiperspaces are virtual storage structures. The available memory with 31 bit addressing allows to address 2 GB of memory. This also became a short resource. In order to overcome this limitation expanded storage was introduced. Expanded storage extended the main memory. The biggest difference was that in Expanded Storage only pages and no bytes could be addressed. Be-

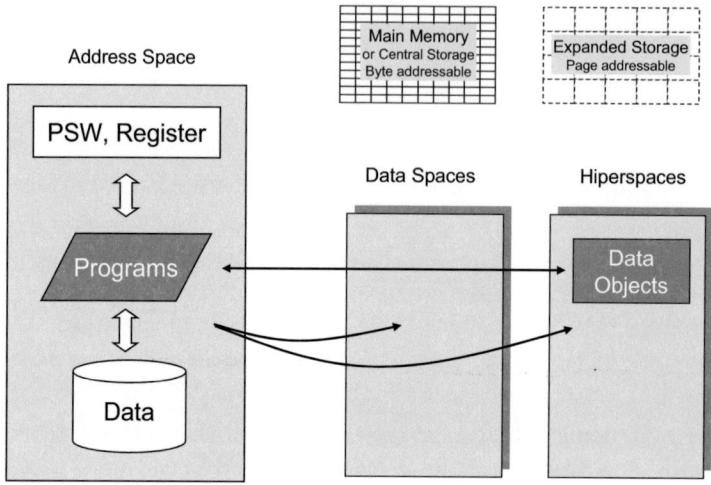

Figure 3.3.: Address Space and Storage Types

cause of this limitation Expanded Storage established as a fast paging device. Especially functions like TSO could make very efficient use of it. For TSO users typically only require very short periods of time when they are active in storage. Most of the time the user does editing in the buffer in its terminal or terminal emulation buffer and only when the user presses the ENTER button a request is sent to the system. At that time the user now needs fast access to system resources and storage. On the other hand the processing usually doesn't require much time and after the processing a relative long period starts again where the user is inactive or idle from the point of the system. With expanded storage it is now possible to page or swap the TSO memory fast out of main memory which is a constrained resource with 31 bit addressing and page or swap it fast in again when it is needed. This structure of 2 GB main memory and up to 16 GB of expanded storage allowed to run systems with thousands of TSO users together with Batch and huge transaction systems before 64 bit addressing was introduced.

It should be mentioned that expanded storage also had a disadvantage besides the fact that its extension to the 2 GB main memory was limited because it was also limited to 16 GB. The disadvantage was that a page which needs to be migrated from expanded storage to auxiliary storage, the paging devices, needs first to be brought back to main memory before it can be sent to auxiliary storage and thus amplifying storage constraints. Nevertheless it is a good example to provide a scalability solution which also solved storage constraints for a period of 16 years. Hiperspaces finally made use of expanded storage also for applications and operating system components. Today Hiperspaces are mapped to main memory above 2 GB.

3.2.2. Control Block Areas

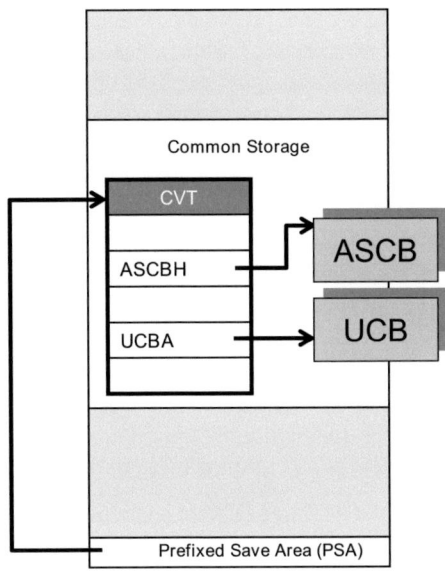

Figure 3.4.: Prefixed Save Area and Common Storage

The common storage area namely the CSA and SQA (also ECSA and ESQA) are used for z/OS control structures. The main table of z/OS is the Communications Vector Table (CVT). It contains the anchor to all operating system components and data structures which need to be accessed by different components. As an example of such structures are the Address Space Control Blocks (ASCB) which represent the address spaces of the system. An ASCB needs to be accessed by multiple operating system components and therefore needs to reside in a common storage area. Another example are Unit Control Blocks

(UCB) which represent the devices of the system (see figure 3.4). The communications vector table is anchored in the Prefixed save Area at the fixed address X10.

3.2.3. Storage Protection

In order to access these control structures the program must run in supervisor state and use storage protection key 0. Storage protection key is available only to operating system programs. The storage keys 1 to 7 are reserved for major z/OS subsystems and key 8 is for user programs. A detailed description of storage protection can be found in chapter ??. Supervisor State is similar of kernel mode of other operating systems and again applies to the operating system. A usual application runs in problem state and then it is not possible to execute operating system tasks. So it is possible to compile and link programs to allow them to switch to supervisor state. The programs need also to be placed in an authorized program library. The concept of authorized libraries (APF) is a key concept because it allows an installation to control which programs can use certain system services and especially which programs can switch to supervisor state and change their storage access keys.

3.2.4. Address Space Creation

Address Spaces can be created in one of three ways in the system:

1. Through a START, MOUNT, or LOGON command
2. During system initialization.
3. From a program by using the assembler interface ASCRE (address space create)

Address spaces are created by the MASTER address space and initialized by the Job Entry System. The only exception is during system initialization. In this case the MASTER address space which is the first address space of the system also initializes the address space. The initialization steps are shown in figure3.5:

- First the virtual storage area is created. This encompasses the control tables to enable addressing. At the same time the first task is created and anchored in the address space control block (ASCB). The task is represented by a task control block (TCB) which resides in an operating system area of the private storage of the address space (LSQA, see page 7 and 8). This step is named Memory Create.

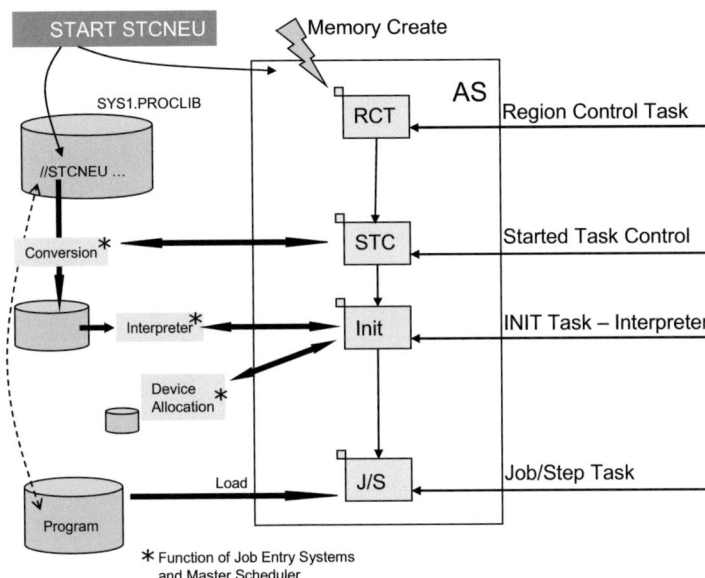

Figure 3.5.: Address Space Creation

- The Region Control Task creates two subtasks:
  - Started Task Control (STC) controls the conversion of the start procedure. The start procedure is located in a library and tells the system which devices and data sets need to be allocated, whether the address spaces requires special libraries and which program should be started initially. A start procedure is a batch job fragment and it is required for every address space creation. The STC task also receives the job id and links to the INIT task on completion.
  - INIT task interprets the start procedure and allocates devices and datasets. Finally it attaches the Job Step Task and loads the program which should be executed.
- The Job Step task executes the program. Now it is possible to attach other subtasks and also to load multiple programs which can be executed in parallel.

Batch Jobs

For batch jobs address spaces are pre-started. These pre-started address spaces are named initiators and they are pre-initialized up to the INIT task. For a batch job the STC and INIT tasks control the conversion and interpretation of the job which is similar to the process for start procedures and then allocate the data sets and devices needed by the batch job. Finally the Job Step task is created to execute the program referred to in the batch job. When the job completes the job step task is detached and the device allocations are reversed so that the initiator can be used for another batch job.

3.3. Program Execution

Programs which run in an address space are executed under the control of a Task. The Region Control and Job/Step tasks are examples for special tasks. A task is represented in the system by a Task Control Block (TCB) (see figure 3.6).

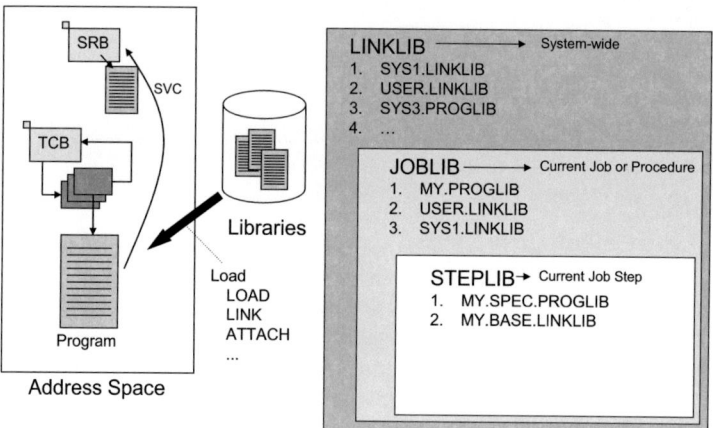

Figure 3.6.: Program Execution

There are not only application programs in the system which need to execute. Very often it is necessary to execute a system function. System functions cover all kind of activities which require special authorities in the system and which need to be performed by application programs as well, for example obtaining and freeing storage for private use. One of the most common ways to call a system function is by issuing a Supervisor Call (SVC). The Supervisor Call also loads a program and executes the requested function and returns to the caller. Because these supervisor call are relative short service requests they are treated differently then the execution of a user, application or regular program.

Instead of creating a task structure a Service Request Block (SRB) is created for the Supervisor Call. The SRB enables some special features for example that it gets executed before all other tasks which are similar to the calling task. Also most Supervisor Calls are non preemptable and therefore execute rather fast in the system.

Programs are loaded from system libraries. System libraries are concatenated in a search concatenation. For example the standard libraries of the system which are available to any user program are concatenated as LINKLIB. A start procedure or batch job can now define its own library concatenations by defining its own STEPLIB or JOBLIB.

3.3.1. Reentrant Programming

Reentrant programming is required to invoke programs which are used by multiple callers at the same time and which are loaded only once into common storage. The link pack areas of common storage are reserved for such programs. The example in figure 3.7 shows the data areas and register conventions used for standard linkage to a reentrant program in 31 bit addressing mode. The convention for 64 bit addressing is similar.

The example starts with the caller which already has a save area created. Before the caller calls the new program it follows the following conventions:

- Register 1 points to the parameters which are required by the calling program

- Register 13 points to the caller save area

- Register 14 will receive the return address within the caller's program when the BASR (or BALR) instruction is executed. That means the current content of R14 is destroyed.

- The entry point address is loaded to to register 15

- The BALR (or BASR) instruction[1] branches to program 15 and before that saves the return address (the address where the instruction pointer will point to after the current instruction has been executed in R14)

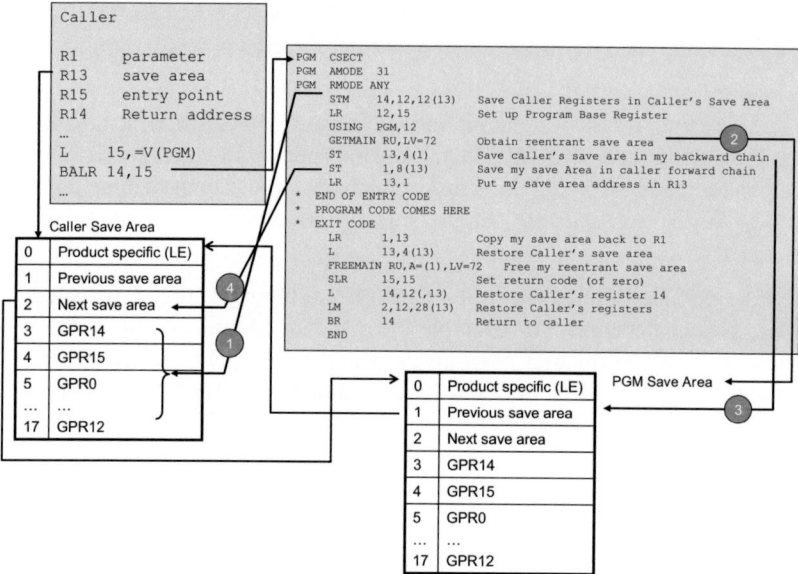

Figure 3.7.: Reentrant programming for 31 bit Programs

Then the new program (PGM) receives control. In our example the new program runs in address mode of 31 bit (AMODE 31) and can reside anywhere in virtual storage below the 2GB line (RMODE ANY). The following steps are important at entry of the new program:

1. The registers of the caller are saved to the caller's save (beginning at word 3, offset 12). Notice that word 3 (offset 12) of the callers save area now points to the return address of the caller's program

2. The caller loads the entry point address in register 12 and uses register 12 as base register to address all further code sequences. If the caller provided parameters in register 1 this parameter pointer must now be saved too (not shown) before PGM allocates its own save area which is required to call another reentrant program. The GETMAIN macro is

---

[1]BALR = Branch and Link, BASR = Branch and Save, see Appendix ??

used to allocate the save area and the address of the save area is placed in register.

3. PGM saves the caller's save area in the previous pointer of its own save area.

4. Finally it saves its save area address in the next pointer of the caller's save area. The two save areas now point to each other. Finally the address of PGM save area is stored in R13. R13 is typically not used during program execution.

At the exit the steps 1. to 4. are reversed and the save area of PGM is freed before the program returns to the caller (BR 14). Notice that only registers 0 to 12 are restored. Register 14 has been fetched from the save area to set the return address for the branch instruction correctly and register 15 is used as return and reason code.

3.3.2. Program Recovery

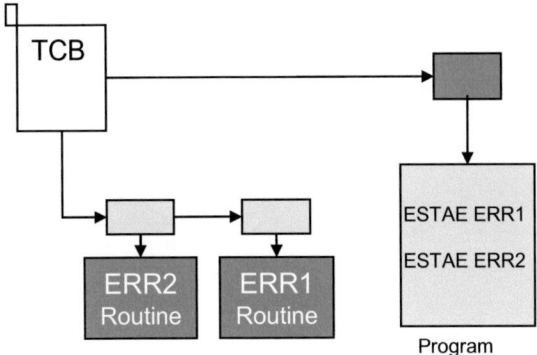

Figure 3.8.: Problem Mode Error Recovery Routines

One critical aspect of z/OS especially with respect to High Availability is error recovery. A lot of effort is undertaken for all kind of system routines to protect the system against failures. The same is the case for the major subsystems and middleware and is also offered for application programs. The motivation is simple: If a standalone programs abends usually not much damage is created but if a server program terminates by error this can immediately affect hundredths of end users. Therefore error recovery is essential for server applications and the underlying operating system which process hundredths or even thousandths of users simultaneously. The overall idea for all error recovery is to process the error and to continue processing of at least not affected parallel tasks as much as possible. In addition it is necessary to capture diagnostic information which will later allow the development and service organization to analyze the problem and solve it

Error recovery distinguishes between Problem state and Supervisor state programs. Problem state programs have limited access to system resources (restrictions concerning storage access and program invocation). The error recovey must be within the same scope. A problem state program typically sets up an ESTAE (Extended Specified Task Abnormal Exit) which is called by the Recovery Termination Manager if a program ends abnormally. An ESTAE routine always maintains the scope of the application program. Supervisor State programs have usually access to everything. The corresponding error recovery routine is an FRR (Functional Recovery Routine). This type of recovery routine an enabled unlock task which protects code that is not disabled, locked and in system mode.

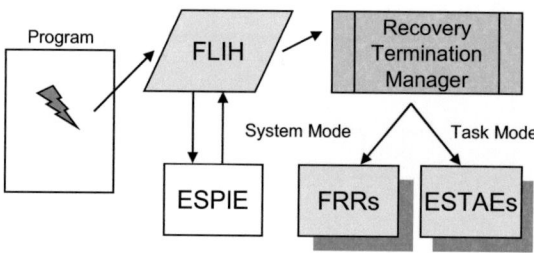

Figure 3.9.: Error Recovery Components

Error recovery as well as program interruption in general is handled in two steps: Step 1: is the First Level Interrupt Handler. This usually saves the program registers. Usually there is no error recovery at this point. Nevertheless for special cases it is possible to invoke an error recovery exit already at this point (Extended Specified Program Interruption Exit (ESPIE)). Step 2: the Recovery Termination Manager (RTM) calls the routine which handles the program interruption and this can be an error recovery routine in case of an abnormal software interrupt.

Figure 3.8 shows the stacking of error recovery routines for problem mode programs protecting code parts and figure 3.9 the various versions of error recovery routines for supervisor and problem state programs.

Table 3.1 depicts typically ABEND codes and their meanings. Typically, a program gets control, performs its function, and terminates normally (via SVC 3, EXIT). However, there are ways a program can terminate abnormally: Program checks, System and application detected errors resulting in ABEND macro calls, and Program Checks like Application logic error, System-detected software errors (incorrect value specified to a system service), and Hardware-detected errors.

ABEND Code	Description
0C1	(Privileged) Operation exception
0C2	Invalid instruction, read to not closed file, invalid subroutine call, ...
0C4-4	Protection exception: Invalid Storage Key
0C4-10	Segment Table translation exception (storage not obtained)
0C4-11	Page Table translation exception (storage not obtained)
0C5	Addressing exception: storage location not available in configuration
0C7	Various data exceptions
0C9	Fixed point divide exception

Table 3.1.: Abnormal Termination Codes

3.3.3. Recovery Processing

Figure 3.10 setup of an error recovery routine and the instrumentation which can be done to protect special code areas. It is not unusual that a program might expect that an abnormal termination may occur during certain parts of its processing. If this is the case it is standard practice to set footprints which will allow an error recovery routine to handle various types of errors depending on where they occur during processing. The recovery routine is usually appended to the main program and its initialization is also usually the first program activity. During mainline processing the program might now turn on various footprints to signal the error recovery routine the state where the program ended abnormally. Such footprints can influence whether and to which extent the error recovery routine collects diagnostic data (writing error logs and initiating dumps). A special diagnose area (System Diagnostic Work Area (SDWA)) is set up and passed to the error recovery routine. The error recovery routine can

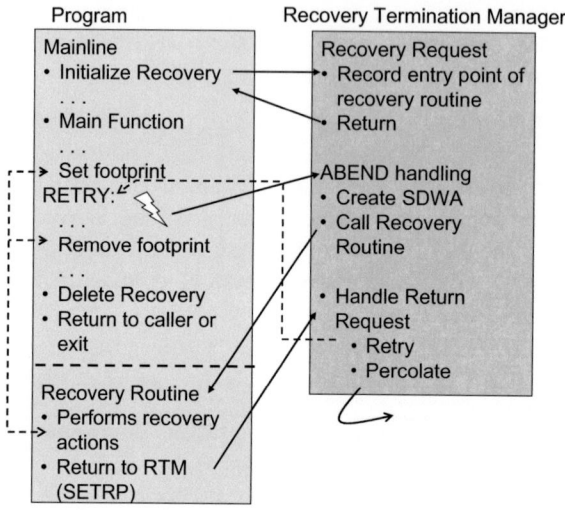

Figure 3.10.: Error Recovery Processing

set information in this area which then controls the follow on activities performed by the recovery termination manager. This can result in writing dumps and error logs or suppressing them. It is possible to return to a retry address or to continue with the next higher level of error recovery (percolate).

3.4. Program Data Exchange

So far we looked at address spaces, how programs are being executed and protected against errors. One very important aspect is how data can be exchanged between address spaces. The address space concept provides high level of isolation between different users of the operating system. Except for system or authorized programs it is not possible to access common storage easily. Therefore data exchange is not that simple between different address spaces.

Three classical techniques to exchange data have been developed in MVS and z/OS and with the introduction of UNIX system services also shared memory objects were introduced which can be protected through semaphores to share data between programs running in different address spaces. The latter technique is available through UNIX system service calls. In the following we want to take a closer look at the three classical techniques to exchange data:

- via common storage

- via cross memory

- by directly addressing data of other address or data spaces.

3.4.1. Data Exchange via Common Storage

The start situation is that program A running in address space A wants to copy data into address space B so that this data can be used by programs of address space B.

Steps, see figure 3.11:

1. Program A copies the data into common storage. It must be noted that program A needs to obtain the permission (key=0) to copy the data to common storage.

2. Program A now schedules an SRB to Address Space B. It must be noted that this is a push solution where program A initiates the data transfer. At the end of this step the program is interrupted and the dispatcher receives control.

3. When the SRB is dispatched it is then able to copy the data from common storage to local storage for address space B.

This technique has one advantage. At the time when program A wants to provide the data to address space B it doesnt know whether address space B is swapped in. By scheduling the SRB to address space B the address space is automatically swapped in in case it wasnt. On the other hand this technique also has disadvantages: Common storage is a limited resource and therefore cant be used to exchange large amounts of data. Also scheduling an SRB for this purpose costs CPU cycles and therefore induces overhead for the copy or move activity.

Programming Notes

The z/OS Assembler Services provide a service SCHEDULE which allows to schedule a program as an SRB to a target address space. The identification of the target address space is done via an Address Space Token (STOKEN) which can also be obtained via an assembler service.

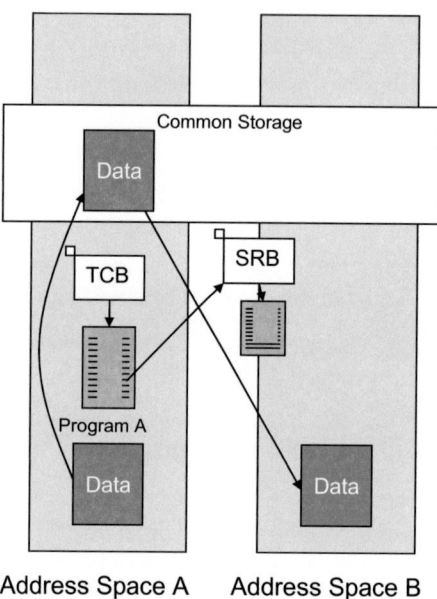

Figure 3.11.: Data Exchange via Common Storage

Above we discussed the way that program A initiates the data exchange to an arbitrary address space to which no other connection exists. If the address spaces are already connected in some way and know about each other it is possible to initiate the data transfer through other ways. For example z/OS also allows to setup event lists on which one address space can wait and which can be triggered by the initiating address space. But this requires that both address spaces are related to each other.

3.4.2. Data Exchange via Cross Memory

The cross memory method is very efficient for cases where a system component or middleware offers services to application programs. By using the service it is very often necessary to pass input data to the service or to pass result information back to the caller when the service activity is completed. This can be quite substantial amounts of data for example for storing or retrieving data in a database. The service provider can now provide his service routines as Program Calls. This is an architectural interface which creates a program call table and the corresponding assembler instruction (PC) can invoke the service routine by its program call number.

Accessing Address Space

For invoking a program call and using cross memory services it is important to understand how address spaces can be accessed on System z The System z architecture uses an ASCE to describe an address space. The ASCE provides access to the primary region or segment table origin of the address space and it is the anchor point for address translation, see section 2.11.2. The layout of the ASCE is depicted in figure 3.12.

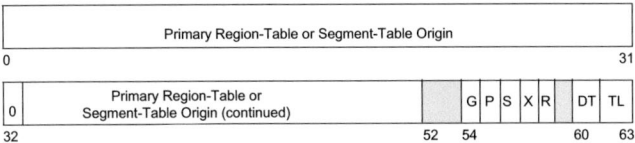

Figure 3.12.: Address Space Control Element

The ASCE is contained in control registers 1, 7, or 13 depending to which address space it refers to:

1. Home is always the address space from which the original activity was started. This always remains the same address space even if consecutive activities change the following address spaces. The ASCE of the home address space is contained in CR13. The home address space is important in a consecutive address space switching sequence to find the original point where the sequence has started.

2. Primary is the address space where the current program is executing. Its ASCE is contained in CR1.

3. Secondary the address space to which the executing program can easily get access to. This can be the target address space for copy operations and its ASCE can be contained in CR7.

The architecture (see [31]) provides an explicit assembler instruction SSAR to set the secondary address space to CR7 and also to clear the value which means set it back to the primary address space number. CR7 is also modified by other assembler instructions which can be used to transfer the program control between address spaces, like PROGRAM TRANSFER, PROGRAM RETURN and PROGRAM CALL. For detailed description see [31].

Program Calls

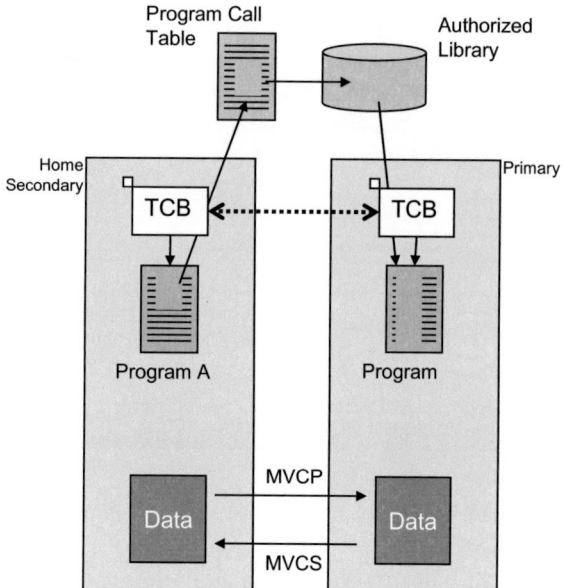

Figure 3.13.: Data Exchange via Program Call

Figure 3.13 shows the data exchange via Program Call and Cross Memory. The technique is very efficient for system components and middleware components which provide application interfaces (API) which can be used by programs to obtain a service. How program call tables can be established is described in detail in [31]:

1. Program A calls a service through a PC which is offered by a system component or middleware. The Home AS remains address space A. The primary (**) address space now becomes address space B which belongs to the system component. The calling address space A is now also treated as secondary address space in this constellation.

2. Home, primary, and secondary address spaces are now accessible for the service routine through its control registers. Also the assembler instruction MVCP (Move Character to Primary) moves data from the secondary to the primary address space without any additional setup.

3. MVCS (Move Character to Secondary) is the corresponding instruction which allows the service routine to copy result data back to the target address space.

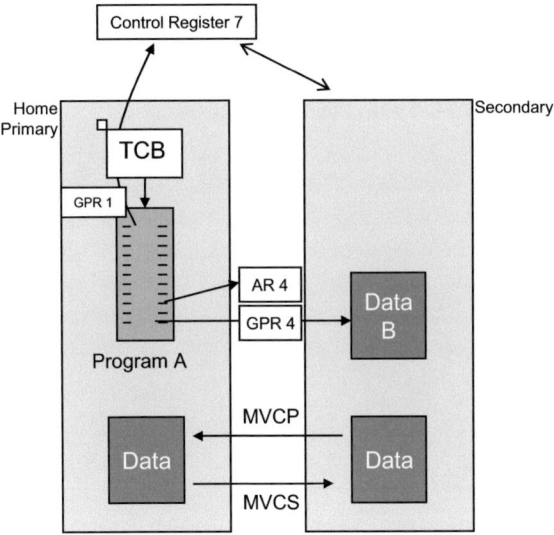

Figure 3.14.: Data Exchange via Access Registers and Cross Memory

This example assumes a space switching PC call. For a non space switching PC call the service routine would execute in address space A and address space A would remain the primary AS. But in our example we want easily access data in both address spaces which results in implementing the service as a space switching PC call.

3.4.3. Access Registers

Figure 3.14 shows a technique similar to the previous but without having a service call. This technique was introduced when data spaces were implemented for OS/390 because now the need increased to move data between different spaces. The technique is again primarily used by system components and middleware which require to keep high amounts of data in virtual storage.

The program which wants to copy the data to the other space does this directly and therefore needs the address space number of the target address or data space. With the address space identification token (ASIT) the calling program is able to modify control register 7 to define the secondary address space (SSAR (Set Secondary Address Space) instruction (1). Now the program can copy data from the secondary to the primary address space (2) with the MVCP instruction and backwards (3) with the MVCS instruction.

Another possibility is to address data in the target address space directly (4) without using the instructions MVCP and MVCS which make use of control register 7. For this purpose a program can use access register mode. For each general purpose register in the system an access register exists. In access register mode the access register must contain an ALET (Access List Entry Token). In AR mode the content of the access register is used to resolve an address of the general purpose register in the target address space which is denoted by the ALET (see also section 2.8.2 and [31]).

3.5. Storage Management

As we already discussed in section 2.11.2 the address spaces together own much more virtual storage than real storage or memory is installed on the system. As a result the operating system must decide which portions of virtual storage are moved into real storage and are immediately accessible and which portions are moved out to external storage devices. The portions which are moved between the different storage areas described in figure 3.15 are 4 KB blocks which are named pages when their virtual storage representation is referred to, frames when they reside in real storage and slots when they are on external devices. The external devices are page or swap data sets and generally referred to as auxiliary storage. With large page support a page can also be 1 MB in size.

3.5.1. z/OS Storage Managers

Central storage frames and auxiliary storage slots, and the virtual storage pages that they support, are managed by separate components of z/OS. These components[2] are known as the real storage manager, the auxiliary storage manager, and the virtual storage manager.

Real Storage Manager

(RSM) keeps track of the contents of central storage. It manages the paging activities such as page-in, page-out, and page stealing and helps with swapping an address space in or out. RSM also performs page fixing, which is marking pages as unavailable for stealing.

Auxiliary storage manager

(ASM) uses the system's page data sets to keep track of auxiliary storage slots. Specifically:

- Slots for virtual storage pages that are not in central storage frames

- Slots for pages that do not occupy frames but, because the frame's contents have not been changed, the slots are still valid.

When a page-in or page-out is required, ASM works with RSM to locate the proper central storage frames and auxiliary storage slots.

Virtual storage manager

(VSM) responds to requests to obtain and free virtual storage. VSM also manages storage allocation for any program that must run in real, rather than virtual storage. Real storage is allocated to code and data when they are loaded in virtual storage. As they run, programs can request more storage by means of a system service, such as the GET-MAIN macro. Programs can release storage with the FREEMAIN macro. VSM keeps track of the map of virtual storage for each address space. In so doing, it sees an address space as a collection of 256 subpools, which are logically related areas of virtual storage identified by the numbers 0 to 255. Being logically related means the storage areas within a subpool share characteristics such as:

- Storage protect key

---

[2]Extracted from [36]

- Whether they are fetch protected, pageable, or swappable

- Where they must reside in virtual storage (above or below 16 megabytes)

- Whether they can be shared by more than one task

Some subpools (numbers 128 to 255) are predefined by use by system programs. Subpool 252, for example, is for programs from authorized libraries. Others (numbered 0 to 127) are defined by user programs.

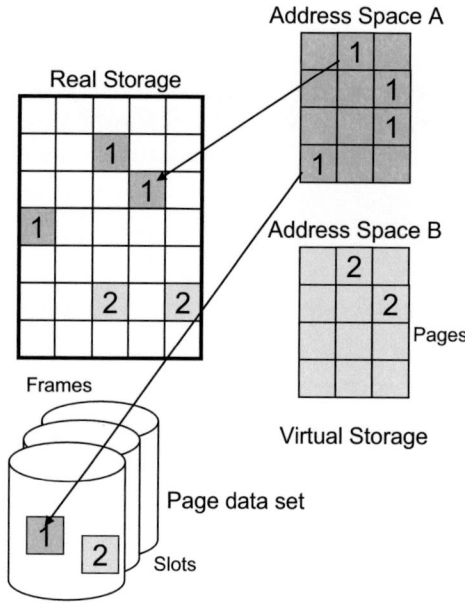

Figure 3.15.: Real, Virtual and Auxiliary Storage

3.5.2. Managing Storage

For managing storage and how and why it evolved over time we must first take a look at storage sizes. For System /390 only 2 GB of real storage and up to 16GB of expanded storage could be installed. Meanwhile it is possible to to install up to 3 TB of real memory. Even if no z/OS system really uses that much storage, it can easily use storage sizes of 128 GB or more.

Managing storage for the operating system means to determine which pages should stay in real storage and which should be sent to expanded storage and auxiliary storage on System /390 and to auxiliary storage only on System z. Virtual storage is part of the address spaces therefore managing storage can be achieved in two ways [3]:

1. By swapping a complete address space out of storage. That means all pages and control structures except those which are required to bring the address space back into storage are sent to auxiliary storage. Swapping is the most drastic way for freeing up storage. On System z an address space could be logically and physically be swapped out. We will discuss this in more detail in chapter 5 when we take a look at the corresponding management algorithms. It must also be mentioned that because of the huge storage sizes which are available on today's systems physically swapping is no longer be done.

2. By paging pages to auxiliary storage. Paging requires to understand which pages are more often needed than others in order to avoid that a page which just got swapped out will be swapped back in immediately. Paging is also a good example how storage algorithms must adapt to a growing system. We will see that System /360 to System /390 developed very sophisticated storage measurements which became problematic when the memory size grew to 10 or 20 times of the memory being available for 31 bit addressing.

Classical Storage Management

The classical method of managing storage counts how often and frequent pages are referenced. The measurements are taken by a system component named System Resource Manager (SRM) which is predecessor and today part of the z/OS Workload Manager. The hardware provides for each page information for the access authority, whether the page is write protected (F), whether it has been referenced (R) or modified (C). We already discussed the access bits which are used for storage protection in section 2.11.4.

Figure 3.16 shows the usage of the reference and change bit for managing storage. When ever a page is referenced, the reference bit (R) is set to '1'. When

---

[3] see also section 4.2.1 for Address Space States for CPU and Storage Management

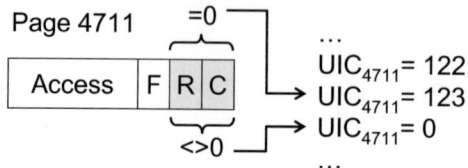

Figure 3.16.: Page Statistics

the page is changed the change bit (C) is set to '1'. SRM[4] continuously monitored all pages and counts for each page whether it has been accessed or not. If the reference or change bit is set a counter named the Unreferenced Interval Count (UIC) which exists for each page of an address space was set to '0' and when the flags are zero the counter was incremented. The highest original value of the counter was 256 because it it was an 8 bit field. For later versions the sampling frequency has been decreased and the counter could reach a value of 2560 at maximum.

Paging means that the RSM must steal pages from address spaces which are swapped into the system. In addition RSM maintains a queue of unused pages named the available frame queue. As long as little activity exist in the system enough unreferenced pages are queued off the Available Frame Queue but when contention starts, the number of frames available to resolve immediate storage requests shrinks. If it falls below a threshold paging starts and RSM must decide which pages it can take first. For this reason the pages are queued by their UIC in Last Recently Used (LRU) order for each address space and the address spaces by their highest UIC. Stealing pages now obtains pages first from address spaces with a high UIC. The overall UIC for the system was also a good indicator how much contention existed on the memory subsystem.

Scaling Problems

The classical method for managing storage is very precise and works quiet well for systems with 31 bit addressing. A similar technique was developed for managing pages in expanded storage but also expanded storage only consisted of 16 GB. The classical technique showed scalability problems when the in-

---

[4]System Resource Manager is part of the operating systems and monitors and manages resource access

stalled memory grew with 64 bit addressing to 10 to 20 times of its original size of 2 GB. Especially if address spaces need to be swapped in it is necessary to steal pages from address spaces in storage for the address space which is swapped in. The address spaces now have very long page queues and searching through all these queues, finding the best pages to be paged out and updating the UICs became very expensive and could last multiple seconds. This causes significant reduction in system throughput and thus requires a different method which might not be as precise as the original memory management technique but better adapted to large memory sizes.

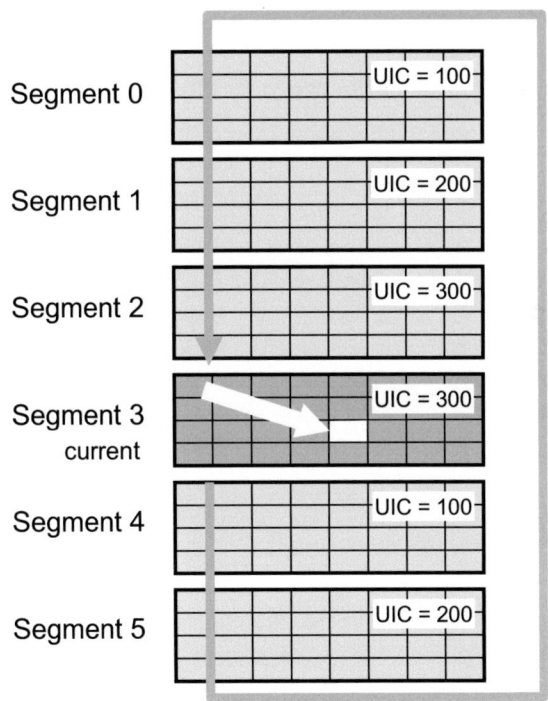

Figure 3.17.: UIC Calculation on current z/OS Systems

New Storage Management

Figure 3.17 depicts the new storage management. It introduces a new way to calculate the UIC. The storage is split into segments depending on the amount of storage installed for the z/OS system. SRM and RSM calculate a UIC for each logical segment. The UIC is calculated by moving a cursor through the storage. Every segment UIC segment UIC represents the time in seconds the cursor spent in the other logical segments and in the current segment. Pages are simply stolen from the segment with the highest UIC if the reference bit is turned off. The system calculates three UICs:

$$MinimumUIC = Minimum(Segment_0, Segment_1, ..., Segment_n) \tag{3.1}$$

$$MaximumUIC = Maximum(Segment_0, Segment_1, ..., Segment_n) \tag{3.2}$$

$$CurrentUIC = \frac{1}{n} \bullet \sum_{k=1}^{n} Segment_k \tag{3.3}$$

The new storage management is not as precise as the old technique was but it is much better suited for large memory sizes. It is also a good example that very accurate book keeping might be necessary if a resource is very constraint and more relaxed algorithms are sufficient if enough resources are available. The newer storage management algorithms are important to remember because they resolve a scalability concern for z/OS growing beyond the limits of 31 bit addressing.

3.6. z/OS Data Sets

On z/OS files are called data sets. The reason for this is that the construct which is used to store data on a disk or tape may consist of multiple single files.

Disks on z/OS are named Direct Access Storage Device (DASD). The I/O architecture is a record oriented architecture as opposed to I/O architectures on UNIX or Windows systems which are byte oriented. Therefore data sets are typically structured files and not just sequences of bytes. The I/O architecture is also named Extended Count Key Data (ECKD) architecture which refers to the way data sets are structured on a DASD. A data stream usually consists of a data count, a data key and the data record (see figure 3.18).

DASD	Bytes/Track	Tracks/Cylinder	Cylinder/Volume	Bytes/Volume
3380	47476	15	885-2655	630-1890 MB
3390	56664	15	1113-3339	946-2838 MB
9345	46456	15	1440-2156	1000-1500 MB

Table 3.2.: Sizes of last physically build z/OS DASDs

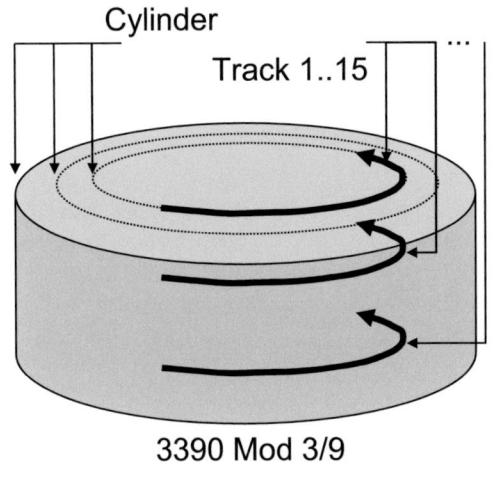

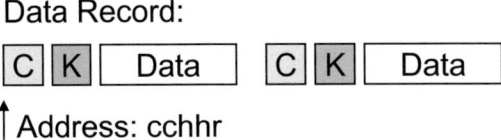

Figure 3.18.: Structure of a Direct Access Device and Count Key Data

DASDs in the original way do not exist anymore. Today a DASD just exists as a logical volume which is mapped to standard disks in a storage controller. The last physical DASDs were 3390 Model 3, Model 9 and 9345. Such DASDs consisted of tracks and cylinders. A track is a single disc and a 3390 consisted of 15 tracks per cylinder. The cylinder refers to the read write position of the head on the track. A 3390 and also the preceding model 3380 had 15 read write heads each and were able to save between 630MB and 2.6 GB (see table 3.2). Today logical volumes can meanwhile get to nearly any size of capacity. But this required many changes to the architecture.

Another architectural specialty is that z/OS allows for 216 = 65536 device addresses. The simple reason for this is that a device address is made of a 2 byte word. Again something which cant be changed in the system anymore. To overcome this limitations the device addresses are now pooled in multiple sub-channel sets, see section 2.13.5.

3.6.1. Sequential Data Sets

z/OS data sets are a collection of multiple files. The basic data sets are sequential or partitioned data sets. A sequential data set consists of one file which is organized in multiple records. A sequential data set can have a fixed record size up to 32768 bytes. The records can be blocked or unblocked. Also variable record lengths are possible.

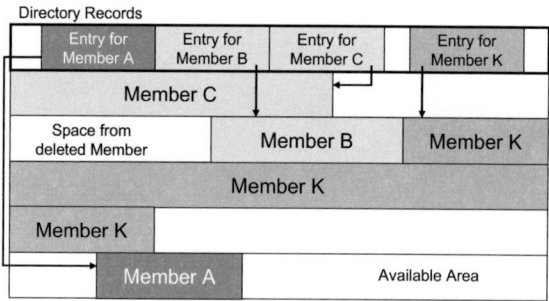

Figure 3.19.: Structure of a Partitioned Data Set

3.6.2. Partitioned Data Sets

A partitioned data set (PDS) consists of an index and multiple members (see figure 3.19). The directory blocks define the size of the index and thus the number of members which can be allocated. The index contains a reference to the member of the data set. If a member is changed the old member is deleted and a new version is appended at the end. This will lead over time to a situation that a partitioned data set is full while there is still a lot of unused space in the data set. If that is the case the data set must be compressed. With PDSE (Partition data Set Extended) this is no longer necessary and the garbage collection runs automatically.

```
   Menu  RefList  Utilities  Help
   --------------------------------------------------------------------
                          Allocate New Data Set
   Command ===>

   Data Set Name   . . . : VAUPEL.SAMPLE.CLIST

   Management class . . . NOMIG        (Blank for default management class)
   Storage class  . . . . STANDARD     (Blank for default storage class)
   Volume serial . . . . LABEL0        (Blank for system default volume) **
   Device type . . . . .                (Generic unit or device address) **
   Data class . . . . . .               (Blank for default data class)
   Space units . . . . . MEGABYTE      (BLKS, TRKS, CYLS, KB, MB, BYTES
                                         or RECORDS)
   Average record unit                 (M, K, or U)
   Primary quantity  . . 3             (In above units)
   Secondary quantity    10            (In above units)
   Directory blocks  . . 100           (Zero for sequential data set) *
   Record format . . . . FB
   Record length . . . . 80
   Block size  . . . . . 6160
   Data set name type    PDS           (LIBRARY, HFS, PDS, LARGE, BASIC, *
                                         EXTREQ, EXTPREF or blank)
   Extended Attributes                 (NO, OPT or blank)
   Expiration date . . .               (YY/MM/DD, YYYY/MM/DD
   Enter "/" to select option          YY.DDD, YYYY.DDD in Julian form
      Allocate Multiple Volumes        DDDD for retention period in days
                                         or blank)
```

Figure 3.20.: Allocating a z/OS Data Set via ISPF

While it seems pretty old fashioned to allocate data sets with a fixed size and also sometimes with a fixed block length it is very efficient to use such data sets by application programs especially batch programs. It must be understood that z/OS is not primarily an operating system for an on-line user but an operating system to process multiple applications simultaneously as efficient as possible and also to access external data as fast as possible.

3.6.3. Allocating a Data Set

Figure 3.20 shows the ISPF (Interactive Programming Facility) screen to allocate a data set. In this example a partitioned data set is created. When a data set is allocated it is necessary to specify the record length, whether it is blocked or unblocked and the space of the dataset. The space of the dataset can be defined in a classical way as multiples of cylinders, tracks or blocks or in a newer version as bytes, KB or MB. In our example we must specify directory blocks because this data set should contain multiple members. For a sequential data set we would define 0 in this field which distinguishes the allocation process for a sequential and a partitioned data set.

3.6.4. Virtual Storage Access Method

The most important data set type for application usage is Virtual Storage Access Method (VSAM). The most important subtypes are:

Key Sequenced Data Set
> (KSDS) are sorted by an ascending key. A KSDS data set is organized in control intervals (CI) which consists of records (R1, .., Rn), Free Space (FS), Record Definition Files (RDF2, , RDFn) and the Control Interval Definition Field (CIDF). The CI is the smallest data unit which is carried between disk and main memory. CIs are organized in Control Areas and the are split when the free space is not sufficient to save new logical records.

Entry Sequenced Data Set
> (ESDS) is a data set organization where the records are sequentially created. A record is never deleted but invalidated. Also a key exists to access specific records but the access is always sequentially.

Relative Record Data Set
> (RRDS) consists of a pre-defined number of of formatted data records. The records can be accessed by a sequence number. A formatted entry may or may not contain data.

Variable RRDS

(VRRDS) can have variable length records. Because of that it is no longer possible to pre-define the records. So a VRRDS is really organized like a KSDS with the record number as key.

Linear Data Set

(LDS) consists of byte streams of 4KB records.

ESDS, RRDS, and VRRDS are specialized data sets for sequential processing. The most important data set is the KSDS which allows to implement data bases. The first data bases on MVS were all implemented based on KSDS data sets. A KSDS also always consists of 2 files: an index file and a data file. A KSDS as well as the other VSAM data sets can be allocated via storage management utilities.

Another set of data sets are available for UNIX System Services. There are basically two UNIX file systems on z/OS: HFS and zFS. They are internally mapped to linear data sets (and earlier to partitioned data sets).

3.6.5. Data Set Organization

Data sets on z/OS can consist of up to 44 characters with qualifiers of up to eight characters which are separated by dots. The highest level qualifier (HLQ) has an entry in the master catalog of the system with a pointer to its user catalog which contains entries for all data sets of this qualifier. Typically each TSO (Time Sharing Option) user has a high level qualifier but the system administrators can also create high level qualifiers which can be accessed by multiple applications. The system usually has the high level qualifier SYS1.

The user catalogs then contain a list of all data sets which belong to this HLQ. For each data set a reference to the DASD on which it is located exist. On the DASD the data set is also listed in the Volume Table of Content (VTOC) with the address where it is located on the disk. Data sets can also span across multiple DASDs.

3.7. Starting z/OS

Starting z/OS from disk and loading it into main memory is named Initial Program Load (IPL). As a preparation the microcode of the physical system must be initialized already. This step is named Initial Microcode Load (IML). The

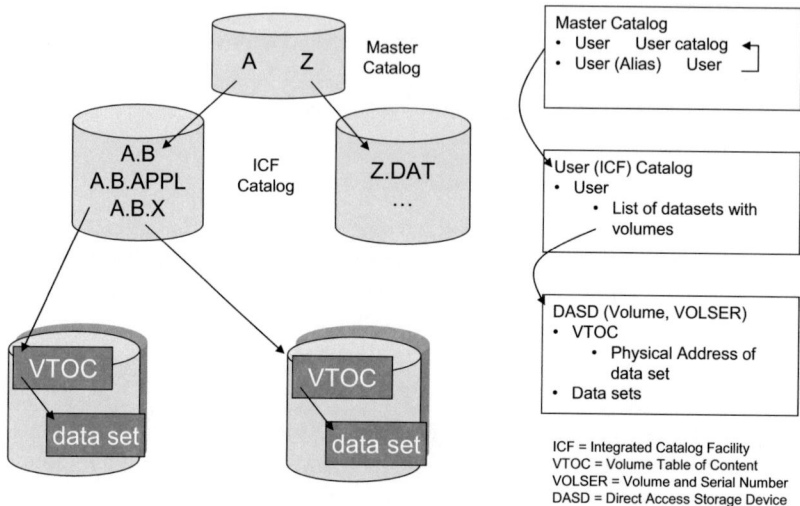

Figure 3.21.: Data Set Index

operating system initialization (IPL) is initiated either from the Hardware Support Element (SE) or the Hardware Management Console (HMC).

The figure 3.22 shows the informatiuon required to start a z/OS system. The LOADPARM is set on the HMC and the address of the disk on which the operating system programs are located. In the example above this disk has the address 705 and it is named SYSRES (system resident disk). The LOADPARM parameter consists of the following information:

- The address of the disk where the I/O definition is stored. z/OS requires a pre-defined I/O definition which needs to be generated prior to the IPL. The I/O definition contains definitions for each I/O device and it is the base for the operating system to create the internal control structures. The I/O definition is stored in an IODF (I/O Definition File) and the data set name is SYS1.IODF. The address in the example above is 206.

- The suffix of the initialization file. The initialization file contains references to all attributes of the operating system. The file is contained in a partitioned data set SYS1.IPLPARM on the SYSRES volume and always has the prefix LOAD with a two digit suffix. The LOADxx member defines which configuration attributes are loaded

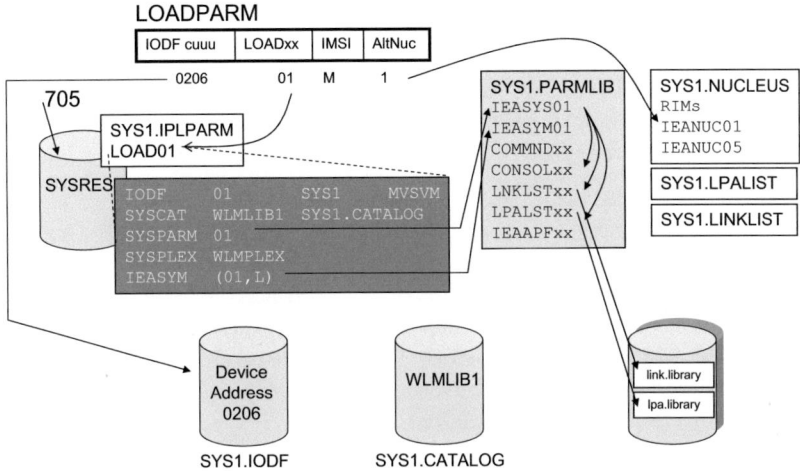

Figure 3.22.: Information to IPL a z/OS System

- In case an alternate nucleus should be started the LOADPARM allows to specify the suffix of the alternate nucleus. The IMSI value is no practical importance.

The LOADxx members now defines the first level of information required to start the system:

- The IODF line defines the IODF suffix (01), the high level qualifier of the IODF data set (SYS1) and the name of the system to be started (MVSVM). The IODF data set resides on the disk defined at the IODF address of 206. This shows the full flexibility of the system start which allows to define multiple configurations and then describe the actual configuration by composing them based on different aspects. This flexibility is available to all parts of the system definition for every aspect.

- The SYSCAT row names the primary system catalog data set and the Volume Label on which it resides.

- The SYSPARM row now points to the main member IEASYSxx of the SYS1.PARMLIB. This is the main parameter library for all z/OS system components. The suffix now points to the main member which then has refernces to all other members of the system.

- The SYSPLEX line defines the name of the cluster in which the z/OS system is started.

- The IEASYM line defines similar to the SYSPARM line the suffix of the member which defines generic values for system generation. These are variables which can then be used in other system definitions.

SYS1.PARMLIB is the main parameter data set of z/OS. As mentioned before every system component has its own parameter members in this data set. For example the CONSOLxx member defines the consoles of the system, and the COMMNDxx member system commands which need to be executed at a certain point of the IPL process. Other important members are LNKLSTxx and LPALSTxx which describe the default library concatenation for executable programs and programs which can be loaded permanently in the LPA areas of common storage (See Program Execution).

The IPL process can be separated in 3 steps:

Step 1 Initialization

- Only 1 processor is enabled

- Load of I/O Configuration

- Load of Resource Initialization Modules (RIM) which create system control structures

- Load of nucleus

- Start of master address space

Start 2 System Start

- Activate all processors

- Switch to master console, Step 1 only showed a limited NIP (Nucleus Initialization) console

- Start of system address spaces. Many system functions have their own address spaces which are started and initialized by the master address space

- Start of Job Entry System. Now z/OS BCP (Basic Control Program) is completely initialized and ready

Start 3 Start of Subsystems and Applications

3.8. Job Entry System

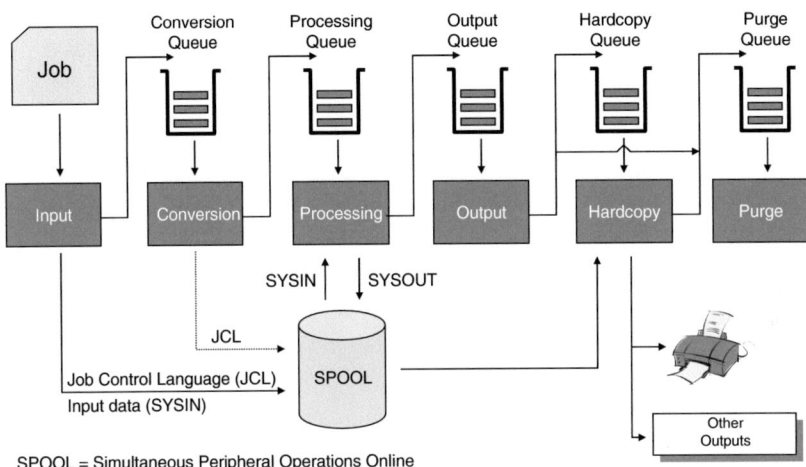

Figure 3.23.: Steps of Job Execution

We already discussed that the Job Entry System is necessary to create address spaces in the system but the main functionality is controlling the program execution of batch work: Accepting the Job Control Statements Providing the resources for the job to run (data sets, devices) Controlling job execution with the possibility to define check point at which the job execution can be resumed if necessary Buffering of data in and output. This process is named spooling. Freeing the resources after program execution

Figure 3.23 depicts the steps of job execution:

Input   JES accepts the control statements from a card reader. There are no physical card readers anymore therefore program which functions as a card reader is named Internal Reader. Internal readers are defined by the system programmers and they are initialized at start of JES. Starting an address space also uses an internal reader which receives the control statements from SYS1.PROCLIB.

Conversion
translates the control statements and provides error checking. If the control statements are correct they are placed on the spool dataset.

Processing

A batch job is selected from a processing queue by an initiator (see Creation of Address Spaces). Batch jobs are defined to classes and initiators are started for each class. With this technique an installation can control how many jobs of a certain class are being executed. By using Workload Manager Batch Management it is also possible that the installation delegates the starting and stopping of initiators to the z/OS internal function Workload Manager. A job can only be executed if it can access to all required resources (data sets, tapes, disks). In a multi system environment it is also possible to define that a job should only be executed on a certain system if for example certain resources (like a data base for example) is only available on that system.

Output The output which is generetaed during job conversion and execution is saved in a virtual data set which is passed to the JES output queue.

Hardcopy

After end of execution the virtual output data set is passed to a printer. Usually there is no physical print step anymore and the hardcopy output is just placed in another virtual data set.

Purge   Also after end of execution the virtual data sets can be purged in order to free the spool space.

3.9. Time Sharing Option

The classical interface for interactive users is TSO/E (Time Sharing Option/-Extended). Similar to a UNIX shell it allows access to resources of the system and provides editors and command interpreters.. TSO is a line and page oriented user interface. In order to use it efficiently a menu oriented interface ISPF (Interactive System Productivity Facility) can be started when the TSO environment has been established.

Two command interpreters are provided on TSO: CLIST which is an abbreviation for Command-List. This is the original interpretative language for combining multiple commands together. With REXX (Restructured Extended Executor) a modern command interpreter exists which provides powerful string manipulation capabilities. Figure 3.24 shows how a TSO user is embedded in the MVS system and how a TSO user address space is created and how a connection to the terminal is established. Today there are no real terminals available anymore instead a terminal emulation runs on a workstation.

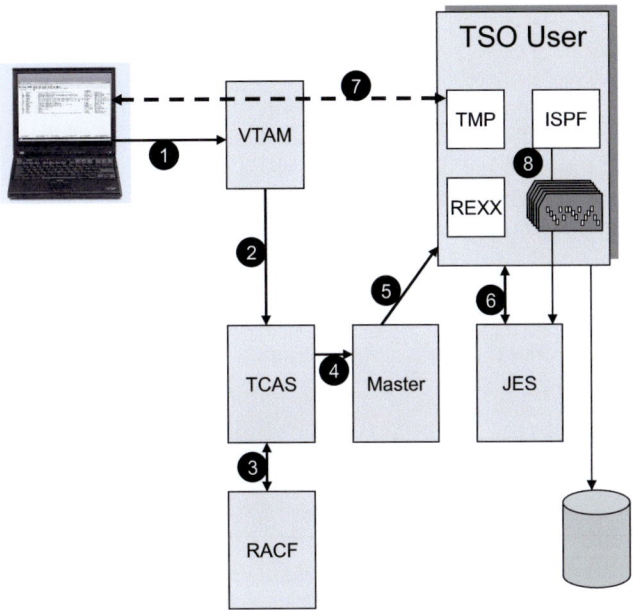

Figure 3.24.: Initializing a TSO Address Space

The steps for initializing a TSO address space as shown in figure 3.24 are described below:

1. User Requests LOGON

2. VTAM passes LOGON to TSO Control Address Space (TCAS)

3. TCAS verifies the request with RACF® (Resource Access and Control Facility)

4. If successful TCAS passes request to MASTER address space

5. MASTER creates the TSO user address space

6. INIT task initializes the address space with JES

7. Connection established between Terminal Monitor Program (TMP) and end user thru VTAM

8. User can start ISPF, use command languages (e.g. REXX, access devices and edit and submit jobs, etc)

A detailed description on TSO and how it can be used is available in [4].

3.10. Unix System Services

UNIX System Services are part of the operating system and it is about 35% of the code base of z/OS. USS follows POSIX standard 1003.2 and the XPG/4 proting rules of the X/OPEN Group. The kernel is integrated in the basic control program and the kernel functions can be used by any process of the z/OS system. For end users three possibilities exist to use UNIX functions:

1. UNIX Shell: A user can connect to z/OS via telnet or rlogin and start directly a UNIX shell.

2. A special IShell exists which provides an ISPF interface to use UNIX System Services

3. UNIX functions can also be directly invoked from ISPF and TSO.

Figure 3.25 shows how UNIX System Services are integrated in z/OS. The abbreviation internally is OMVS because USS was former named Open MVS. Member BPXPRMxx is the parameter member for UNIX system services in SYS1.PARMLIB. It defines the start procedure of the USS kernel address space (usually OMVS), the name of the root file system and the file system organization. Other important address spaces are BPXONIT which is PID(1) and it is the mother process of /etc/rc. All orphaned processes are assigned to it for garbage collection.

A new UNIX process is usually created by a fork() or spawn() operation. In z/OS this would mostly result in creating a new address space. In order to reduce the startup overhead for new address spaces UNIX address spaces are also pre-started similar to initiators for batch jobs. These address spaces are named BPXAS and they are pre started by the z/OS Workload Manager component.

Unix System Services[5] is today a significant part of z/OS which accounts for more than 1/3 of the operating system. A set of shell environments allow the end user to logon to USS either through a telnet, rlogin or directly from an ISPF session. USS also builds on top of the language environment which provides C++ and Java language on z/OS, it is integrated with TCP/IP and security

---

[5]Unix System Services was formerly named Open MVS and abbreviated as OMVS. These terms still exist inside the system

services and supports multiple file systems. In figure 3.25 we saw that the file system type for the root file system is HFS which means Hierarchical File System. In addition another file system named zFS and Network file systems can be used from USS.

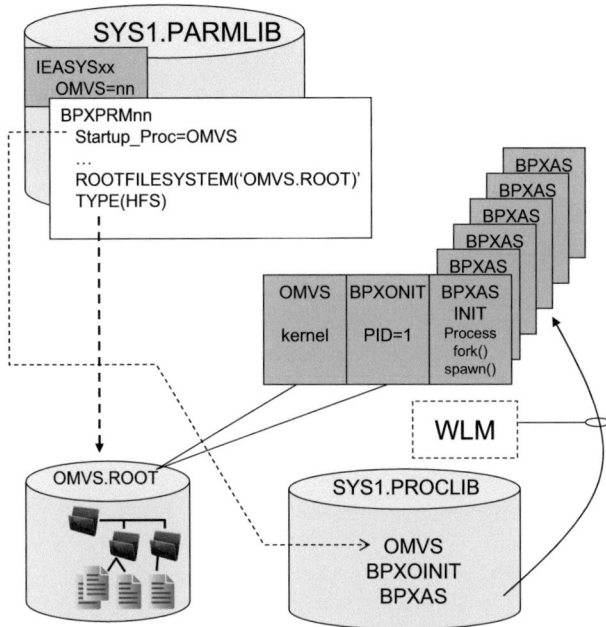

Figure 3.25.: Unix System Services

3.11. Summary

At this point we complete our overview of z/OS. We can observe that z/OS combines both: the heritage of a mature operating system with constructs going back to the 1970s and adaptations and enhancements which provide a a very flexible, powerful and efficient system.

Two major functions were not discussed and because they are very important for both scalability and high availability we will discuss them extensively in the two following chapters: Dispatching and Workload Management.

4. Dispatching

All operating systems on System z run in a virtualized environment. This always requires two dispatching processes for the executing work, one of the operating system which assigns a logical processor to the unit of work and one of the virtualization layer which assigns a physical processor to the logical processor. In this course segment we will discuss the dispatching processes for z/OS and PR/SM. We will further discuss how they act together and which parts became problematic for allowing an environment with many physical and logical processors to scale and to exploit the high processor frequency of System z10 and z196.

For System z10 the processor frequency grew by a factor of 2.5 compared to the previous System z models. We already discuss in section 2.5 that more cache structures were required to accommodate the speed difference between memory and the processor. But this is not enough. The complete section 2.8 discusses techniques to speed up the execution within the processor and how it is possible to reduce cache accesses. We will now see that the two separate dispatching processes are also problematic for gaining maximum performance out of the system. The solution is a new modified and combined dispatching mechanism named Hiperdispatch which synchronizes the activities of the PR/SM and the z/OS dispatcher to also provide high efficient execution on System z10 and z196.

4.1. Dispatching Requirements

We discussed virtualization and how it is supported in the hardware already in section 2.14. Now we want to take a look what requirements exist for dispatching in the virtualization layer of the hardware, the Process Resource and Systems Manager (PR/SM) and the z/OS operating system.

Figure 4.1 depicts a possible virtualized environment on System z. The graphic assumes that many different virtualized operating systems and potential further virtualization layers are running on System z. This is possible and it needs to be considered that up to 60 LPARs may run on a System z CEC. That also means that many small can share the computing hardware. It is also independent of the number of active physical processors on the systems. But more often large installations divide the CEC in few partitions with some very big z/OS systems. Very often 2 or 3 big partitions share the CEC together with some number of smaller systems for test and maintenance. Figure **??** shows such a typical LPAR environment which can be found in large customer installations. The graphic shows a CEC with four partitions, one very large systems and 3 smaller LPARs.

In addition a z/OS system may support more than 1 processor type. z/OS allows to run processors on which Java workload and processors on which service oriented work can be offloaded from regular processors. This is primarily done for cost effectiveness but needs to be considered too.

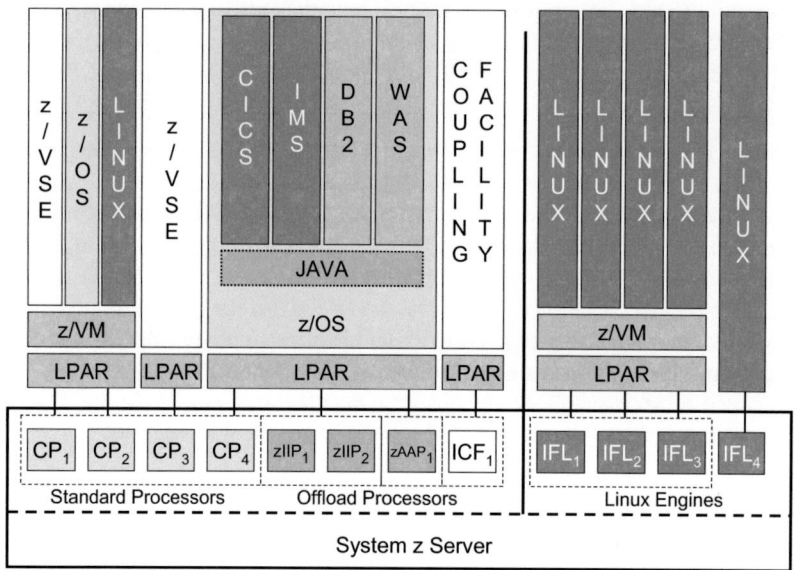

Figure 4.1.: Logical Partitioning supported on System z

Typically many different applications share the same z/OS system. Figure 4.3 takes a look into the large partition named SYS1 which is shown in figure 4.2. The graphic shows a two day period of the system and we can observe many different applications as well as changing utilization requirements over time. During the night time different types of batch jobs use up to 100% of the system resources and during day time *On-line Transaction Processing* work together with DB2 are the dominating workloads.

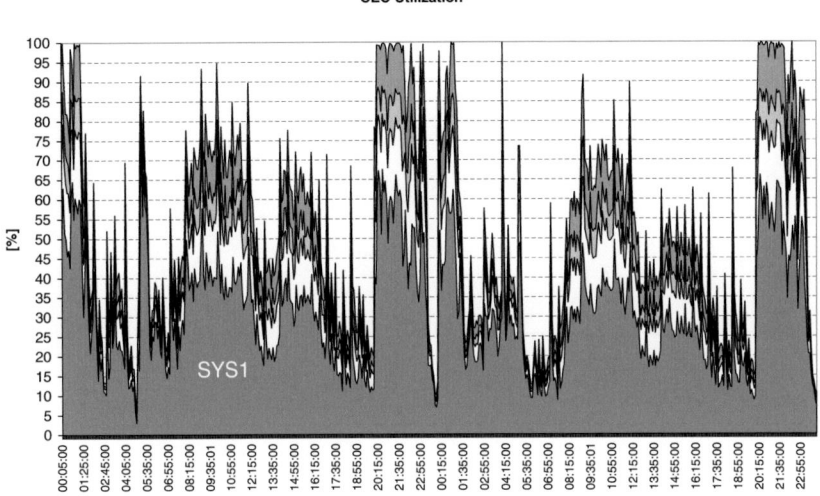

Figure 4.2.: Typical Partitioning of a System z CEC

This is a difference of z/OS to other operating systems which typically host mostly a single middleware or application and it is based on history. In the 1970s and 1980s business hosted all of their applications on the mainframe. As a result the mainframe and especially the predecessors of z/OS developed techniques which allowed them to host applications with very different resource and runtime requirements. An example of such techniques is the possibility to assign different dispatching priorities to different types of work. This allows to distinguish short running OLTP work from long running batch jobs which do not have the same short response time objectives. In the end these requirements led to the development of z/OS Workload Manager (see chapter 5) which assured that the access to system resources is oriented towards business goals and reflects changing workload usage of the system.

PR/SM needs to ensure that the partitions can share the system resources efficiently and guarantees that a defined amount of resources is always available to the partitions as well as allowing the partitions to use unused resources. We will discuss both dispatching processes of PR/SM and z/OS in detail and how they interact with each other.

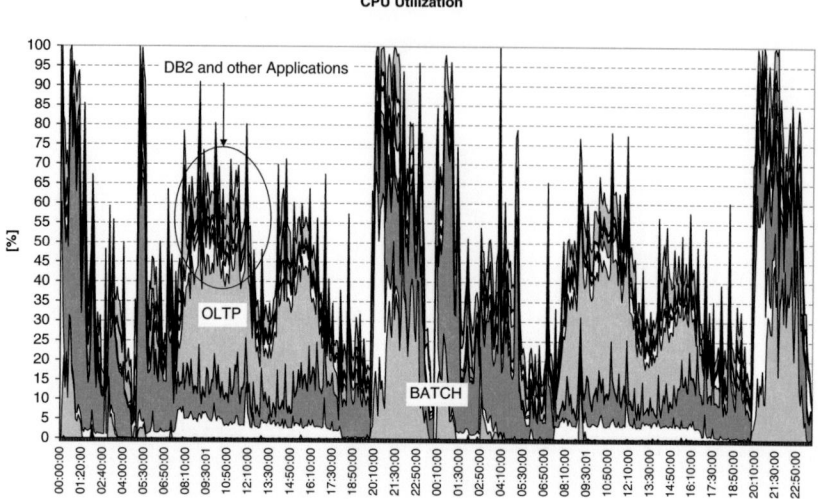

Figure 4.3.: Typical Workload Utilization on z/OS

4.2. z/OS Dispatching

Before we start to look into dispatching we want to take a look on the work which executes on z/OS and how z/OS differentiates these types of work. Basically we can distinguish work in 4 categories:

- Address spaces of which z/OS does not know much. Address spaces are just in the system and request access to CPU and other resources.

- On-line users, like TSO or UNIX System Services users. The corresponding address spaces are instrumented and whenever the user presses the ENTER button the address space signals the system that a transaction begins which ends when the result of the command is returned to the output device (terminal) of the user.

- For Batch or APPC (Advanced Program to Program Communication) a new transaction starts when the address space selects the batch job or receives the communication task and it ends when the batch job or communications tasks are finished.

- Finally On-line Transaction Processing which is recognized in two ways:

1. As address spaces, also named application regions. These are the processes which receive the work requests and process them.

2. The individual work requests. They are not automatically visible to the operating system but the operating system provides application interfaces which allow the OLTP manager to inform it when a transaction starts and when it completes. A more detailed discussion on how transactions are recognized and managed follows in chapter 5.

As a summary we must notice that z/OS runs very short living on-line requests in parallel to potentially very long running batch jobs. We can also observe that everything which is more than just an address space requires instrumentation and therefore requires cooperation of the z/OS subsystem, or the middleware with the operating system.

4.2.1. CPU and Storage Management

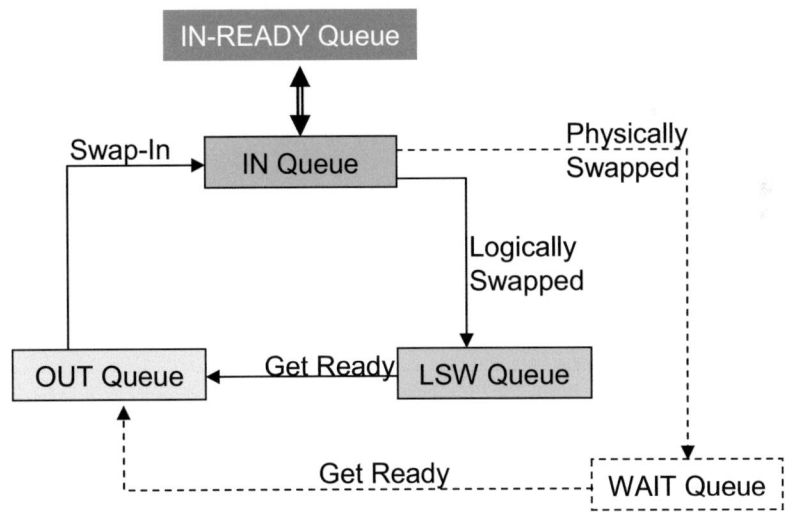

Figure 4.4.: Address Space States

The next step is to take a brief look in the intersection between storage and CPU management. It is only meaningful to dispatch a unit of work if the corresponding address space is in storage so that it is possible to access at least its major tables and minimum working set. In order to understand the state of address spaces a simple state machine exists which tells the system about an address space state and what has to be done next.

- If an address space is on the IN-Queue and gets ready the TCBs and SRBs which want to process data can be placed on the System Work Unit Queue of the dispatcher. All address spaces which are on the IN-Queue and which have ready TCBs or SRBs are logically placed on the IN-READY-Queue which represents all address spaces which currently execute or request execution. The IN-READY-Queue is just a logical queue.

- If an address space gets swapped out it can be swapped out in two ways:

  - It can be physically swapped out and is then placed on the WAIT-Queue. A physical swapped address space is just represented by its major control block in the system and all working set pages are moved to the page and swap datasets. In todays environments address spaces are no longer physically swapped out but the state still exists. The main reason is that the main memory is so big that it is not necessary to completely move all pages of an address space to disk (see section 3.5).

  - If the address space is logically swapped out the in storage parts are trimmed but some pages remain in storage to resume the address space faster.

- An address space is moved to the OUT-Queue when it is either physically or logically swapped out and a work unit (TCB or SRB) signals that it needs to run. The next step is to swap the address space in, place it on the IN-Queue and the ready TCB or SRB on the System Work Unit Queue.

4.2.2. Dispatcher Queue

All work elements which need to run on a processor are anchored on the System Work Unit Queue[1]. Each work element is represented by a Work Element Block (WEB) and the order on the System Work Unit Queue is defined by the major and minor priority of the TCB or SRB. The minor priority just describes a graduation within the priorities for an address space. The major priority is

---

[1]More than one work unit queue exist in z/OS but for the moment we will simplify this to only one work unit queue

calculated by z/OS Workload Manager (WLM) based on service goals defined by the installation. Work units are queued by dispatch priority. The graphic also shows enclaves to which we also referred on the page What is Work?. An enclave encapsulates a TCB or SRB and thus allows to give the unit of work a different dispatch priority than the address space to which it belongs to. All other TCBs and SRBs have the major dispatch priority of the address space. In chapter 5 we will discuss how the system calculates dispatch priorities for the work.

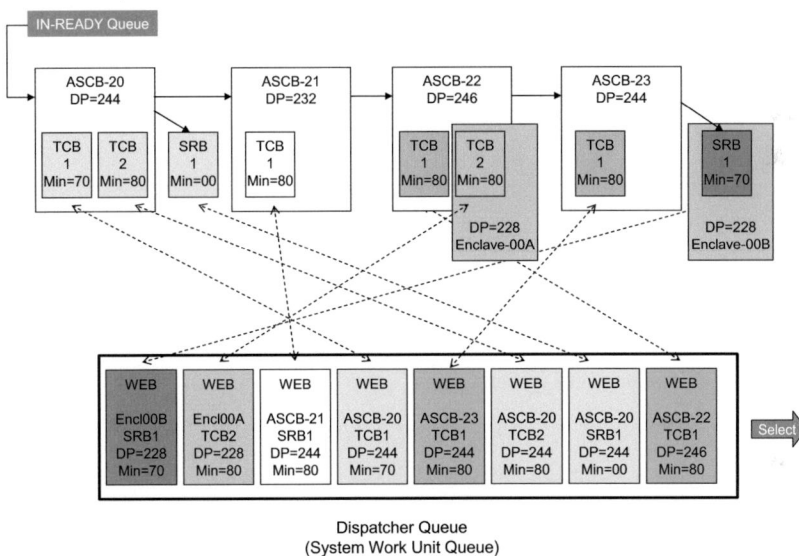

Figure 4.5.: Dispatcher Queue

4.2.3. Dispatching Work

The dispatcher is the central function in the system which will always run on a processor after an interrupt has occurred or the processor was waken up. Figure 4.6 depicts steps of work processing:

1. The First Level Interrupt Handler (FLIH) is loaded after an interrupt or when a unit of work ends. It saves the program state and registers and

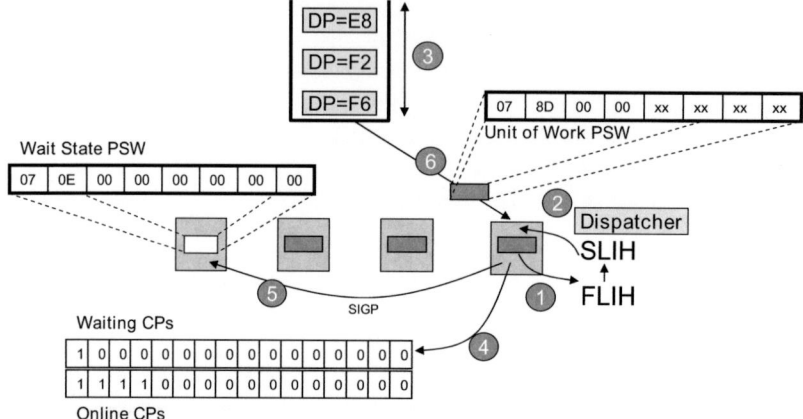

Figure 4.6.: Dispatching Work

then selects the necessary action to process the interrupt (Second Level Interrupt Handler (SLIH) see section 3.3.2).

2. At the end always the dispatcher gets control.

3. The dispatcher examines the System Work Units Queue. One of its tasks is to provide some queue maintenance which runs prior to the next dispatches.

4. Another important task is to observe how long the dispatcher queue is and how the elements have to wait on it. If this exceeds certain thresholds the dispatcher examines whether it can wake up Waiting processors. Processor masks provide the information which processors are on-line and which processors are waiting. If the current processor which executes the dispatcher decides that it should wake up another processor it examines this masks and if it finds a waiting processor it sends a Signal Processor (SIGP) to wake up the processor.

5. Finally the dispatcher selects the next unit of work from the dispatcher queue. If no units of work are on the queue anymore goes into an enabled WAIT state. This means the processor mask flips on that the processor is waiting and a WAIT-State-PSW (Program Status Word) is loaded.

As a summary we can remember that the tasks of the dispatcher are

- To select a work unit to run on a processor
- To load state information
- To control how long a work unit runs
- To save state information
- To load a no-work wait PSW if no work is ready to run

4.2.4. Preemption and Time Slicing

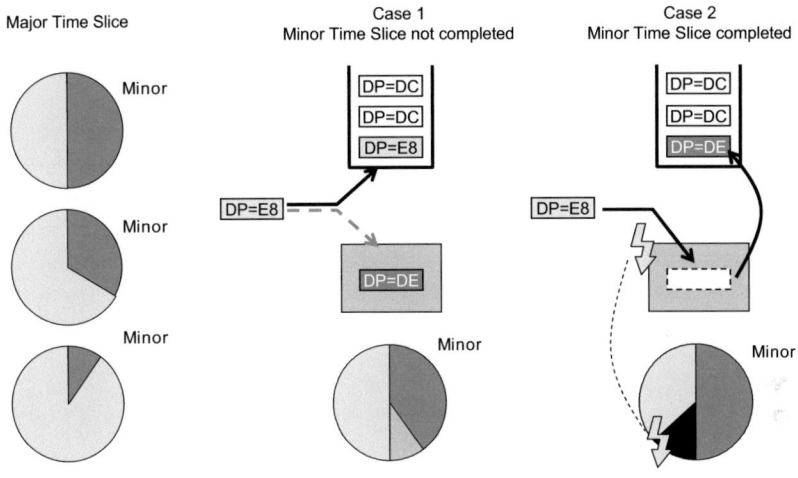

Figure 4.7.: Time Slicing

How long a work unit runs is today determined by time slices. The z/OS dispatcher is a reduced preemption dispatcher and the time slices define how long a unit of work run at a minimum and at a maximum on the processor. Older versions of the MVS and OS/390 dispatcher were full preemption or partially full preemption dispatchers.

Full preemption means that the currently running unit of work is always interrupted when a new unit of work with higher dispatch priority is ready to run. A reduced preemption dispatcher defines two time slices, see figure 4.7:

Case 1 The minor time slice defines the minimum time a unit of work can always stay on the processor before it must leave it because a higher prioritized unit of work is ready to run.

Case 2   If the minor time slice has expired already then the unit of work can be interrupted at any time when a higher unit of work wants to process.

A partially full preemption dispatcher observes the units of work and depending on pre-defined conditions it changes workloads from reduced to full preemption. Such conditions may favor work which may require high responsiveness. Such an observation technique was implemented for the MVS dispatcher when the dispatching algorithms was moved away from a full preemption dispatcher. On current systems even this is not really efficient anymore and it is the best to let all work units run in reduced preemption mode which favors system throughput. Only for system tasks it is sometimes advantageous if they can immediately interrupt all other units of work.

The Major Time Slice defines the amount of time a unit of work can run at a maximum before the dispatcher examines the work unit queue whether an equal prioritized unit of work is waiting to run. If that is the case the current unit of work is paused and placed back to the dispatcher queue. The major time slice is a multiple of the minor time slices and in z/OS environments on a z196 in the range of multiple hundredths of milliseconds. Minor time slices are between two to ten times smaller than the major time slice(see figure 4.7).

4.2.5. Interrupt Processing

An interrupt is an event that alters the sequence in which the processor executes instructions. An interrupt might be planned (specifically requested by the currently running program) or unplanned (caused by an event that might or might not be related to the currently running program). z/OS reacts on the six types of interrupts as described in section 2.9.

Figure 4.8 shows the flow of interrupt processing.

1. When an interrupt occurs the system state, and Program Status Word are saved.

2. The First Level Interrupt Handler then saves the registers (STM, MVC) and selects the service routine or interrupt handler to process the specific interrupt.

3. The new PSW and state to process the interrupt is loaded.

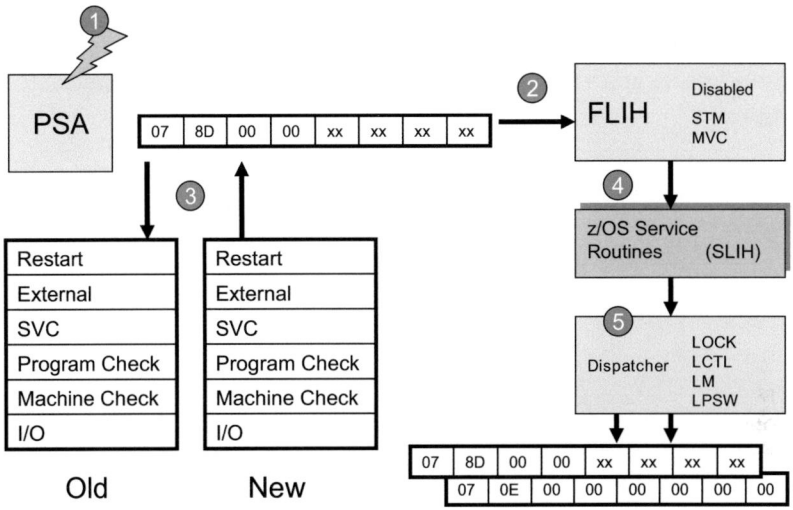

Figure 4.8.: Interrupt Processing

4. There is one major interrupt handler for each of the six interrupt types which can occur. In the section 3.3.2 we looked at this processing when a program check occurs and discussed the invocation of error handling routines which are setup by the application or a system routine.

5. At the end of the interrupt processing the dispatcher becomes control, selects a unit work, locks it and loads its new Program Status Word.

4.2.6. I/O Enablement

The last function we want to take a look at is I/O processing. Most of the I/O request is processed directly by the I/O channel and the System Assist Processor, see section 2.13.4 but when the I/O is completed the I/O must get back to a regular processor. An I/O interrupt is an interrupt which will always interrupt the running process therefore it is not wise to enable all processors of a multi processor environment for I/Os. It is much better to limit the I/O interrupt processing to as few processors as possible. In order to achieve this the I/O interrupt rate and how many I/Os are processed as a result of a Test Pending Interrupt (TPI) are observed. A TPI is always issued at the end of every interrupt processing by the dispatcher therefore it is a good indicator whether I/O interrupts wait for execution. An installation now has the possibility to specify thresholds at which point a new processor is enabled for I/O processing (see figure 4.9).

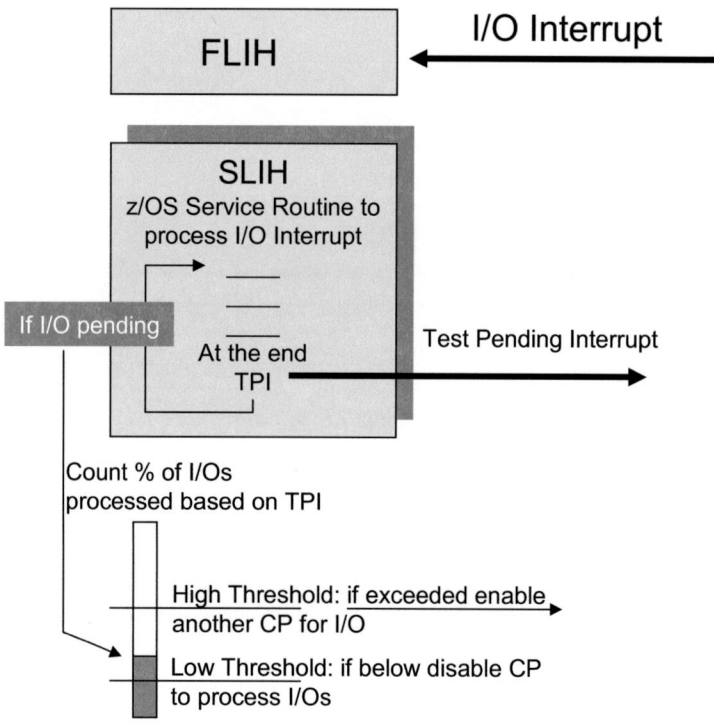

Figure 4.9.: CPU Enablement for I/O

This function conceptually belongs to the z/OS dispatcher but like processor WAIT processing and adjusting of time slices it is not performed by the dispatcher. The reason is that these functions require a permanent data collection and that is not done by the dispatcher. In z/OS another function called the System Resource Manager (SRM) executes such functions on behalf of the dispatcher and provides the results in control areas so that the dispatcher can react on them. The System Resource Manager is since 1995 part of the z/OS Workload Manager and we will discuss these functions in more detail

in chapter 5. The parameter CPENABLE defined in member IEAOPTxx of
SYS1.PARMLIB for the System Resource Manager specifies the low and high
thresholds for enabling and disabling I/O processors.

4.2.7. CPU Report Example

At the end of this section we want to take a look how the information which
we just discussed is presented to the installation. The standard monitoring
and reporting program of IBM to present such data is Resource Measurement
Facility[TM] (RMF[TM]). RMF provides various reports. Performance analysts typically use RMF Postprocessor reports for detailed analysis to understand the
behavior of past events and to tune the operating system.

The example in figure 4.10 shows a CPU Activity report from RMF. The CPU
Activity report displays the MVS view of the logical processors being used on
the system. The depicted system is a small partition with 4 logical processors.
The report shows information for a 5 minute time interval. The reporting length
can be adjusted between 1 minute and 1 hour and is typically 15 minutes for
most installations. All 4 processors were on-line during the reporting period.
The columns LPAR Busy and MVS Busy show how the logical processors are
being used by z/OS (MVS Busy) and how often they were dispatched on a
physical processor of the z System (LPAR Busy). We can observe that on all
processors during this 5 minute period for more than 98% of the time work
has been processed. On the other hand only for 53% of the time the logical
processors were really dispatched on a physical processor (LPAR Busy). When
we look at the "LOG PROC SHARE %" column we can observe that each
processor has a share of 32.6% for using a physical processor. As a result the
partition exceeded its share by more than 20%. We will take a closer look at the
dispatching process of PR/SM to understand how, why, and when a partition
can use more than its share.

Finally processor number 1 is highlighted. When we take a look at the I/O
rate column we can observe that more than 93% of all I/Os were executed on
this processor. So this is the I/O enabled processor of the system. The installation uses the default setting for enabling I/O interrupts processors: CPEN-
ABLE(10,30) which means that a new processor is enabled for I/O when the
rate of handling I/Os via *Test Pending Interrupt* (TPI) exceeds 30%. A processor is disabled when it falls below 10%[2]. During this interval only 25% of the

---

[2]One processor is always enabled for I/O interrupts.

```
1    z/OS V1R9          SYSTEM ID SMPA                   C P U   A C T I V I T Y
                        RPT VERSION V1R9 RMF             START 10/27/2008-20.50.00
-CPU 2097   MODEL 704   H/W MODEL E40                    END   10/27/2008-20.55.00   CYCLE 1.000 SECONDS
                                       SEQUENCE CODE 000000000002610F                HIPERDISPATCH=NO
0---CPU---               ------- TIME % -------                       LOG PROC       --I/O INTERRUPTS--
 NUM TYPE   ONLINE    LPAR BUSY    MVS BUSY    PARKED    SHARE %       RATE           % VIA TPI
 0   CP     100.00    53.42        98.95       -----     32.6          16.46          61.24
 1   CP     100.00    53.42        98.69       -----     32.6          5286           25.15
 2   CP     100.00    53.40        98.63       -----     32.6          19.69          55.70
 3   CP     100.00    53.42        98.93       -----     32.6          330.1          16.93
 TOTAL/AVERAGE        53.41        98.80                 130.4         5652           24.88
```

Figure 4.10.: CPU Report Example

I/Os were processed after executing a TPI instruction and therefore it is not required to enable another processor for I/O.

RMF is not the only reporting function available for z/OS. Many other software vendors provide similar reporting functions. Performance monitoring and reporting is also an important business because performance reports are crucial to run a system efficiently.

4.3. PR/SM Dispatching

The first decision for defining a partition is whether the partition should share the physical processors with other partitions or whether it should use dedicated processors. On System z a partition can only use either shared or dedicated processors with one exception. We will later see that a special partition can use both dedicated and shared processors. Also it should be mentioned that prior to System z competitors also built hardware for S/370 and S/390 architecture. The concept of logical partitioning existed at that time already and both Hitachi and Amdahl the two main competitors supported so call L-shaped partitions which could use dedicated and shared processors.

Partitions with dedicated processors own the physical processor to 100%. The physical processor is not available to any other partition. Partitions with shared processors compete for the shared physical processors. By definition a partition cannot have more logical processors than physical processors which are active on the box. The only exception exists when a physical processor is malfunctioning and must be configured off-line and no spare processor can take over the function of the physical processor. In such cases partitions may have more logical than physical processors.

Each partition which uses shared processors also has a weight defined. The weight defines the share of the physical processor pool which is guaranteed to the partition assuming the number of logical processors is high enough to support this share. PR/SM dispatches the logical processors on the shared physical processors. It uses a time slicing algorithms and determines the priority of logical processors based on the partition share and the time the logical processors have used their share. A system layout with 3 partitions of which two use shared physical processors and one has a dedicated processor is shown in figure 2.48 and figure 4.1 which depicts a more complex environment which also includes offload processors.

When a logical processor is dispatched on a shared physical processor it is possible to complete the dispatch cycle in one of two modes:

Weight Completion = Yes A logical processor must complete its guaranteed share even if the wait state PSW is loaded. This option is a CEC (Central Electronic Complex) wide control and effects all partitions. It guarantees that all partitions have always their share available to it but it doesn't allow partitions to use more than its share.

Weight Completion = No (standard mode of operation): If the logical processor loads the WAIT State PSW the SIE is exited and the control is returned to PR/SM to dispatch another logical processor. Nearly all installations use this mode of operation because it allows to effectively use the available capacity of the CEC.

4.3.1. Dispatching Logical Processors

Metric	Physical or Total	LPAR A	LPAR B	LPAR C
Processors	4	4	3	2
Weight	1000	500	300	200
Weight/LCP		125	100	100
Percent Logical to Physical Processor		50.0%	22.5%	10.0%
3.6% of Share		4.5	3.6	3.6
Resulting Weight Range		120.5-129.5	96.4-103.6	96.4-103.6
Resulting Utilization Range		48.2-51.8	28.9-31.1	19.3-20.7

Table 4.1.: Example for Processor Shares of three Logical Partitions

Table 4.1 shows a very simple partitioning example with 3 partitions. The CEC has 3 shared physical processors (PCPs). Each PCP supports 25% of the total capacity of the CEC. The weights and number of logical processors (LCP) for the 3 partitions are chosen with the following criteria:

- The weight should represent how much capacity the partition can always use from the CEC

- The logical processors should at least support the partitions weight

- At least 2 logical processors should always be defined. There are exceptions for partitions which run really low utilizations or which are not critical for an installation

- The number of logical processors should also assure that the time slice of a logical processor does not become too small

- The number of logical processors should also allow the partition to use more capacity than its guaranteed share

PR/SM guarantees that a processor meets its share within 3.6% precision. The share of each logical processor depends on the partition share and the number of logical processors of the partitions. The resulting weight range for each processor and based on this the resulting utilization range for each partition is calculated in the table above. The following basic equations for determining the share of logical processors are used:

$$\text{Weight per LCP} = \frac{\text{Weight(LPAR)}}{\text{Online LCPs(LPAR)}}$$

$$\text{LCP\% per PCP} = \frac{\text{Weight(LPAR)}}{\text{Total Weight}} \bullet \frac{\text{PCPs Online}}{\text{LCPs Online}}$$

$$\text{Total Weight} = \sum_{LPAR=1}^{N} \text{Weight(LPAR)}$$

$$\text{Res. Weight Range} = \text{Weight per LCP} \pm \text{Weight per LCP} \bullet 3.6\%$$

$$\text{Res. Util. Range} = \text{Res. Weight Range} \bullet \frac{\text{Online LCPs(LPAR)}}{\text{Total Weight}}$$

The example in table 4.1 also shows that the logical processors (LCPs) can't be mapped 1 to 1 to physical processors (PCPs). This is no surprise because the example has 7 LCPs defined by only 4 PCPs. PR/SM will always try to re-dispatch a LCP on the same PCP but the example already shows that this is not always possible. We will discuss this problem in more detail when we look at limitations of the existing dispatching processes.

PR/SM calculates the time slice based on the number of partitions, logical and physical processors of the CEC (see figure 4.11). The resulting value is then capped in the range from 12.5 to 25 ms. For each logical processor PR/SM keeps a history table of 32 entries of cumulative dispatch time. For each time a logical processor has been dispatched the effective dispatch time is filled in the current entry of the history table. The sum of all entries is the Total Effective Dispatch Time. The Total Effective Dispatch Time now determines the priority of a logical processor for the next dispatch interval. A lower value results in a higher dispatch priority.

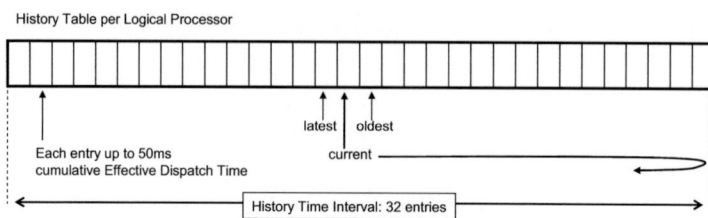

Figure 4.11.: History Time Interval per Logical Processor

The effective dispatch time is the dispatched time multiplied by an expansion factor. The expansion factor is calculated from the number of logical processors and the weight of the partition, the sum of all weights and the number of shared physical processors. The effect is that a partition with a small share and higher logical processor number also gets a higher expansion factor and therefore accumulates more effective dispatch time for the same amount of absolute dispatch time and thus will probably less often dispatched than a partition with a high processor share:

$$
\text{Expansion Factor} = \frac{\text{Total Weights}}{\text{LCP Weight} \bullet \text{\# of Shared PCPs}}
$$

$$
= \frac{\text{Total Weights} \bullet \text{\# of LPAR LCPs}}{\text{LPAR Weight} \bullet \text{\# of Shared PCPs}}
$$

$$
\text{Effective Time} = \text{Effective Time}
$$

$$
+ \text{Dispatched Time} \bullet \text{Expansion Factor}
$$

$$
\text{Total Effective History} = \sum_{i=oldest}^{current} \text{Effective Time Interval}(i)
$$

As an example we will use the partitions from table 4.1. Table 4.2 shows the resulting effective dispatch time for 10 ms dispatch time. Based on the configuration the expansion factor for LPAR A is the smallest because it has the highest weight definition. The processors for LPAR B and C have the same expansion factors and therefore also accumulate the same amount of effective time for the 10 ms dispatch time. This shows a positive effect of defining only 2 logical processors for partition C instead of 3. For 3 logical processors for partition C the expansion factor would be smaller because the weight of partition C is smaller. On the other hand with 2 LCPs partition C can use only up

Metric	Physical or Total	LPAR A	LPAR B	LPAR C
Processors	4	4	3	2
Weight	1000	500	300	200
Weight/LCP		125	100	100
Expansion Factor		2.0	2.5	2.5
Dispatch Time [ms]		10	10	10
Effective Time [ms]		20	25	25

Table 4.2.: PR/SM Dispatching Example

to 50% of the CEC if the other partitions only have little demand while with 3 LCPs it could use 75% of the total CEC capacity.

4.3.2. LPAR Report Example

We will take a look how the information of logical partitions is presented to an installation. We will use the same example for the z/OS system SMPA when we discussed z/OS dispatching. Figure 4.12[3] shows a part of the RMF Partition Data Report which is printed together with the CPU Activity report shown in figure 4.10.

The report shows the partition information. System SMPA runs in a partition with the name LPARA03. Please note that SMPA is the short name of the z/OS system and LPARA03 the name defined on the Hardware Management Console (HMC) for the partition. The CEC has 4 physical shared processors. In the column Number of Physical Processors we can also see other processor types and we will discuss them in the following sections. Altogether there are 9 logical partitions defined on the CEC which share the 4 regular physical processors. Column WGT shows the weight definitions for each partition. The total weight for all partitions is 2198.

On the CPU Activity report we observed that SMPA logical processors use 53.4% of the physical processors and that they were entitled to use 32.6% of them. For SMPA (or LPARA03 respectively) the logical processor usage matches the physical processor usage because 4 logical processors are defined for this partition. For partitions which have fewer logical processors defined

---

[3]Some report columns have been deleted for presentation purposes

```
1        z/OS V1R9            P A R T I T I O N   D A T A   R E P O R T
                       SYSTEM ID SMPA        START 10/27/2008-20.50.00   INTERVAL 000.04.59
                       RPT VERSION V1R9 RMF    END   10/27/2008-20.55.00   CYCLE 1.000 SECONDS

         MVS PARTITION NAME              LPARA03   NUMBER OF PHYSICAL PROCESSORS  12    GROUP NAME   PROD
         IMAGE CAPACITY                 401                                       4  CP  LIMIT      401
         NUMBER OF CONFIGURED PARTITIONS  23                                      2  AAP
         WAIT COMPLETION                NO                                        4  IFL
         DISPATCH INTERVAL              DYNAMIC                                    0  ICE
                                                                                  2  IIP
```

NAME	S	WGT	MSU DEF	MSU ACT	CAPPING DEF	CAPPING WLM%	NUM	TYPE	TOTAL	TOTAL (UTIL)	LPAR MGMT	EFFECTIVE	TOTAL
LPARA03	A	718	0	214	NO	0.0	4.0	CP	00.10.40.461	53.41	0.16	53.26	53.41
LPARA01	A	116	0	21	NO	0.0	2.0	CP	00.01.03.875	10.65	0.14	5.19	5.33
LPARA02	A	222	0	35	NO	0.0	2.0	CP	00.01.44.974	17.51	0.11	8.64	8.75
LPARA04	A	390	0	68	NO	0.0	2.1	CP	00.03.24.603	33.24	0.14	16.93	17.06
LPARA06	A	228	0	17	NO	0.0	0.0	CP	00.00.50.105	16.71	0.05	4.13	4.18
LPARA07	A	224	0	21	NO	0.0	2.0	CP	00.01.01.749	10.30	0.13	5.02	5.15
LPARA1F	A	100	0	4	NO	0.0	1	CP	00.00.11.583	3.86	0.06	0.91	0.97
LPARA11	A	98	0	4	NO	0.0	1.0	CP	00.00.13.233	4.41	0.03	1.07	1.10
LPARA13	A	102	0	3	NO	0.0	1.0	CP	00.00.10.226	3.41	0.03	0.82	0.85
PHYSICAL									00.00.26.151	2.18			2.18
TOTAL									00.19.46.965	3.02		95.97	98.99

Report Columns Deleted

Figure 4.12.: RMF Partition Data Report Example

then physical processors exist, the physical processor usage is the LCP per PCP fraction of the logical processor usage (see LPARA01 for example).

We can also observe that the CEC is really busy because the Total Utilization for all partitions is 98.99%. The report also shows how much of the dispatch time is used for managing the partitions. The column LPAR MGMT shows the time which can be directly attributed to the partitions and *PHYSICAL* shows the processing time of PR/SM.

4.3.3. CEC Utilization Example

LPAR	Logical Processors	Weight	Percent Share	Maximum Share
SYP1	5	700	61%	100%
SYT1	5	300	26%	100%
SYW1	3	150	13%	60%

Table 4.3.: LPAR Configuration Example

The previous example showed a CEC with 99% utilization and also that some of the partitions, like LPARA03, used more than their guaranteed share. Table 4.3 shows a small CEC with only 3 partitions for a 9 hour period from 8:00 to 17:00. This is a typical "Day" or "Prime" shift period for an installation with on-line transaction processing as the dominating workload on the system. The CEC has a main z/OS partition with OLTP workload and a second partition for development and testing purposes.

Figure 4.13 shows the physical processor utilization of the 3 partitions and in dark gray the system overhead for PR/SM management. Figure 4.14 shows the used share of all partitions. We can observe that the maintenance partition SYW1 usually doesnt use much of its share. We can also see that SYT1 tries to get as much CPU cycles as possible. Most of the time it exceeds its share whenever SYP1 does not require all of its capacity. During the morning peak hours we can also see that real contention exists on the CEC. At that time SYP1 and SYT1 are around 100% of their share and the CEC is at 100% busy.

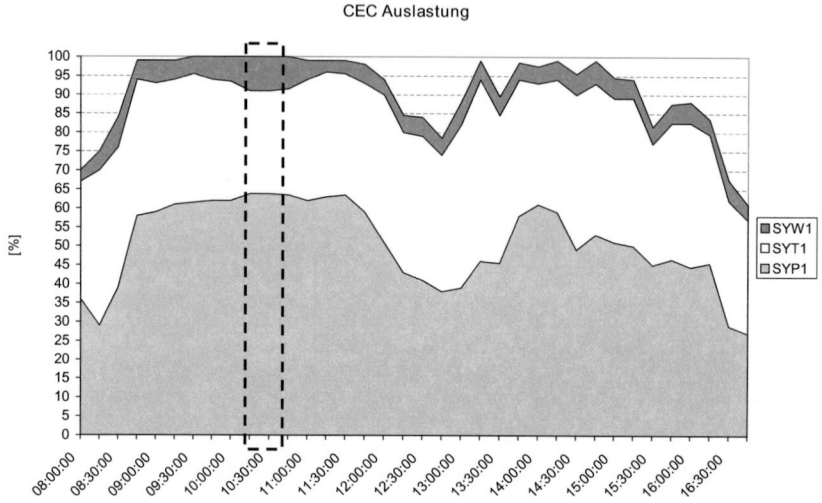

Figure 4.13.: Physical Utilization for a CEC with 3 Partitions

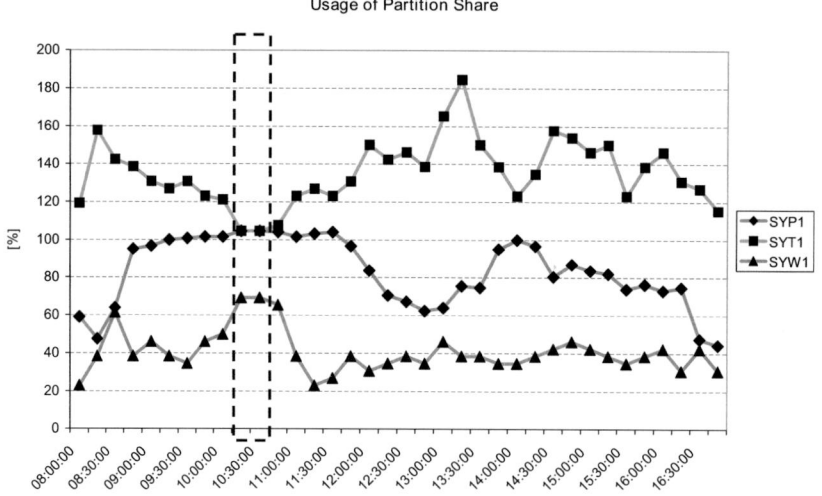

Figure 4.14.: Used Share for the CEC with 3 Partitions

4.4. Offload Processors

A general purpose processing platform supports a wide range of applications but it may not support all types of applications with the same efficiency. Reasons for offloading work to special purpose processing platforms are

- The special purpose platform is designed to run the special application with the highest possible efficiency. Examples for such cases are systems especially designed to run JAVA work or to process XML messages. Datapower is an example for offloading XML messages. If an XML message needs to be processed within a Websphere transaction the message is offloaded to a special network device which is rack module of a ZBX extension to a zEnterprise. Another example is Smart Analytics Optimizer which is a database acceleration rack module to perform business analysis tasks.

- The specialized architecture allows to process work at a much cheaper price for an installation. This is the main reason for using System z internal offload techniques. This has two flavors:

  - Integrated Facility for Linux (IFL) and Integrated Coupling Facility (ICF) are System z processers which run a specialized microcode to only allow either the execution of z/VM and Linux systems or the Coupling Facility Control Code. The specialized microcode allows to provide an execution environment on System z especially for Linux applications which is price performance competitive to other platforms. A coupling facility is a part of the infrastructure and therefore running coupling facilities with reduced or no costs is similar to the fact that installations also need to run firmware in order to host their applications.

  - Application Assist Processors (zAAP) and Integrated Information Processors (zIIP) are not intended to host own operating systems. They can be defined as assist processors to z/OS allowing z/OS to offload either JAVA or DB/2 work for price performance reason. This option became necessary because z/OS hosts many different applications and it is especially effective to run all these applications on the same image. This allows to reduce network as well as cluster connections and still provides the most efficient way to run most workloads.

It should be noted that the primary reason for introducing different flavored processors is price performance but it also allows System z installation to scale their environments while using newer technologies like JAVA, and modern database facilities. Another offload mechanism which is not discussed is cryptographic processing. Cryptographic processing is performed by cryptographic co-processors or offloaded to special attached processors.

4.4.1. Using zIIPs and zAAPs

The next step is to examine how System z and z/OS handle different types of processors and how this effects dispatching. PR/SM creates separate processor pools for offload processors. Figure 4.15 shows how execution units move between regular and offload processors. z/OS uses up to two additional processor pools for offload processing:

- Application Assist Processors (zAAP) which are primarily to execute Java work and some XML related work

- Integrated Information Processors (zIIP) which were introduced to process DB2 related work but which can also process all kind of offload eligible workloads including Java and XML related work if zAAPs are not installed on the CEC.

z/OS defines Work Unit Queues for each processor type. We already saw that work is schedule on the System Work Unit Queue (SWUQ) which is accessed by all general purpose processors. It is also the case that work always first arrives on the SWUQ first and a general purpose processor will first select the unit of work (1).

- Different possibilities exist to tell the dispatcher that it should switch the work to an offload processor (2): The entry of a special code segment can be instrumented and tell the operating system that the following instructions are allowed to be executed on an offload processor. This solution is used when JAVA processing starts. The dispatcher then puts the unit of work not back to work unit queue for general processors but places it to the work unit queue for zAAPs.

- After a predefined execution time the unit of work is placed on the work unit queue for zIIPs. Alternatively it is also possible to run some units of work completely on zIIPs and others completely on regular processors. In both cases a certain percentage of work should be able to run on the offload processor (2).

At some point the unit of work must return to the regular processor. Either if a system call is processed which isnt supported on the offload processor (3)

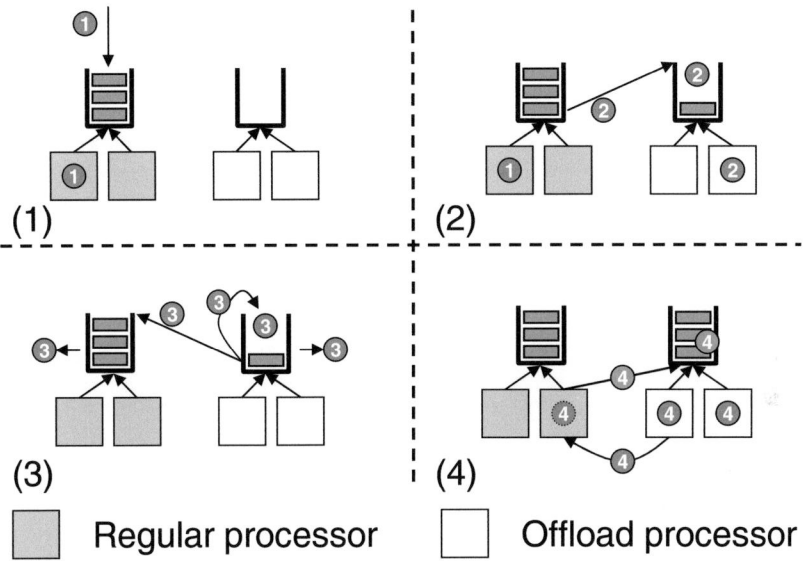

Regular processor ▢ Offload processor

Figure 4.15.: Executing Work on 2 Processor Pools

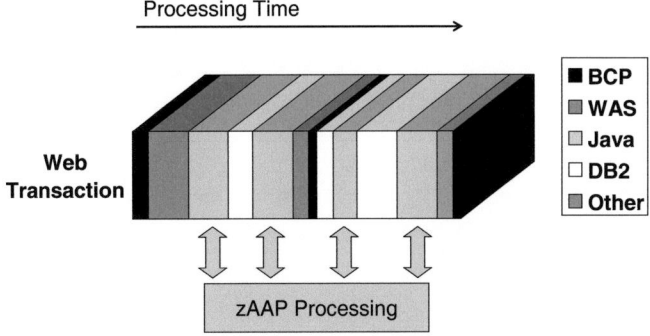

Figure 4.16.: Websphere Transaction Phases

or if the time interval the work should run on the offload processor is expired (3). Finally we have to discuss what happens if too few offload processors are configured on the system or the amount of work which can run on the offload processors is too much. In that case the general purpose processors need to have the ability to also select work from the Alternate Work Unit Queues (AWUQ) (4). But they will not start with that until the z/OS dispatcher observes a bottleneck. The z/OS dispatcher will then enable regular processors individually to select work from the AWUQ. The general purpose processors which are enabled as helper processors will then test dispatch priority order whether it should select work from the SWUQ or AWUQ. The help processing automatically ends when the general purpose processor sets the WAIT State PSW.

Figure 4.16 shows how a sample Websphere transaction is executed on regular CPs and zAAPs. First the operating system gets control (BCP) which dispatches the Websphere Application Server. Some part of the processing is executed by infrastructure code of Websphere (turquoise) before the real application code written in Java (blue) gets control and the work can be processed on a zAAP. DB2 (red) requests and Java native interface calls (yellow) require to switch back from the zAAP to a regular processor. Finally the transaction completes and BCP gets control to end the processing.

4.4.2. Processor Pools

PR/SM creates separate processor pools for regular CPs, zIIPs, zAAPs, IFLs, and ICFs, see example in figure 4.17. That means a z/OS partition can have up to three weight definitions one for regular CPs, one for zIIPs and one for zAAPs. Also different numbers of these processor types can be defined to z/OS partitions. The only restriction is that it is not possible to define more zIIPs or more zAAPs to z/OS then regular processors have been defined. IFLs can be used by Linux systems and also by z/VM because Linux is most often hosted as a guest operating system under z/VM.

A specialty exists for Coupling Facilities. Coupling Facilities can use ICFs but they can also use at the same time regular processors. The idea is to define regular processors as an overflow mechanism for coupling facilities in case the traffic to the cluster data storage is that high that it requires more processing power then the available ICF processors can provide. Also coupling facility partitions can use dedicated and shared processors. The shared processors are only used if the dedicated processors are not sufficient to execute the requests

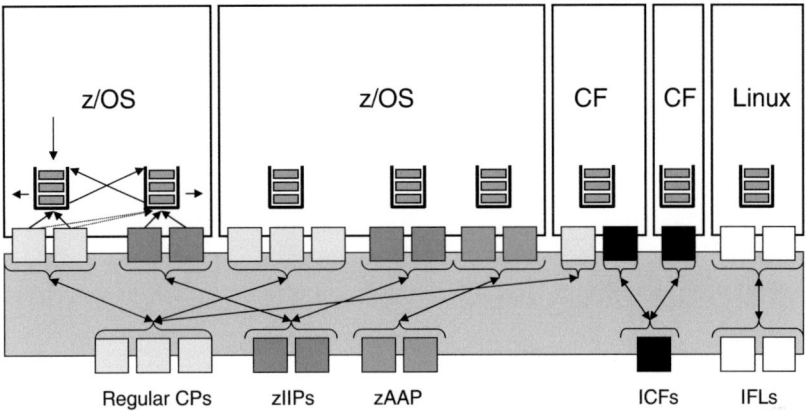

Figure 4.17.: Processor Pools on System z

in the coupling facility. We will discuss coupling facilities in detail in chapter 6.

Finally the number of regular processors, plus offload processors, IFLs, ICFs, System Assist Processors and Spare processors cannot exceed the maximum number of processors installed across all books of the z system.

4.4.3. LPAR Report Example including Offload Processors

We can now complete our example from section 4.3.2: The reporting example for the z/OS system SMPA and the CEC on which it is hosted. We already observed that AAP, IFL, and IIP processors exist on the CEC. Figure 4.18[4] shows the complete list of partitions across all processor pools:

- System SMPA which runs in partition LPARA03 uses regular processors and also zIIPs.

- Partition LPARA02 even uses all three types of processors which can be configured to z/OS. The example above shows that the three pools are distinct and that different weight definitions for the partition exist for each pool. As a result we can observe that LPARA02 has a share of 10%

---

[4]Some rows and columns have been deleted for presentation purposes

of the regular processor pool, 22% of the zIIP pool and even 67% of the zAAP pool. LPARA02 can use up to 50% of the regular processor pool because it has 2 regular CPs defined out of 4 installed regular CPs on the CEC. For the zAAP and zIIP pool it can theoretically use up to 100% of the installed CPU resources because it has each 2 offload processors defined out of 2 installed offload processors.

- LPARA09 runs on the IFLs. From this report we can't determine which operating system is running in this partition but it is most likely z/VM with Linux guests.

4.5. Example on how z/OS and PR/SM Dispatcher work together

Up to this point we discussed the different dispatching technologies for z/OS and PR/SM. We can summarize that both are very efficient with respect to their objectives: running many different applications in parallel on z/OS and hosting multiple operating systems with as little as possible overhead on System z. We also found out that multiple processor pools exist on System z, primarily for price competitiveness but also for scalability reasons.

Now it is necessary to take a look how the two dispatching algorithms work together. As an example we will take a side step to serialization and locking on z/OS and then discuss what happens when a processor has to wait for completion of a lock request on another processor and how z/OS and PR/SM can work efficiently together for such cases.

4.5.1. z/OS Serialization

The basic instruction for serialization in z/OS is Compare and Swap. This is an atomic instruction which can't be interrupted, see section 2.12. It compares two values with each other and if they are equal it stores the content of a third value in the location of the first. This technique is used to implement most locking functions especially spin locks. A spin lock means that the requester processes the lock obtain instructions as long as it gets the lock. Then it processes the critical path and releases the lock again. Another possibility is a suspend lock. In this case the requester asks for the lock and if it is not available the requester is suspended. A lock manager will resume the requester when the lock becomes

```
1                      P A R T I T I O N   D A T A   R E P O R T
          z/OS V1R9    SYSTEM ID SMPA         START 10/27/2008-20.50.00   INTERVAL 000.04.59
                       RPT VERSION V1R9 RMF    END   10/27/2008-20.55.00   CYCLE 1.000 SECONDS
-
MVS PARTITION NAME               LPARA03      NUMBER OF PHYSICAL PROCESSORS  12      GROUP NAME   PROD
IMAGE CAPACITY                   401                   CP                    4       LIMIT        401
NUMBER OF CONFIGURED PARTITIONS  23                    AAP                   2
WAIT COMPLETION                  NO                    IFL                   4
DISPATCH INTERVAL                DYNAMIC               ICF                   0
                                                       IIP                   2
-
--------- PARTITION DATA -------  ---MSU---  -CAPPING-   -----------AVERAGE PROCESSOR UTILIZATION PERCENT--
0                                                                    ---- PHYSICAL PROCESSORS ----
NAME     S  WGT  DEF  ACT  DEF  WLM%  NUM  TYPE   TOTAL         TOTAL  LPAR MGMT  EFFECTIVE  TOTAL
0LPARA03 A  718   0   214  NO   0.0   4.0  CP   00.01.40.461   53.41    0.16      53.26     53.41
LPARA01  A  116   0    21  NO   0.0   2.0  CP   00.01.03.875   10.65    0.14       5.19      5.33
LPARA02  A  222   0    35  NO   0.0   2.0  CP   00.01.44.974   17.51    0.11       8.64      8.75
.. Rows deleted . . .
LPARA13  A  102   0         3  NO   0.0  1.0  CP  00.00.10.226    3.41    0.03       0.82      0.85
*PHYSICAL*                                        00.00.26.151            2.18                2.18
                                                                        ------    ------    ------
   TOTAL                                          00.19.46.965            3.02     95.97     98.99

LPARA02  A  400                            2  AAP  00.00.01.503   0.25    0.00       0.25      0.25
LPARA06  A  200                            2  AAP  00.00.00.617   0.10    0.00       0.10      0.10
*PHYSICAL*                                        00.00.00.071            0.01                0.01
                                                                        ------    ------    ------
   TOTAL                                          00.00.02.192            0.02       0.35      0.37
-
. . . IFL Section deleted . . . .
-
LPARA03  A  400                            2  IIP  00.00.02.455   0.41    0.00       0.41      0.41
LPARA02  A  400                            2  IIP  00.00.23.789   3.97    0.04       3.93      3.97
. . . Rows deleted . . .
LPARA07  A  400                            2  IIP  00.00.23.767   3.96    0.05       3.92      3.96
*PHYSICAL*                                        00.00.01.473            0.25                0.25
                                                                        ------    ------    ------
   TOTAL                                          00.01.08.977            0.39     11.11     11.51
```

Report Columns Deleted

Figure 4.18.: RMF Partition Data Report with Offload Processors

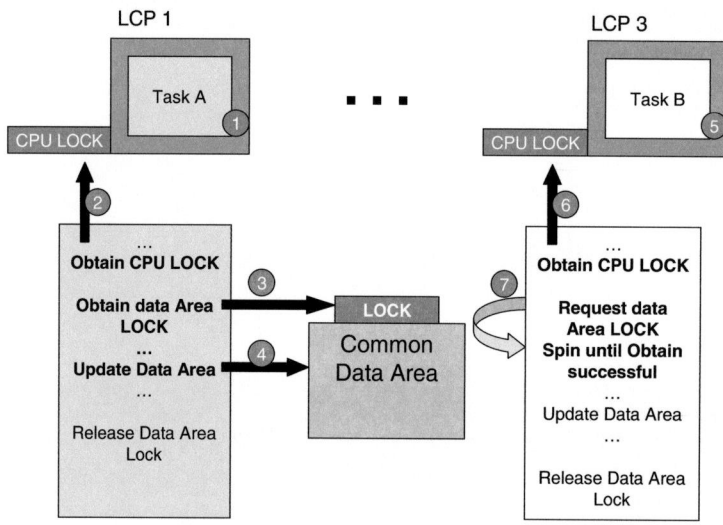

Figure 4.19.: Two Logical Processors requesting the same spin lock

available again. The advantage of a suspend lock is that the processor is not occupied but the disadvantage is that it takes too many instructions to obtain the lock. Also it always requires a lock manager as a referee. Therefore within the operating system most locks especially all really resource critical locks are implemented as spin locks.

4.5.2. z/OS Spin Lock Processing

Figure 4.19 shows an example where two logical processors request the same spin lock in z/OS:

1. The dispatcher dispatches a system task on LCP1

2. The system task first obtains the CPU lock of the processor because it doesn't want to get interrupted

3. The task wants to update a common data area which is also protected by a lock and requests and obtains the system resource lock

4. Then it starts to update the common data area

5. Little later task B is dispatched on LCP3

6. Task B also wants to access the same common data area and it performs the same steps as tasks A: To obtain the CPU lock of the logical processor it is running on.

7. Requesting the system resource lock to update the same common data area. Because the lock is held by tasks A, task B starts to spin and continuously runs through the same instructions to wait until the lock is released and can be obtained by B.

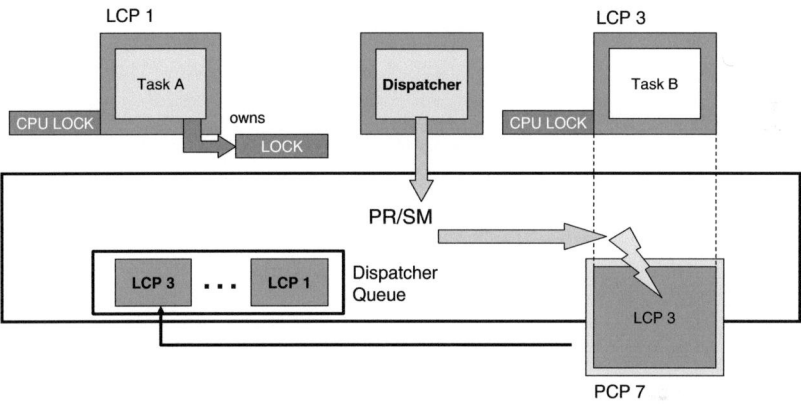

Figure 4.20.: z/OS and PR/SM Spin Lock Synchronization

When the dispatcher gets control it periodically tests whether spin lock processing is running. Eventually it recognizes that the task is in a spin loop and it also recognizes which processor is holding the lock. The z/OS dispatcher and PR/SM can communicate and the z/OS dispatcher is able to find out whether LCP1 is really processing, meaning that it is dispatched by PR/SM on a physical processor. If that is the case the dispatcher returns control to the spinning task which continues to request the lock.

The other case is that the dispatcher finds out that LCP1 is not running meaning that it is not dispatched by PR/SM on a physical processor. Locking the logical processor does not guarantee that the logical processors is really dispatched on a physical processor. In this case the situation is very unfortunate. It does not only hamper the current partition in completing its tasks it also effects other partitions because LCP3 is dispatched on a physical processor (otherwise the z/OS dispatcher couldn't find out that no progress takes place).

The z/OS dispatcher sends a signal to PR/SM to inform PR/SM that the currently dispatched LCP3 can't complete its processing because it is waiting on the completion of LCP1, see figure 4.20. PR/SM takes the logical CP off the physical processor and queues it back to its dispatcher queue behind LCP1 of the partition which sends the signal. Now it is possible for other LCPs or other partitions to use physical processors. Once LCP1 is re-dispatched a great chance exists too that the critical path processing will end soon so that task B can obtain the system resource lock and complete its processing.

At this point we can summarize that interaction between the operating system and the virtualization layer is desired to speed up the processing within the partition but also to increase the throughput across all partitions on the hardware.

4.6. Limitations of Dispatching

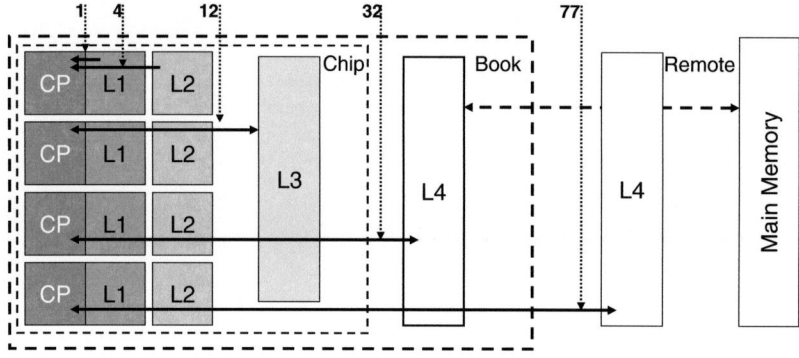

Figure 4.21.: Relative Access to Data in Cache Structures for System z196

At first question we have to take a look again how big System z is. A System z starting with z10 can have up to 77 physical processors which are distributed across 4 books and System z196 has up to 96 and the zEC12 up to 120 processors. 64 processors on z10, 80 on z196, and 101 on zEC12 can be used for production work. On such systems it is possible to host up to 60 logical partitions or very few big partitions may use all of the physical processors. Especially z/OS is designed to run multiple workloads concurrently and z/OS is also able to use dozens of logical and physical processors. The discussion of the z/OS dispatcher showed that it is possible for for work to get selected from any logical processor. This can mean that a unit of work which was selected on a processor on book 1 is the next time selected on a different processor on a different book. This shows us that it is possible that work crosses the boundaries of chips and books and that the access to data depends heavily where it resides and on which logical and physical processor the work is being dispatched.

Figure 4.21 shows the book structure and relative latencies for accessing data in different cache structures on System z196. System z196 as well as its predecessor z10 and successor zEC12 have such high clock frequencies that it is necessary to deploy multiple cache hierarchies to reduce the access time to data. Another reason is that the high clock frequencies shrink the level 1 caches which allow to access data within 1 cycle. As a result another cache which allows to access data in 4 cycles (L2) is placed very close to the core and starting with z196 a shared cache for all cores on the same chip (L3). Finally all cores on the same book share a common Level 4 (L4) cache.

The access times shown in figure 4.21 are relative access times, not exact cycle times. For a z10 they are slightly better because the clock frequency of the z10 is lower and for a zEC12 slightly worse. On the other hand the zEC12 has bigger caches as listed in table 2.1. By looking at these access times and especially we can observe that it is very expensive to fetch data from a remote book or even the memory which is even more expensive. It becomes obvious that the performance of the systems can be optimized if work can be kept locally on the same book or on the same chip. The best situation would be if it is possible to re-dispatch a logical processor always on the same physical processor so that it can find its local L1 or L2 cache content with a high probability. That's the base and motivation for Hiperdispatch which exactly tries to achieve that units of work are re-dispatched on a small subset of processors so that the cache content which was once loaded doesn't require expensive re-fetches from remote cache structures or even main memory.

4.6.1. Large System Effects

Before we want to discuss Hiperdispatch in detail we will take a look at Large System Effects. Table 4.4 shows examples of Relative Capacity Indicators for z196 systems. The data is based on the Large System Performance Reference (see [22]) which is a benchmark executed by IBM for all System z processors. The benchmark encompasses different workloads and different system configurations. It also utilizes the CEC to 90% load. The result are curves which show the capacity change depending on workload and configuration. The typically or most likely scenario for a customer is captured with the Average RCI. The *High RCI* depicts the worst case and the *Low RCI* the best case. We can observe the following:

- Adding another physical processor does not linearly increase the capacity. This is no surprise because we can expect additional overhead. For example cross cache invalidations and locking will reduce the effect of a linear increase. Nevertheless we can see that the effect is not that bad. The 50 way system is only 5.39% below the ideal curve when we increase the capacity by 20 processors from a 30 way system. Adding one processor for systems with less than 10 processors shows a capacity reduction of less than 2% and for systems with more than 30 processors of less than 1%.

- On the other hand we can also observe that the spread between the best and the worst case becomes bigger when we run a system with more processors. While a 1 way only shows a spread of 4% it is already by 27% for a 30 way system. This increases the planning uncertainty and makes a system more prone to workload and configuration effects while the number of processors increases.

Processors	Low	Average	High	Spred: Low/High
1 Way	2.02	2.03	1.94	4.12%
10 Way	17.86	16.51	15	19.07 %
30 Way	46.4	40.35	36.6	26.78%
50 way	72.09	61.86	55.97	28.80%

Table 4.4.: Relative Capacity Indicators for System z196

These observations which can be based on measurements are another good motivation to improve the dispatching in order to get high scalability for large n-way systems.

All these measurements are executed on systems with Hiperdispatch active. Without Hiperdispatch the RCI increase would be worse as well as the spread between High and Low RCI. At the end of our discussion we will discuss the benefit for using Hiperdispatch for selected installations.

4.7. Hiperdispatch

Based on the observations and analysis of the z architecture we derive the following design objectives for Hiperdispatch (see figure 4.22):

PR/SM Keep logical processors as long as possible running on the same physical processor. Also try to re-dispatch a logical processor always to the same physical processor whenever possible. The technique which is developed by PR/SM is named "Vertical CPU Management".

z/OS Do not allow that work can be dispatched freely on every logical processor. Instead try to group work together and try to re-dispatch it only on a subset of logical processors. This technique is named "Dispatcher Affinity" because it creates affinities of work to a subset of logical processors. Hiperdispatch now is the combination of dispatcher affinity in z/OS and vertical CPU management in PR/SM.

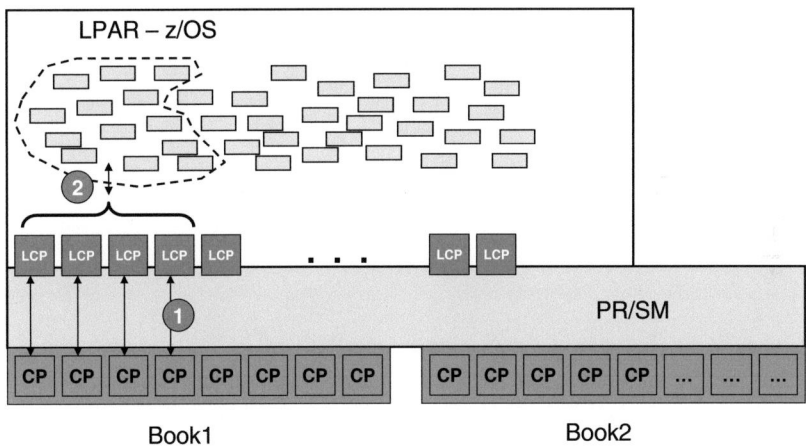

Figure 4.22.: Hiperdispatch Objectives

The first question which may arise is why it isn't possible to assign work just to one logical processor. This is done on other platforms which also have the difficulty to scale out across many processors. The answer is simple: z/OS runs very diverse workloads. These workloads have very different requirements on responsiveness and CPU access. Also z/OS provides a comprehensive mechanism to calculate dispatch priorities for the work (see chapter 5). Other platforms are mostly dedicated to a single type workload with very similar resource requirements. Therefore z/OS and PR/SM need to develop a different technique to address the need of more localized CPU access.

4.7.1. Vertical CPU Management

We will start with a simple example. Lets assume we have a CEC with two partitions: LPAR A and LPAR B. There are 5 PCPs on the CEC and each LPAR has 5 LCPs. LPAR A has a weight defined of 350 and LPAR B a weight of 150. Based on these definitions the guaranteed capacity for LPAR A results to 3.5 PCPs and for LPAR B to 1.5 PCPs.

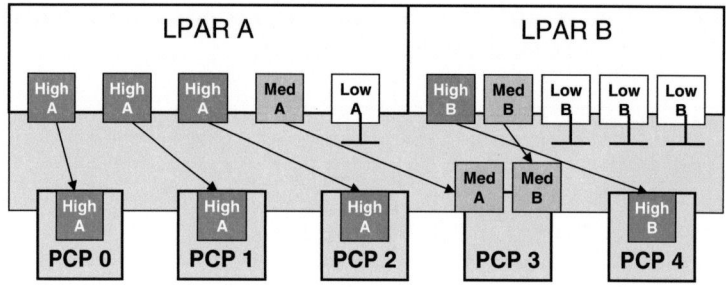

Figure 4.23.: Vertical CPU Management with High Demand

The idea is to use this capacity as efficiently as possible. Therefore we assign 3 of the 5 LCPs for LPAR A to a fixed PCPs and give them a share of 100%. That means whenever one of these LCPs has demand it is always re-dispatched on the same PCP. These logical processors also have the highest shar in the configuration and therefore they can always displace logical processors from other partitions from their physical processors. These logical processors are named *Vertical High Processors* (VH or High). For LPAR B the calculation results to 1 vertical high processor. Both partitions have a guaranteed share of 50% for another PCP. A processor with a share of less than 100% is named *Vertical Medium Processor* (VM or Medium). Each partition gets one vertical medium processor in the current example. We cannot assign a fixed PCP to these processors but can let them compete for the unused PCPs. If both partitions have high demand there is only one unused PCP and the two Medium processors from both partitions will compete for it, see figure 4.23.

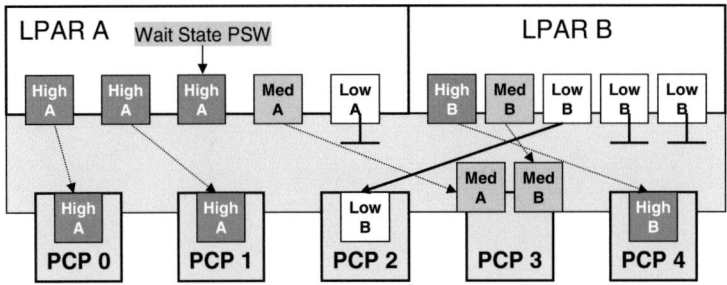

Figure 4.24.: Unparking of Low Processors

Finally both partitions have additional logical processors which are not covered by the guaranteed share of the configuration. These LCPs are named *Vertical Low Processors* (VL or Low) and they have no initial share of the PCP pool. Also they are not used and placed in a *parked* state. That means no work is being dispatched on them. But they are required if one partition has high demand and can use CPU resources which are not used by the other partition. For example if LPAR A loads a WAIT State PSW on any of its high processors it means that no work is available for it and not all processor resources are being used. Now it would be possible for LPAR B to use these resources if there is enough demand. LPAR B can then un-park one or multiple of its vertical low processors and dispatch work on them. The vertical low processors can now use the unused physical processor resources of LPAR A until LPAR A receives more work and the high processors start to execute work again, see figure 4.24.

4.7.2. Processor Shares

We already discussed that a vertical high processor has 100% share of a physical processor and that it is re-dispatched always to the same physical processor. The share for the vertical medium processor is the fraction of this calculation. The share of vertical medium processors is also used as share for unparked low processors. That means all unparked low and the medium processors depend on the same share fraction. If this fraction is smaller than 50% of a high processor than it is too small to allow multiple unparked low processors to compete for processing resources. Under this circumstance a high processor is converted to a medium processor. Both medium processors now get now get half of the share which in sum is above 100%. Figure 4.25. shows how the share of one medium processor is divided between the medium processor and an unparked low processor.

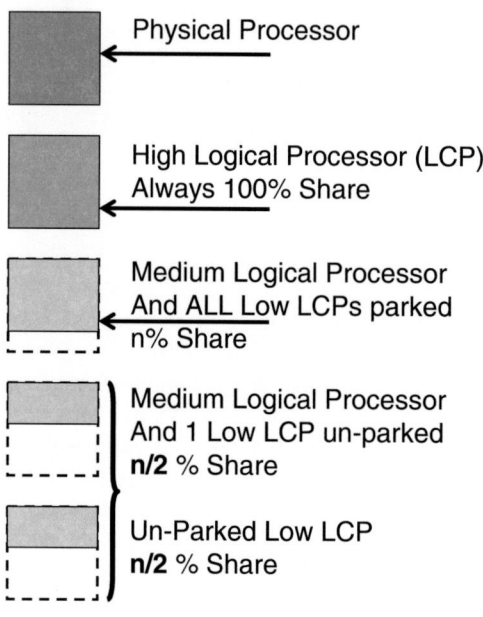

Figure 4.25.: Vertical CPU Management and Processor Shares

The processor share calculation for low and medium processors divides the total share of the medium processors by the sum of all medium and unparked low processors:

$$\text{Share of VM and unparked VL processors} = \frac{n}{\sum \text{VM} + \sum \text{Unparked VL}} \%$$

The share of the medium processors is used to fuel the unparked low processors and the share of VM and VL processors gets smaller when more VLs are unparked. The LPAR Share is calculated as:

$$\text{Share of LPAR(i)} = \frac{\text{Weight of LPAR(i)}}{\sum_{j=1}^{n} \text{Weight of LPAR(j)}}$$

Based on the LPAR Share the Number N of VH processors and the share M of the VM processor is calculated by:

$$\text{Phys. Proc. Share of LPAR(i)} \quad = \quad \text{Share of LPAR(i)} \bullet \text{Total Number of PCPs}$$
$$= \quad N.M$$

A VH is converted to a VM if M < 50% and N, and M change to N_{NEW} and M_{NEW}:

$$N_{NEW} = N - 1; M_{NEW} = \frac{1 + M}{2}$$

M_{NEW} is the share for each of the two VMs.

4.7.3. Example for Unparking Low Processors

Figure 4.26 shows a RMF CPU Activity Report for a Partition which runs HIPERDISPATCH=YES. The z/OS system named R71 has a physical processor share of 5.32 PCPs on a CEC with 16 PCPs. The partition is defined with 16 logical processors and based on the previous discussion this results in 4 VHs, 2 VMs and 10 VLs for R71. The processor share of each VM is 66.4% as long as no VL is unparked.

The RMF reporting interval for this report is 1 minute and we can observe that up to 2 VL processors were unparked. The processor share for the 2 VM and 1 unparked VL is 44.3% for each shared processor and when 2 VLs are unparked 33.2%.

There were two partitions on the CEC:

R71 has a physical processor share of 5.32 PCPs. This partition is depicted in figure 4.26 and 4.27. The partition is very highly utilized for the complete test run. Figure 4.27 shows all logical processors of partition R71, the park and unpark activity of the low processors and the MVS Busy value.

R72 has a physical processor share of 10.67 PCPs resulting to 10 VH, 1 VM and 5 VL processors. The partition and its park and unpark activity is depicted in figure 4.28.

Both graphics depict the MVS utilization or *MVS Busy* value. This value tells how much demand exist on the systems. We can observe that partition R71 has a very high demand and always tries to unpark low processors. Partition R72 has high and varying demand which is always lower than 100%. Usually partition R72 can process the work with the existing number of high and medium processors and we only see two short unpark activities. We can also notice that

```
1                                        C P U   A C T I V I T Y

                z/OS V1R9     SYSTEM ID R71        DATE 01/28/2009          INTERVAL 00.59.753
                                                   TIME 11.02.00            CYCLE 1.000 SECONDS
-CPU  2097      MODEL 716     H/W MODEL E26    SEQUENCE CODE 00000000000A73A2   HIPERDISPATCH=YES
0---CPU---      ---------------- TIME % ----------------                   --I/O INTERRUPTS--
NUM TYPE        ONLINE    LPAR BUSY    MVS BUSY    PARKED    LOG PROC SHARE %    RATE    % VIA TPI
  0  CP         100.00      99.50       100.0       0.00        100.0          29.40      0.00
  1  CP         100.00      99.88       100.0       0.00        100.0          18.14      0.00
  2  CP         100.00      99.83       100.0       0.00        100.0          31.71      0.00
  3  CP         100.00      99.78       100.0       0.00        100.0          16.82      0.00
  4  CP         100.00      72.24       100.0       0.00         66.4           0.00      0.00
  5  CP         100.00      72.30       100.0       0.00         66.4           0.00      0.00
  6  CP         100.00      35.16       100.0      46.14          0.0           0.00      0.00
  7  CP         100.00      52.22       100.0      24.06          0.0           0.00      0.00
  8  CP         100.00       0.00       -----     100.00          0.0           0.00      0.00
  9  CP         100.00       0.00       -----     100.00          0.0           0.00      0.00
  A  CP         100.00       0.00       -----     100.00          0.0           0.00      0.00
  B  CP         100.00       0.00       -----     100.00          0.0           0.00      0.00
  C  CP         100.00       0.00       -----     100.00          0.0           0.00      0.00
  D  CP         100.00       0.00       -----     100.00          0.0           0.00      0.00
  E  CP         100.00       0.00       -----     100.00          0.0           0.00      0.00
  F  CP         100.00       0.00       -----     100.00          0.0           0.00      0.00
TOTAL/AVERAGE               39.43       100.0     532.8                        96.08      0.00
```

Figure 4.26.: RMF CPU Activity Report Example

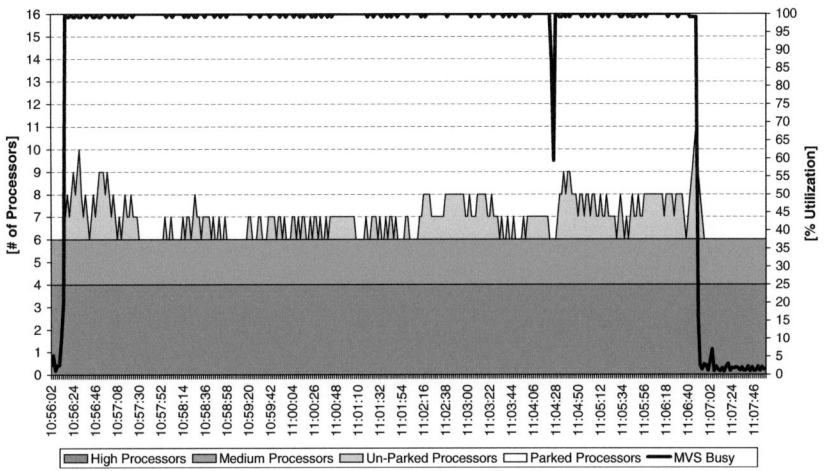

Figure 4.27.: R71: Park and Unpark

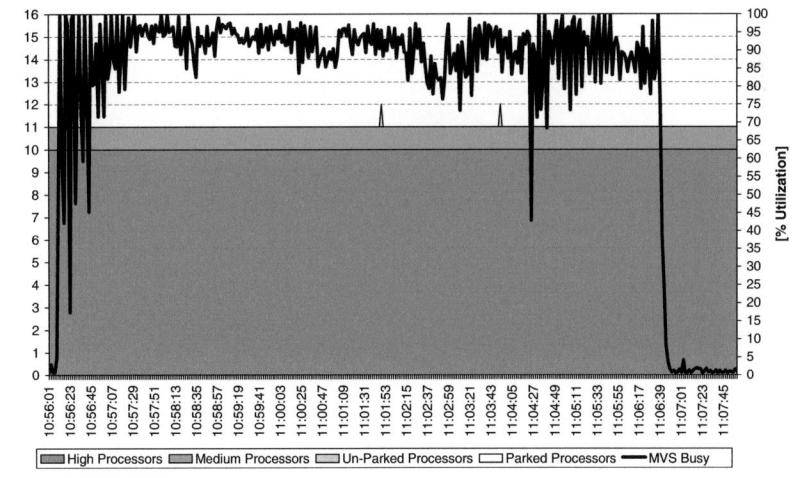

Figure 4.28.: R72: Park and Unpark

R71 must sometimes park all of its low processors. These periods get together with higher demand periods on R72 so that the low processors of R71 can't be efficiently used. The parking and unparking takes place every 2 seconds and it is controlled by the z/OS component Workload Manager. The following pages will now discuss the implementation of Hiperdispatch in z/OS.

4.7.4. Hiperdispatch in z/OS

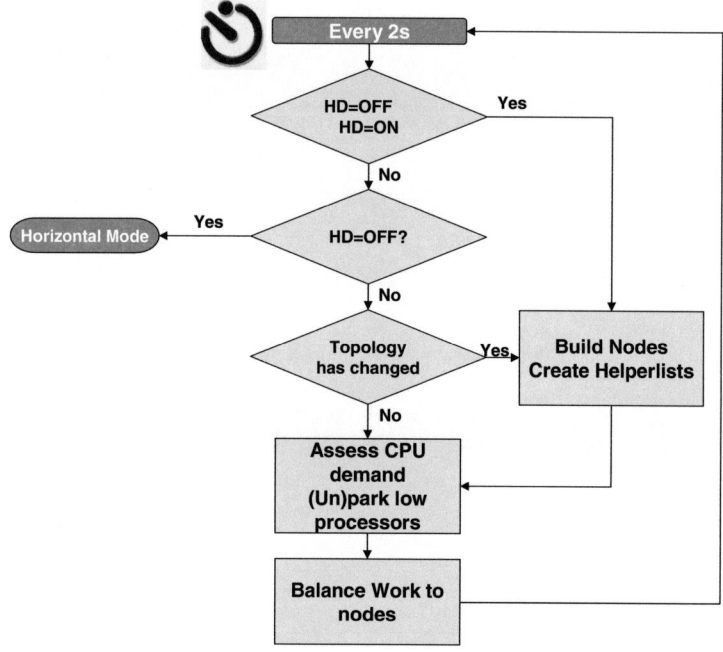

Figure 4.29.: Hiperdispatch Processing in z/OS WLM

Hiperdispatch is implemented in z/OS across the two operating system components Workload Manager (WLM) and z/OS Dispatcher. WLM usually deals with workloads, the user defined performance objectives for such workloads and the resource demand of these workloads. It also deals with how resources are utilized. Because WLM knows which workloads and work units execute in the system it is suited to control how the work is distributed across processors.

For Hiperdispatch WLM performs the following functions every 2 seconds, see figure 4.29:

- It tests whether the configuration has changed from HD=OFF to HD=ON or whether Hiperdispatch has been turned off completely (HD=OFF). In the latter case Hiperdispatch is not used and all work is queued to a single Work Unit Queue for each processor type. Also all LCPs are treated equally by PR/SM.

- WLM obtains configuration information from PR/SM if Hiperdispatch has been turned on (HD=ON) or if the topology has been changed. This configuration information tells WLM about the polarization (High, Medium, or Low) of every logical CP and on which chip and book the logical processor is located. Based on this information WLM creates affinity nodes and helper lists. Each affinity node has a work unit queue.

- Then WLM assesses the demand of the partition and how effective the medium and low processors are running. Based on this information it either parks or unparks low processors.

- Finally the work is distributed across the affinity nodes. After this step each unit of work in the z/OS system has an affinity to one or multiple affinity nodes depending on how many processor types are used by z/OS.

4.7.5. Affinity Nodes

The easiest way to explain how affinity nodes are created is by using a real example. The configuration depicted in table 4.5 shows a CEC with 20 regular physical processors, 1 zIIP and 4 partitions. The CEC is a z196 with 2 books.

Partition	Number of logical processors	Weight	Weight expressed in processors	zIIPs
SYS1	20	595	11.9	1
SYS2	9	200	4	1
SYS3	9	155	3.1	1
SYS4	2	50	1	0

Table 4.5.: LPAR Definition Example

The big partition SYS1 has a share of 59.5% of the regular physical resources which results in 11.9 physical processors. WLM now attempts to create affinity nodes with a minimum of 3 vertical high processors. As a result SYS1 gets 11 high, 1 medium and 8 low processors. In addition one medium is created for the zIIP. Based on this results WLM creates 3 nodes with 3 to 4 high processors each. Then the medium and low processors are distributed across the affinity nodes based on their initial placement on books and chips.

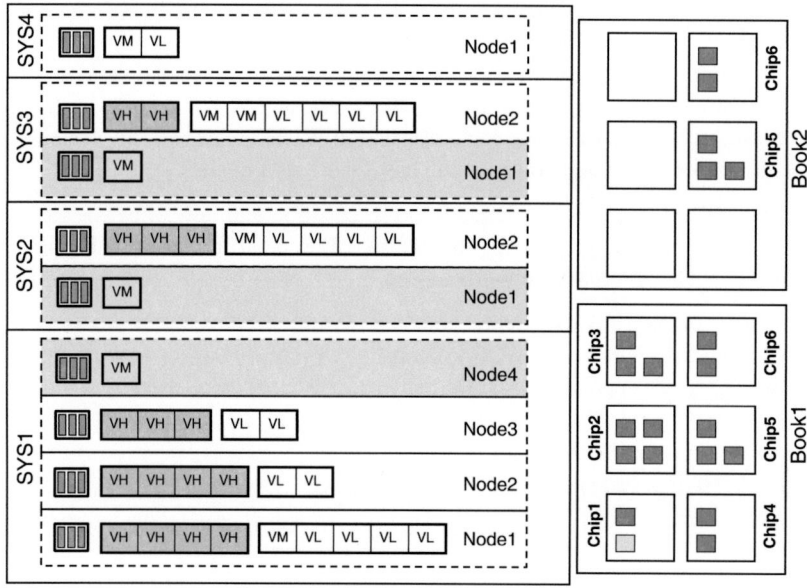

Figure 4.30.: Affinity Nodes on a z196 System

PR/SM assigns a high processors to a physical processor. This assignment is fixed and not changed as long as the whole configuration does not change. PR/SM also assigns physical processors to medium and low processors but it can't be guaranteed that this assignment doesn't change. Nevertheless WLM uses this information to add the remaining processors to the affinity nodes. For such a big partition and a CEC which consists of two books it is very likely that big partitions span multiple books. WLM tries to minimize the nodes which have processors from multiple books and usually adds processors from different book just to one affinity node. On the other hand low processors which are located on the same book are added alternating to nodes with high processors of the same book.

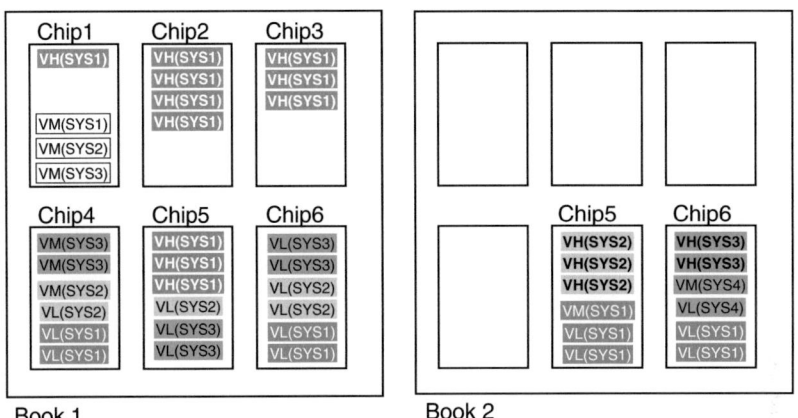

Figure 4.31.: Assignement of Logical to Physical Processors

Figure 4.30 shows the LPAR layout and the affinity nodes created in each LPAR. For the two books the physical processors are depicted. There are 21 physical processors in the configuration of which most are located on Book 1. Five of the physical processors are on Book 2 on chips 5 and 6. Figure 4.31 shows the assignment of logical processors to the chips on each book. This information determines that Node 1 of partition SYS1 in figure 4.30 gets all the VL and the VM processor which are assigned to the second book. The VL processors which are assigned to Node 1 and 2 are all located on Book 1 like the VH processors of these nodes. In addition to the regular processors the partitions SYS1, SYS2, and SYS3 each have a logical zIIP and one physical zIIP is located on Chip 1 of Book1.

Finally a separate node is created for the zIIPs on each partition which has a logical zIIP. The logical zIIPs are all assigned to the same physical zIIP on Chip 1 on Book 1.

4.7.6. Assessment for Parking and Unparking Low Processors

Unparking of a low processors depends on the demand of the partition and whether it is possible to efficiently execute the processor. The worst scenario is that too many low processors are unparked all with very little share and they can't be dispatched anymore because processors with higher shares from other partitions occupy the physical processors. So if both conditions mentioned above are fulfilled a low processor is unparked. This does not depend on a special threshold because additional factors are considered, for example how busy the CEC is. If the CEC is not highly utilized it is possible to unpark low processors already at lower demand levels. Therefore the threshold to unpark a low processor is dynamically adjusted based various factors.

Parking a low processor is the opposite activity. It is primarily driven by the situation that WLM observes low processors not getting enough access to physical processors or if they are just no longer needed. Again this is also dynamically adjusted and the various conditions change on environmental conditions.

4.7.7. Balancing Work

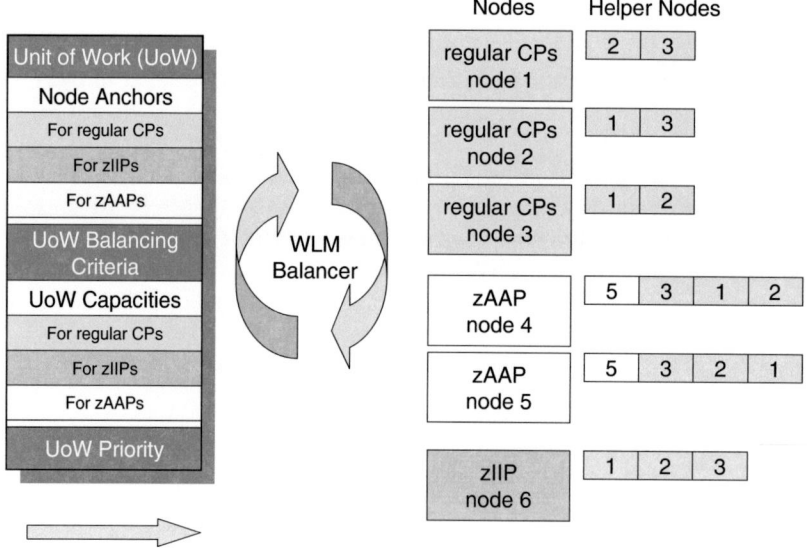

Figure 4.32.: Balancing Work

The main task of WLM for Hiperdispatch is to balance the work across the existing affinity nodes. Balancing the work attempts to distribute the work by dispatch priority as well as by CPU consumption. This should avoid that on one node only high important work is executing while on another node only high CPU consuming work executes. Each unit of work is described by its dispatch priority and the capacity it has used on general purpose CPs, zIIPs and zAAPs. For zIIPs and zAAPs separate nodes are created in the same way as for regular CPs. The balancing algorithm then distributes all units of work across the three CPU resources so that each unit of work receives a location for a regular CP node, a zIIP node and a zAAP node[5], see figure 4.32.

The second step is to define helper nodes. So far we discussed that WLM unparks low processors and evaluates these conditions every 2 seconds. But 2 seconds is a very long time interval. It can't be avoided that a node might get overloaded before WLM can react to it. For this purpose helper lists tell the dispatcher from which node it should enable processors to help the overloaded node. We discussed helper processing already for the case when zIIPs or zAAPs were not able to process all the work which should be offloaded. The technique being used here is the same with the simple restriction that only regular CP nodes can help zIIP and zAAP nodes.

4.7.8. Helper Processing

Node	Type	Processors			Book	Helper Nodes		
		High	Medium	Low	Crossing	left most first		
Node 1	CP	4	1	4	Yes	Node 2	Node 3	
Node 2	CP	4	0	2	No	Node 3	Node 1	
Node 3	CP	3	0	0	No	Node 2	Node 1	
Node 4	zIIP	0	1	0	No	Node 1	Node 2	Node 3

Table 4.6.: Nodes of System SYS1

Table 4.6 shows the helper nodes defined for the sample configuration shown in figure 4.30. We remember that Node 2 and Node 3 were fully contained on Book 1 while Node 1 has its medium and low processors located on Book 2. The helper lists now try to define the preferred helper nodes for a node also on the same book and if possible no book crossing node. That results in Node 2 and 3 being the preferred helper nodes. Node 1 is the helper node for the zIIP node and it is listed as second best choice for Node 2 and 3.

---

[5]Assuming zIIPs and zAAPs are installed.

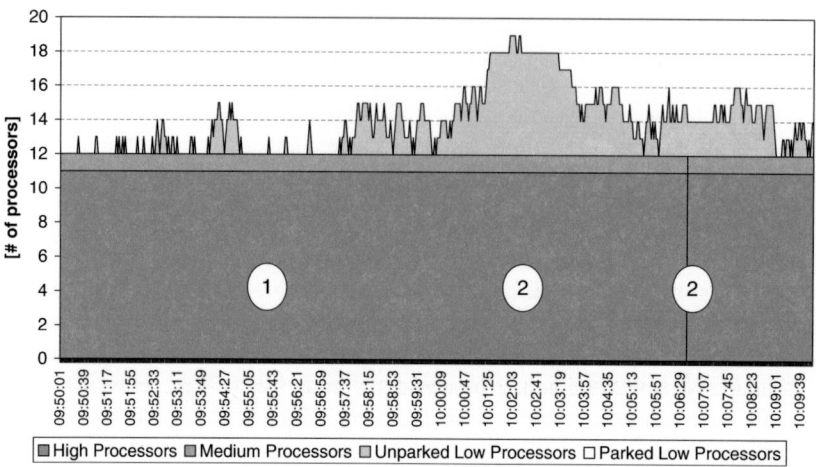

Figure 4.33.: Unpark Processing for System SYS1

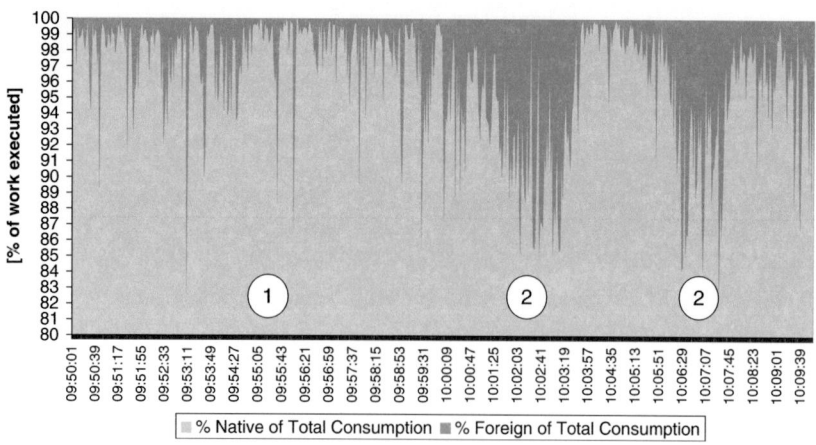

Figure 4.34.: Helper Processing for Node 1 of SYS1

Figure 4.33 shows the park and unpark activity for system SYS1 in the 20 minute time frame around 10 o'clock. Figure 4.34 focuses on Node 1. The dark gray shaded area is the percentage of work being executed on a helper processor that means not on Node 1. We can observe that helper processing always takes place at least to a small extent. If the helper processing is less than 5 to 10% then we have little unpark activity. Node overload conditions were very temporarily and resolved quickly. For more than 10% helper processing the conditions remain longer and eventually WLM reacts and unparks low processors. Helper processing is requested by the z/OS dispatcher when the dispatching queue for the node is too long. The dispatcher first asks one logical processor from the preferred helper node to also select work from the overloaded node. If that is not sufficient another processor is being asked and so forth. Also only high processors are used as helper processors.

The correlation of unpark and helper processing is annotated by bullets 1 and 2 in figures 4.33 and 4.34. Bullet 1 shows that little unpark activity takes places when the helper processing is also small. Bulltes 2 show high helper processing followed by high unpark processing.

4.7.9. System Work

Finally we have to take a look at the kind of work which is being processed in a system. So far we primarily took a look at end user related work from a Hiperdispatch perspective. Nodes are built to guarantee that long running and CPU intensive work does not land on just one node and also not only high important transaction oriented work. We also took a look what can be done to ensure that an overload situation of a node resolves quickly. With helper nodes are an immediate solution and unparking of low processors is a long term reaction of the system. There is still some type of work which requires special consideration, that is system work.

System requests are typically very short running work units. Many of them execute at very high dispatch priority. Putting such requests on a node work queue can potentially result in keeping up system work from completing fast enough. So we need another solution for it. For this reason a special work unit queue is created outside of the node topology. System work is placed on this work queue and one high processor of each node is dedicated to always check this queue before it selects work from its local node work queue. In the example of the installation depicted in figure 4.30 we can observe 3 nodes. One high processor of each node will check the high performance work queue. If that is not sufficient other processors of the nodes can be enabled as additional help processors.

4.8. Hiperdispatch Analysis

At the end of this chapter we will examine of how much performance improvement can be achieved with Hiperdispatch. At this point we should remember that Hiperdispatch was introduced to allow scalability of large systems across many physical processors. The design point is to help large partitions and large CECs. For the comparison we will examine an installation similar to the previous example discussed in section 4.7.4. The CEC in this example is a z10 with 20 regular processors and 1 zIIP. There are 3 partitions on the CEC and we take a look at the biggest partition which also has 3 nodes defined for regular processors and 1 small node for the zIIP. For our analysis we compare three days with Hiperdispatch turned ON (HD=ON) and three days with Hiperdispatch turned OFF (HD=OFF).

We use data from the day time of the system between 08:00 to 16:00. During this period Online Transaction (OLTP) work is running. OLTP work is much more critical then batch work which runs mostly during the night. Also most installations are interested in bets performance for their OLTP workload.

4.8.1. Processor Utilization

Figure 4.35 shows the Partition Utilization (LPAR Busy) for the time frame from 08:00 to 16:00 by processor for each day. At this point we can already recognize a significant difference between Hiperdispatch ON versus OFF. When Hiperdispatch is turned OFF all processors are equal. Hiperdispatch turned OFF is depicted by the gray shades lines in the graphic. Usually the system is not always 100% busy and logical processors load the WAIT State PSW. The z/OS dispatcher tries to put processors with higher numbers more often into a wait. As a result we can observe a curved line for the processor utilization with processors with a high number entering more often a WAIT state than processors with low numbers.

For Hiperdispatch On the graph is very different: We observe a similar behavior for the high processors within the nodes. The utilization drops from the lowest to the highest processor with the difference that the second processor is always a little higher utilized than the first processor. The reason is that the second

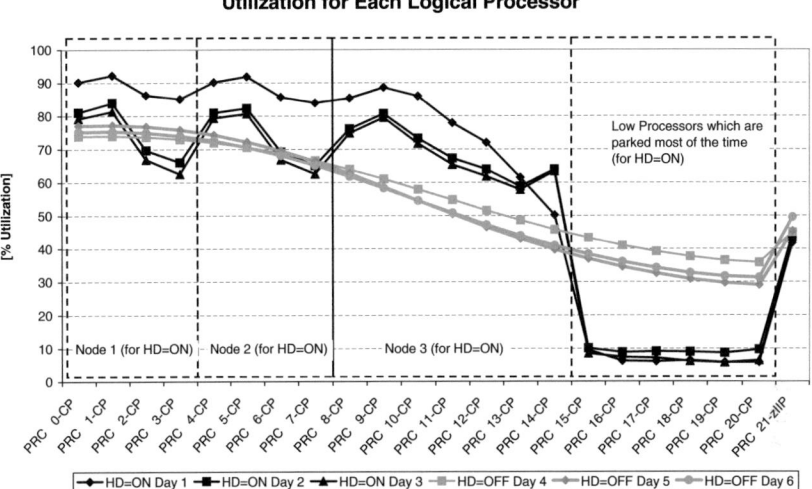

Figure 4.35.: Hiperdispatch Analysis: Processor Utilization

processor of each node is always enabled to select system work from the system work unit queue which is not part of the node topology. The utilization drops for the medium processors and the low processors which are most of the time in a park state show very little utilization.

4.8.2. Cycles per Instruction

For analyzing whether Hiperdispatch improves the performance of the system we will analyze the Cycles per Instructions (CPI) which are required to process the work. The CPI has two components and we will examine both of them:

1. The CPI depends very much on the workload which is processed and the architecture. This values should be the same for the same system running the same workload and it can highly vary between different workload mixes and different systems. We name this value CPI from instruction complexity.

2. The cycles per instructions need to resolve L1 cache misses. This is something we would expect can be addressed better with Hiperdispatch ON because we expect that fewer Cache reloads are required and data

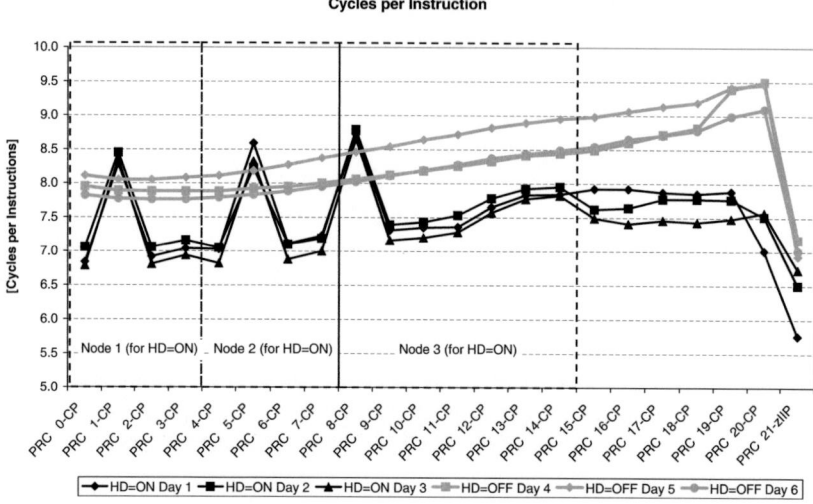

Figure 4.36.: Hiperdispatch Analysis: Cycles per Instructions per Processor

which is not in the L1 cache can at least be found with higher probability in a near by cache structure. This value is named CPI from finite cache and memory system.

Figure 4.36 shows the sum of both components. We can observe:

HD=OFF The CPI is pretty similar between the processors. Higher processor numbers show a slightly higher CPI. The reason is that those processors enter more often a wait state and therefore need to acquire cache content more often than the processors which are less often in a wait state.

HD=ON The CPI is smaller as for HD=OFF. That's what we hoped to see. We also observe that 3 processors make an exception. These are the processors which select the system work. Such work requests are much smaller and have a tendency to encounter more cache misses.

Table 4.7 summarizes the results of the comparison. The average CPI values for the time frame from 8:00 to 16:00 shows smaller values for HD=ON compared to HD=OFF. The differences ranges from 6 to 14% on a day by day comparison with an average improvement of 9% improvement for HD=ON compared to HD=OFF.

Day	CPI	CPI from	
		instruction complexity	finite cache/memory
Day 1 HD=ON	7.54	3.68	3.86
Day 2 HD=ON	7.62	3.69	3.93
Day 3 HD=ON	7.44	3.69	3.75
Day 4 HD=OFF	8.21	3.76	4.45
Day 5 HD=OFF	8.50	3.73	4.77
Day 6 HD=OFF	8.13	3.70	4.43

Table 4.7.: Hiperdispatch Analysis: Cycles per Instructions

We already discussed that we can observe two different components for the Cycles per Instruction and table 4.7 also lists the CPI components. As expected the instruction complexity only varies slightly between the days. The difference between the Hiperdispatch ON to OFF days is about 2%. On the other hand the CPI from finite cache and memory shows the difference between Hiperdispatch ON and Hiperdispatch OFF. The values for Hiperdispatch OFF are between 13 and 27% higher compared to Hiperdispatch ON.

The summary of this analysis is that Hiperdispatch on a large partition of a z10 system gives around 9% better throughput compared to not enabling this function. At this point we have to mention again that the results highly depend on the partition topology and workload characteristics.

4.8.3. Hiperdispatch on z196 and zEC12

The comparison was performed on a z10 system. A z196 provides an additional cache structure and the expectation is that the results or benefits are at least similar to z10. In fact z196 shows advantage for smaller configurations. Book crossing of large partitions on a z10 is the most disturbing effect for system performance. For smaller partitions the positive effect of Hiperdispatch diminishes. Especially on systems with many logical partitions which only have a small share of the physical configuration the effect is small to non existent.

On z196 the additional cache structure allows to create positive effects already within a book. Table 4.8 summarizes the results for z196 models. Again for very small partitions which have a smaller share than 1.5 physical processors no positive effect can be expected. But significant enhancements can be seen

Share of the partition assumes 1.5 logical to physical ratio	Number of physical CPs+zIIPs+zAAPs			
	≤ 16	17-32	33-64	65-80
$0 \leq$ share in processors < 1.5	0%	0%	0%	0%
$1.5 \leq$ share in processors < 3	2-5%	3-6%	3-6%	3-6%
$3 \leq$ share in processors < 6	4-8%	5-9%	6-10%	6-10%
$6 \leq$ share in processors < 12	5-11%	7-13%	8-14%	8-16%
$12 \leq$ share in processors < 24	-	8-16%	10-18%	11-21%
$24 \leq$ share in processors < 48	-	-	11-21%	12-24%
$48 \leq$ share in processors < 80	-	-	-	14-26%

Table 4.8.: Hiperdispatch Benefit for System z196

already for installations with partitions with a share in the range from 3 to 6 physical processors.

On a zEC12 the L3 and L4 cache sizes have doubled compared to a z196. Even with up to 6 processors per chip the cache size is significantly increased for zEC12 processors. This again will result in a positive effect so that Hiperdispatch inevitable function for the newest System z generation. IBM took this into account and with z/OS version 1 release 13 Hiperdispatch is the default setting for System z mainframes.

4.9. Summary

Hiperdispatch deviates from Symmetric Multi Processing (SMP) in a way that it defines a significance for logical processors and based on this significance allows them to compete differently for the physical processors. In addition Hiperdispatch groups logical processors in nodes and thus attempts to reduce the probability that work is re-dispatch across all possible logical processors. This has both positive and negative effects from which the positive effects are stronger.

Pure SMP systems also have two significant disadvantages:

1. The work can run everywhere as discussed and thus reduces the cache value, especially for large systems with many logical processors

2. Even if the work is dispatched in z/OS (or the operating system in gen-

eral) it is not said that it is running. Dispatcher delays of the virtualization layer are not shown at the operating system level and even if the work seems to process (logically) it might still have to wait because the logical processors have to compete for physical resources.

Hiperdispatch addresses these concerns and provides better throughput for the work executing on the systems. So it is highly dependent on the size of the system. Table 4.8 shows the value of Hiperdispatch depending on the partition and CEC size for System z196. Also Hiperdispatch is a very new development on z/OS and its development is not at the end. System z10 was the first attempt and the results shown in the example are already very encouraging that a way has been found to grow and scale systems across many logical and physical processors.

5. Workload Management

Workload Management is a discipline which tries to ensure that different types of work can execute efficiently at the same point in time. MVS was the first operating system which developed a System Resource Manager (SRM) allowing an installation to define resource access for the work running on the system. This has been further developed to a goal oriented approach which now allows an installation to define objectives for the work to the system and the system attempts to meet these objectives. The component is now named z/OS Workload manager (WLM) with SRM as an integral part. We already saw in chapter 4 and section 3.5 that WLM and SRM play important roles for Hiperdispatch and Storage Management on z/OS. In this chapter we will take a closer look at the core functionality of WLM and we will discuss how the function is important for scalability and high availability of the operating system and platform.

5.1. Workload Management Concepts

Industry wide two concepts of workload management components exist.

1. Entitlement based workload or resource management classifies work into groups and then assigns fixed shares to the groups. That means that the work of a certain group always has the same dispatch priority when it gets dispatched. It has access to fix amount or at least a guaranteed amount of memory resources and so on. It might also be possible that work exceeds its shares but as soon as competition starts the workload management component will re-enforce the specified access rights. Examples for such components are the System Resource Manager (SRM) of MVS which was first implemented in 1974. Another example is the AIX Workload manager which also works mainly with static shares.

2. Goal based workload or resource management. The main difference here is that no shares are defined for the work which is classified to groups or service classes. Instead the installation defines goals which is similar a service level agreement which an installation defines with its end

users. The system will then calculate actual resource shares based on the goal definitions and adjusts them based on changing demand. Examples for such functions are the z/OS Workload Manager component which has been introduced in 1994. Another example is the HP-UX Workload Manager component which uses similar techniques.

5.2. Why Workload Management

First we need to ask the question why and to which extend a workload management function is really required. A mainframe environment like z/OS has the characteristic that many different workloads execute at the same point in time. Figure ?? in chapter 4 shows the physical utilization of a z/OS system from a customer installation over a 3 day period. We can observe that many different workloads like On-line Transaction Processing (OLTP), database processing (DB2), customer written applications, Time Sharing users (TSO) and Batch run on the system at the same time and at different times in one partition and also in multiple partitions. Workload Management is now the attempt to optimize the throughput, to satisfy the end user goals for the work on a single system, across a cluster and across a CEC.

The primary motivation for Workload Management is based for easier management of work in a complex environment. We will find out that this encompasses many features which support the scalability of the environment as well the availability of the system and the workloads. In section 4.7 we already discussed WLM's role for Hiperdispatch which is a crucial element for supporting scalability in a large n-way environment.

5.3. Workload Management on z/OS

Figure 5.1 depicts how WLM is integrated in the systems. The installation classifies the work into service classes and defines performance objectives or goals for it. The Workload Manager component (WLM) will use these goal definitions to calculate the access to system resources based on actual demand and work competition on the system. A very important aspect needs to be mentioned at this point: A workload management component on its own can do little to really understand what is happening on the system. Therefore a very important aspect is the coordination and communication with the main software components which execute on the system, mainly the subsystems and

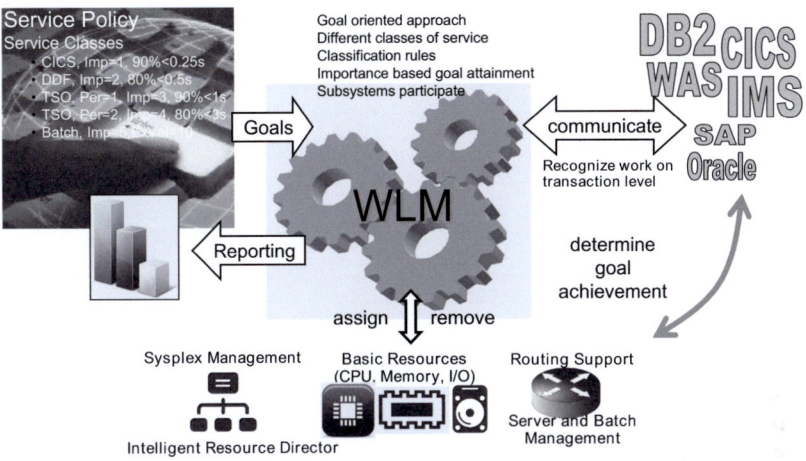

Figure 5.1.: Conceptual View on z/OS Workload Management

middleware. We will find out that this aspect is really the primary strength of the Workload Management implementation on z/OS which distinguishes it from other platforms most.

5.4. z/OS Workload Management Basics

In order to understand Workload Management on z/OS we will first take a look what an installation needs to do to setup a service definition which tells WLM how to manage the work on the system. In this context we also have to understand what types of work can be distinguished on the system and how transactions are recognized and managed. Finally the installation must understand how WLM presents results and how the installation can determine whether its definitions are meaningful and whether they can be achieved.

5.4.1. Work Classification

The first step an installation must perform is to group work into classes with similar attributes. Work Classification is done based on subsystem types. A subsystem in this context is an operating system component or a program prod-

```
    Subsystem-Type  Xref  Notes  Options  Help
    -----------------------------------------------------------------------
                    Modify Rules for the Subsystem Type      Row 1 to 5 of 5
    Command ===> _____  Scroll ===> PAGE

    Subsystem Type . : JES          Fold qualifier names?   Y  (Y or N)
    Description  . . . WLM Batch Rules

    Action codes:   A=After     C=Copy       M=Move      I=Insert rule
                    B=Before    D=Delete row  R=Repeat    IS=Insert Sub-rule
                                                                  More ===>
                -------Qualifier--------              -------Class--------
    Action      Type      Name      Start              Service       Report
                                              DEFAULTS: BTCHDEF      RDEFBTCH
    _____  1   TN        %%COPY%%  ____                BTCHHIGH     RDEFCOPY
    _____  1   TN        DDEB*     ____                BTCHHIGH     RDEFDDEB
    _____  1   TN        TSOS*     ____                BTCHHIGH     RDEFTSOS
    _____  1   TC        X         ____                BTCHCRIT     RDEFCRIT
    _____  1   TNG       JESSTD    ____                BTCHNORM     RDEFNORM
    *************************** BOTTOM OF DATA ***************************
```

Figure 5.2.: Work Classification Example for Batch Jobs

uct which creates work in the system. This can be Started Task Control (STC)
which is responsible for creating address spaces and which is a part of the operating system. Other important subsystems are the Job Entry Systems (JES2
or JES3) which create batch jobs and Time Sharing Option (TSO) for online
users. While STC together with the MASTER address space is responsible for
creating an address space, the work which is scheduled as batch jobs is more
abstract already. The individual batch job receives a classification based on
attributes which are meaningful for the operator, like the Job Class, the Job
Name, or the identification of the TSO user which submitted the job. The job
is not automatically put into execution state but first resides as an entry on the
JES spool data set. Nevertheless after the classification into a service class the
job can already be managed and its retention time in the system already starts
to count. After classifying the work WLM starts to understand the new work
entity and then it is able to measure its retention time and to manage it.

Nearly all major middleware components support WLM, like CICS, IMS, DB2,
and also non IBM middleware like Oracle and SAP. Units of work for these
middleware typically don't result in creating a new address space. The units
of work are typically passed through the existing middleware address spaces.
WLM provides a set of application interfaces which allow to encapsulate the

transactions and which allow the middleware to tell WLM when the transaction starts and when it ends.

Figure 5.2 shows an example for Batch Job classifications. The subsystem type is JES which applies to both job entry systems JES2 and JES3. Both job entry systems support the same attributes, for example TN which is the "Transaction Name" meaning the name Batch job. Various other parameters are also supported and the value of TN can have a different semantic for different subsystems, for example the TN classification parameter is used for the method name on Websphere transactions or used for parameters from CICS commands for the CICS subsystem.

Work classification assigns the units of work to a service class and optionally to a report class. A report class is for fine granular reporting purposes and not used for managing the work. In addition some subsystems require that a default service class is defined which is used if none of the specified classification parameters meet the input data defined in the WLM service definition. For subsystems which do not require a default service class WLM assigns a service class on its own. For this reason three pre-defined service classes exist:

- **SYSTEM** is reserved for system work. System work is recognized by certain start attributes. This service class has a fixed dispatch and I/O priorities which are the highest in the system. It is no target for dynamic Workload Management.

- **SYSSTC** can be used by an installation for work which behaves similar to system tasks. For example lock managers require fast access to CPU resources but typically they do not consume much CPU. The installations are encouraged to define such work to SYSSTC. SYSSTC is also the default service class for all other Started Tasks in the system which have no matching classification rule. But installations are encouraged to define a default service class for subsystem STC to avoid that too much work is classified to SYSSTC and thus runs at a too high dispatch priority outside of the management scope of WLM.

- **SYSOTHER** is the default service class for everything else except for Started Tasks. This service class has no goals and installations are encouraged to ensure that no work is classified to this service class.

A detailed description of work classification can be found in [32] and [33].

```
   Service-Class  Xref  Notes  Options  Help
 -----------------------------------------------------------------------
                          Modify a Service Class         Row 1 to 3 of 3
 Command ===> _____

 Service Class Name . . . . . : BTCHDEF
 Description  . . . . . . . . . Default Batch
 Workload Name  . . . . . . . . BATCH      (name or ?)
 Base Resource Group  . . . . . _____   (name or ?)
 Cpu Critical . . . . . . . . . NO         (YES or NO)

 Specify BASE GOAL information. Action Codes: I=Insert new period,
 E=Edit period, D=Delete period.

            -- Period --  ----------------- Goal -------------------
 Action  #  Duration   Imp.  Description
   __     _  _____    _    _____
   __     1  20000       4    Execution velocity of 10
   __     2  _____    _    Discretionary
 *************************** Bottom of data ***************************
```

Figure 5.3.: Example for a Service Class Definition for Batch Work

5.4.2. Service Class Goals

The next step for the installation is to define goals for the service classes. These goals consist of two aspects:

1. How important the work is. This is required to tell WLM which work requires more attention especially when system resources become tight. WLM will always take care that work with higher importance is able to meet its objectives and if necessary reduces the resource access of lower important work. This doesn't mean that high important work could be throttled in order to help lower important work. This again depends on whether it is meeting its objectives or not. The importance levels are 1 for highest and 5 for lowest. The system work, the service classes SYSTEM and SYSSTC, have better resource access than the managed work in importance levels 1 to 5. Also a level below importance 5 exists which is named Discretionary, meaning that no specific goal is defined.

2. The performance expectation or the performance objective for the work. This expresses what the installation expects how the work should perform on the system and it is expressed as a response time or a throughput oriented value. The performance objective must consider the ability

of the system to execute the work and it must consider the behavior of the work. That means it is not possible to define a goal that work should complete within one second if the runtime characteristics of the work requires at least 2 seconds processing time.

To summarize these aspects it is important for the installation to create a clear picture which work is more important for the business than other work and it requires that the system administrators do understand the basic execution characteristics of the work. The service class is the entity which is used by WLM to manage the work of the system.

Figure 5.3 shows an example for a service class definition for Batch work. The service class is named BATCHMD and it is associated with a workload named Batch. The workload association is just a grouping mechanism. A resource group can be associated with the service class and an attribute CPU Critical can be specified for it. We will discuss this later when we discuss how an installation can minimize the dynamic management capabilities of z/OS WLM.

The service class BATCHMD has two periods. Up to 8 periods can be defined. Periods are another definition which can be used for certain type of work. A period defines for how long a service goal should be used for a unit of work. The idea is that it is sometimes unpredictable how long work will execute. The best example are TSO users or Batch work. Most TSO users probably just do editing which does not require a lot of system resources. Therefore a TSO users may have a very high importance level and very tight goal definitions. But some TSO users may execute a command list or even a long running foreground program. Using the high importance or stringent goal definition for those users would be very unfortunate for the system. Therefore periods define an aging mechanism which tells WLM at what point lower important goals should be applied. The period length is defined as multiple of service units. We will discuss the concept of service units at the end of this section.

5.4.3. Response Time Goals

A response time goal can be used for a service class if the execution or retention time of the work can be measured in the system. Measuring the response time is a task which the subsystem or middleware component must perform. z/OS Workload Manager provides a set of interfaces and constructs which allows these components to encapsulate their units of work and enables the measurement. If these conditions are met it is possible to define either an average or percentile response time goal. The average response time goal assumes that the units of work complete on average within the defined time period. This really requires uniformly behaving work because very few long running units of work can skew the goal achievement and therefore put a big burden on managing the work in the service class.

A percentile response time goal is better suited to manage work which also shows some execution time variations which is the case for most work on a computer system. The percentile response time goal is defined as a certain percentage of the completing transactions which must end within the defined time period. In order to measure this a distribution is defined around the goal value from 50% of the goal definition to 5 times of the goal definition and one bucket for all transactions which need longer to complete.

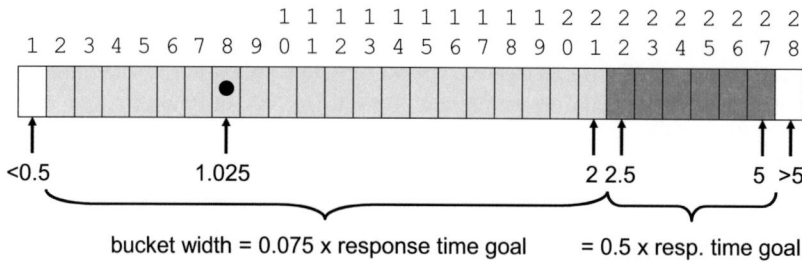

Figure 5.4.: Response Time Distribution Buckets

Figure 5.4 shows the bucket definitions for a response time distribution. The buckets are created in the following way:

- One bucket is defined to capture all transactions which require less than 50% of the time of the goal definition
- Between half the goal to two times the goal 21 equidistant buckets are defined.
- Seven more coarse grain buckets are defined to capture the longer running transactions.
- One bucket is defined to capture all transactions which need more than 5 times of the defined goal to complete.

$$
\text{bucket number} \quad = \quad
\begin{cases}
1 & \text{if } rt \leq 0.5 \times \text{goal} \\
1 + \frac{rt - (\text{goal}/2)}{1.5 \times (\text{goal}/20)} & 0.5 \times \text{goal} < rt \leq 2 \times \text{goal} \\
21 + \frac{rt - 2 \times \text{goal}}{(\text{goal}/2)} & 2 \times \text{goal} < rt \leq 5 \times \text{goal} \\
28 & rt > 5 \times \text{goal}
\end{cases}
$$

Figure 5.5 shows a sample response time distribution for a service class. The distribution is always generated for all service classes with a response time goal. The distribution is created for a specified time period which depends on the number of ending and running transactions. The running or in-flight transactions are also captured in order to make sure that long running and not ending transactions are used for managing the service class too.

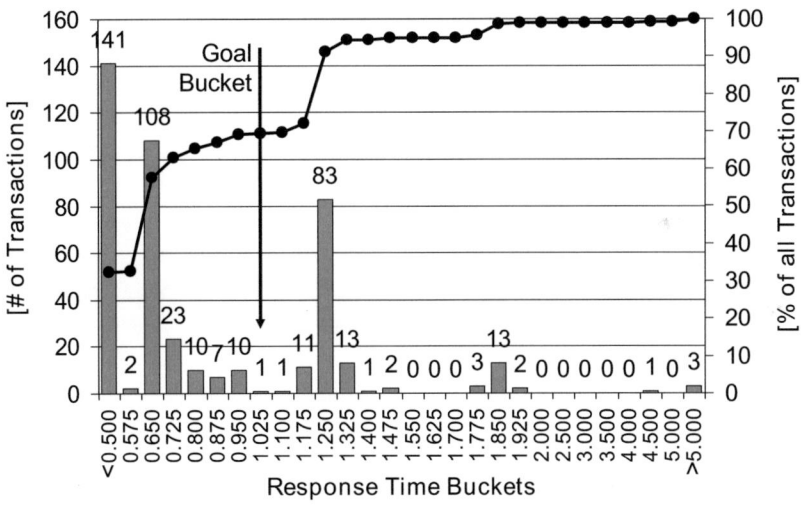

Figure 5.5.: Response Time Distribution for a Service Class

5.4.4. Execution Velocity Goals

It is not always possible to measure the response time of work in the system. For example for most address spaces this is not meaningful. An address space is created at a certain point in time and lives for an unpredictable time period in the system. Also for certain batch work which consists of very long running jobs a response time goal is not suited. In order to capture this work and provide manageability WLM looks at the times when the work can execute and when it must wait in the system. This can best be done by examine the execution phase of work and when it requests a resource. If it must wait for the resource a "delay state" is counted for the execution unit and when it can use it a "using state". This also requires that the system constantly observes all work and all managed resources in the system. In z/OS this is done every 250 millisecond and one of 4 four states is counted for each execution unit in the system:

Idle   The execution unit is doing nothing and does not request any resource

Using The execution unit is using a managed resource like the CPU or an I/O device. Using CPU means the execution unit (a TCB or SRB) is dispatched and executing on the processor. Using an I/O device means that the execution unit waits on the completion of a related I/O request and the I/O request is not delayed in the I/O subsystem.

Delay The execution unit is waiting on a managed resource, like CPU, I/O or memory. It should be noted that memory only shows up as a delay state because all work always uses some amount of memory it is just the question whether this is enough.

Other or Unknown

    Means that the system can't determine the exact state of the execution unit. This is mostly the case because the execution unit is delayed by a resource which is not under the control of the system, for example a subsystem lock.

Measuring the system can be correlated to a traffic system with cameras taking snapshots in defined time intervals at the crossing points of the traffic. If a vehicle passes a crossing point a "using state" is counted and if it must wait a "delay state". The speed of the work in the system can now be defined as the quotient of all measured using states to all managed states in the system (without Idle and Other). This speed is named "Execution Velocity" in z/OS and it is a measure for the throughput of work[1]. It is also used as a goal definition for the installation to define a performance objective for work which is not suited for response time goals:

$$\text{Execution Velocity} = 100 \times \frac{\text{Total Using States}}{\text{Total (Using + Delay) States}}$$

---

[1]A velocity is normally a directed speed but in z/OS it is just used synonymous for speed

5.4.5. Managing Work in z/OS

In section 4.2 we discussed which types of work can be distinguished in a z/OS system. At this point we want to take a look how these workload types can be managed.

Criteria	Started Tasks	TSO OMVS	Batch APPC	On-line Transaction Processing	
				CICS/IMS	WAS, DB2, and all others
Unit of Work Begin/End	Unknown	Press ENTER Terminal Out	Begin of Job End of Job	informed by subsystem	Enclave create Enclave delete
Duration	Indefinite	short medium	medium long	very short	short medium
Management	using and delay states	by response time	by response time and using/delay states	by response time	by response time and using/delay states

Table 5.1.: Possible Goals for Workload Types

Table 5.1 lists the workload types which we already introduced in section 4.2. Furthermore the table lists whether z/OS Workload Manager is able to recognize the begin and end of individual work requests as *units of work* or whether those requests are unknown. z/OS WLM can manage the requests if it is able to recognize their begin and end. Then it is possible to measure the response time of the unit of work or transaction[2].

We can distinguish between work which is instrumented and those which isn't. Started tasks are typically not instrumented and they can only be managed with the help of execution states and towards an execution velocity goal. TSO and OMVS users are instrumented by the system. Whenever the user presses the ENTER button a signal is sent to the System Resource Manager[3] which tells the system that a new transaction has started. When the result is returned to the terminal another signal is sent which informs of the end of the transaction. For batch or APPC work the Job Entry System and the Advanced Program to Program Communication (APPC) Service send the signals when a new work unit starts its processing and also signal when the processing is completed.

---

[2]The term transaction is often used instead of unit of work or work request
[3]SRM is part of WLM

More complex is the situation for transactions of databases and transaction monitoring systems. A transaction monitoring system controls the flow of many end user transactions at the same time. Those requests are typically very short running. The transaction monitor guarantees access to resources like databases which complies the requirements of atomicity, consistency, isolation and durability.

The transactions are often executed in one or multiple address spaces which manage a set of TCBs or SRBs. The TCBs and SRBs are assigned to the incoming work requests. WLM developed a set of application interfaces allowing the transaction monitoring systems and databases to inform WLM when a work request starts and when it is completed. At this point we distinguish for *On-line Transaction Processing* (OLTP) work between CICS and IMS and all other types. This is based on the instrumentation which is used by these transaction monitors. We will shortly discuss the concepts and their implications on managing work in a z/OS system.

5.4.6. WLM Transaction Management

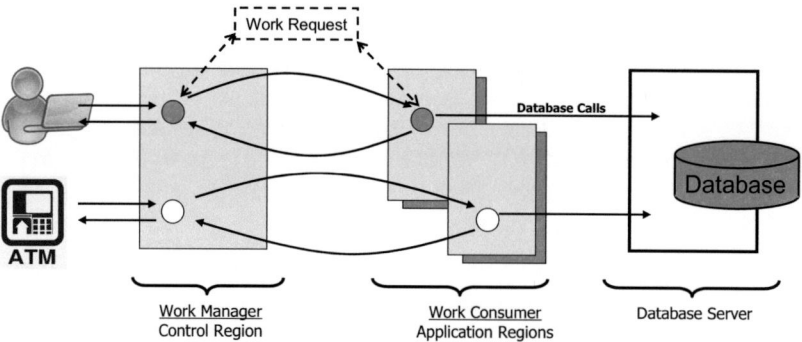

Figure 5.6.: WLM Transaction Management

WLM manages the performance characteristics of transactions. A general model for transactions executing in the system is shown in figure 5.6. Typically transactions are short running requests which get into the system through a network connection. A control region, or daemon receives the requests, validates them and sends them for execution to an application processing region. The application processing region starts a program on behalf of the transaction and usually the transaction accesses a data base on z/OS. This is one model. It is also possible that only one address space does everything and it is possible that multiple application server address spaces are involved. A transaction can also go outside the system again but the simple mode shown in figure 5.6 captures the behavior which can most often found for CICS, IMS, Websphere and DB2 transactions.

The terminology transaction usually refers to its quality attributes, like atomicity, consistency, isolation, and durability. From a WLM point of view these attributes are not visible and for managing the performance characteristics of requests it is not important whether such attributes apply or not. Therefore the term "Business Unit of Work" (BUoW) is often used instead of transaction.

5.4.7. Enclaves

An Enclave is a mechanism to group execution units (TCB, SRB) across address spaces. This allows to classify transactions or business units of work independent from the address spaces to which the TCBs or SRBs belong to. This also allows to apply different goals for the service classes of the enclaves and therefore to manage the enclaves as separate entities in the system. Because enclaves encapsulate individual business units of work they also allow to report those business units of work through on-line or historical monitoring products.

Figure 5.7 shows one processing model for enclaves as it is used by Websphere transactions. The Websphere Ciontrol regions, named Work Manager Address Space A, receives the requests from the network, validates them and classifies them by creating an enclave to WLM. Together with creating the enclave the work unit attributes are passed to WLM which compares them to the installation definitions and associates the enclave with a service class. Finally WLM passes an enclave token back to the control region.

The control region passes the request to a server region. This is done by exploiting a queuing mechanism which is provided by WLM which we will discuss later. A TCB in the server manager address space B eventually selects the request and then joins the enclave. By joining the enclave the TCB is logically moved to the enclave because from now on the performance objectives of the enclave service class apply to it and no longer the performance objectives of the address space service class. The TCB loads a program to process the work request and at the end leaves the enclave. the enclave will finally be deleted either from the server manager or the originating work manager. The work manager which created the enclave is also the enclave owner.

Enclaves allow to apply performance characteristics which are typically not as stringent as the performance objectives of the address spaces of the middleware. the address spaces are part of the infrastructure and they typically require fast access to system resources while the enclaves represent the production work which should follow rules of a service level agreement. Enclaves allow to individually manage transactions therefore it is also possible to create different service classes for different types of work requests, for example work coming from ATM machines might require preferential service to work requests coming from a banking counter.

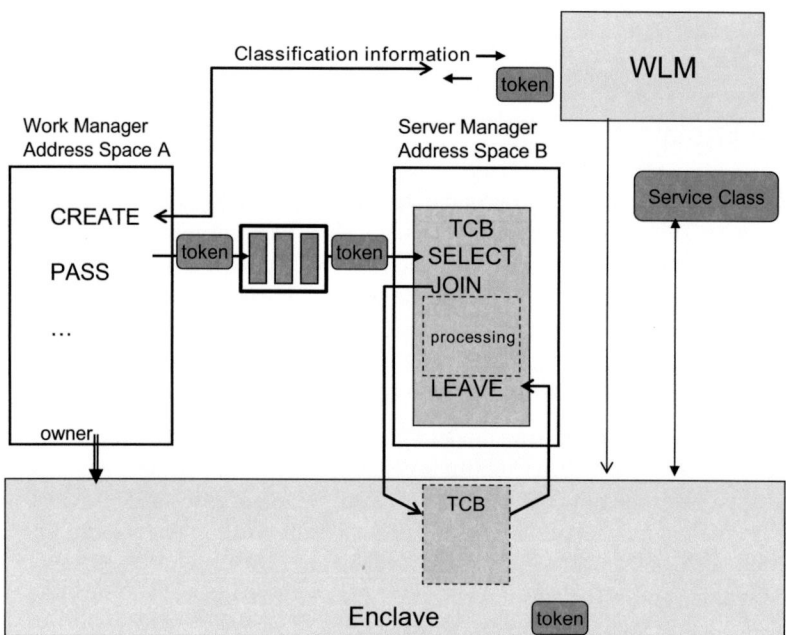

Figure 5.7.: Enclave Processing Model for Websphere

Finally it must be mentioned that the depicted model only applies to Websphere. DB2 Distributed Data Facility (DDF) which also uses enclaves extensively uses a different model. Instead of passing the work request to a server address spaces, DDF creates a special SRB to process it. DDF now uses two different types of enclaves:

1. Short living enclaves which encapsulate just one transaction or user request. This is similar to how Websphere uses enclaves.

2. Long living enclaves. In this case only a certain number of enclaves is created in the system and never deleted. New requests are associated with an enclave and at the end dis-associated from them but the enclave is never deleted. In this case the enclave represents many transactions and it is for example not possible to use response time goals for them because the begin and end of them is not defined.

DB2 Stored Procedures also use enclaves and their processing model is more like the model for Websphere but their are still gradual differences. Other products and components again use either short or long living enclaves with their own processing model.

5.4.8. Managing CICS and IMS Transactions

Another method exists for managing CICS and IMS transactions. This method does not encapsulate the individual work requests it rather counts the types of work requests used in each execution address space and it also provides a tracking mechanism for execution states.

The general flow is similar to the previous example discussed for Websphere. A CICS TOR (Terminal Owning Region) receives work requests from outside the system, verifies them and classifies them to a service class for performance management. But in this case no envelope is created which represents the transaction in the system. Only a control block named performance block (PB) is associated with the transaction and it is used to track execution states. The work request is usually also passed to another region an application owning region (AOR). Based on the previous classification the AOR also associates a PB with the transaction. During execution the AOR now uses interfaces to book keep execution states in the PB, see figure 5.8.

The PB has another more important meaning from a performance management perspective. WLM runs through all PBs in the system every 250 milliseconds and monitors their association to service classes. This gives WLM a picture which transactions are executed by which application region. Based on these measurements WLM creates sets of address spaces which process the same transactions types. For this it is independent of how many transactions of each type are executed by the address spaces, just the type matters. These sets of address spaces are internally used as dynamic internal service classes. For managing the the goal fulfillment of the transaction service classes at some point WLM needs to decide for which associated internal service class it must change the resource access. So finally achieving the goals for CICS transactions means to select the correct internal service class which is associated with the address spaces for which the resource access is adjusted. This also means that transactions of the same type depending on the server address space they are executed in might receive different service depending on other transactions types also executing in those address spaces. It can also be shown that for N external service classes for CICS or IMS transactions up to $2^N - 1$ internal service classes can be created.

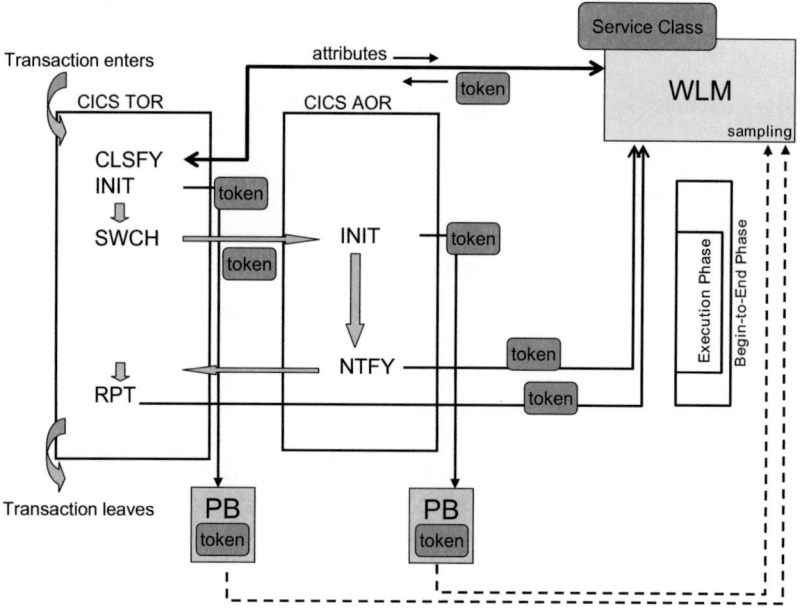

Figure 5.8.: Processing Model for CICS Transactions

When the transaction completes the association to the PB is removed and the execution and end-to-end response times are tracked and book kept. WLM also collects this information on a microsecond basis and updates the service class statistics accordingly. By doing this the statistics of completed transactions and their response times is always correct for the associated service classes.

Detailed descriptions on how WLM manages business units of work can be found in [13], [27], [28], [33], and [34].

5.4.9. Service Definition

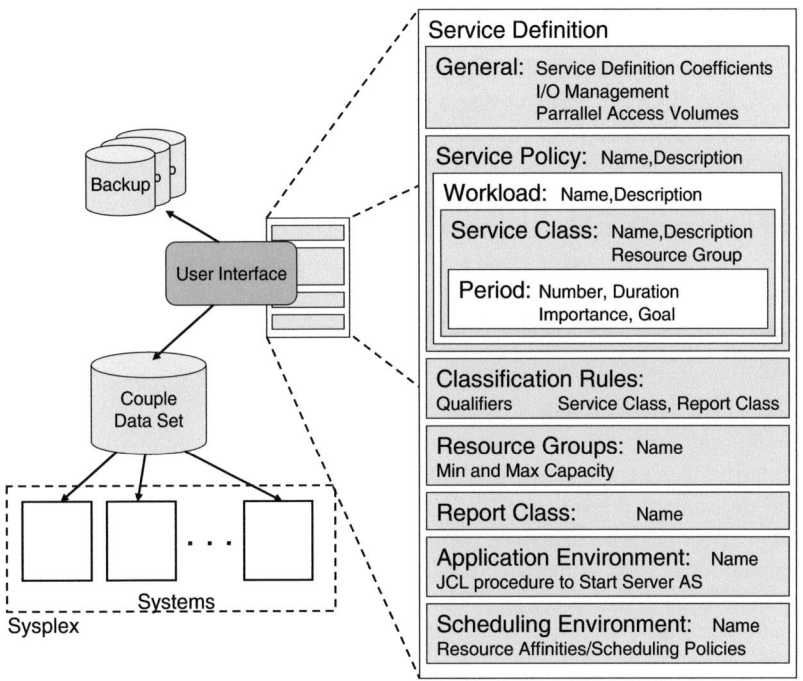

Figure 5.9.: WLM Service Definition

The service classes, goals and classification rules are saved in a service definition together with additional grouping and reporting mechanisms. A service definition consists of multiple service policies which describe modified sets of goals for the specified service classes. A workload is a higher grouping mechanism and in addition it is also possible to specify report classes for more granular reporting purposes. A service class always consists of at least one and up to eight periods.

In addition to service classes, service policies, classification rules and report classes the service definition contains additional constructs like resource groups, application environments and scheduling environments. We will discuss them in section 5.6 when we take a look at advanced topics of Workload Management.

The service definition is defined through a user interface which can either be an ISPF based and therefore host based user interface or a web based application. The result of the definition can either be saved for later use or it can be "installed" on a couple data set. A Couple Data Set is a special data set which contains cluster information for a parallel sysplex. We will discuss them in chapter 6. But this already shows that a service definition applies to all systems in a z/OS cluster which is named a sysplex or parallel sysplex. This concept shows one of design objectives for z/OS Workload Management: by assigning a service definition to all systems of the same sysplex the definition for all these systems must only be made once. Adding additional systems does not require to add a new definition, the existing definition can simply be used for it too. Therefore the WLM definitions support scalability of sysplex environments by keeping and using only one definition for the complete sysplex.

5.4.10. Service Unit

The duration of a period is defined as the amount of consumed service. The units of this service consumption is a Service Unit (SU). Period aging is not the only reason to measure service consumption. Especially in the past service consumption was used in many SRM algorithms. A service unit is composed of CPU and SRB service, memory consumption, and I/O traffic. Service Definition Coefficients are used to weight these factors against each other and the result is the service consumption of a unit of work or a service class:

$$
\begin{aligned}
\text{Service} \quad = \quad & (\text{CPU weighting} \times \text{CPU Service Units}) \\
+ \quad & (\text{SRB weighting} \times \text{SRB Service Units}) \\
+ \quad & (\text{IOC weighting} \times \text{I/O Service Units}) \\
+ \quad & (\text{MSO weighting} \times \text{Storage Service Units})
\end{aligned}
$$

CPU Service Units are the TCB execution time multiplied by an SRM constant which is model dependent. SRB Service Units are basically the same except that SRB execution time is used. The differentiation between CPU and SRB service units allows to distinguish user related from system related work by changing the weighting factors.

I/O Service Units are measurements of individual data set I/Os and JES spool reads. SRM counts the number of EXCPs which give a good indication of the number of I/Os executed. Storage service units are the number of central storage pages multiplied by CPU service units and divided by $\frac{1}{50}$. In fact storage service units were of much interest as long as the memory size was constrained by 2 GB and it is no longer relevant. In z/OS environment the recommendation for the weighting factors are:

$$CPU=SRB=1.0; IOC = 0.3; MSO=0$$

The SRM constant is model dependent. It represents the speed of the processor multiplied by multi processing factors which reflect the number of logical processors configured to the system. IBM publishes SU/sec for all of its System z processor models but it must be understood that these numbers are very rough sizings only and for capacity planning purposes not ideal. Much better suited are values taken from the Large System Performance Reference. It must also be mentioned that IBM publishes different types of Service Units for different purposes. The System z IBM web pages give more information to these subjects.

5.4.11. Goal Achievement

Finally we have to take a look how an installation can evaluate whether the goals for their service classes have been achieved or not. This also leads over to the next section where we will discuss the basic algorithms for z/OS Workload Manager.

Goal achievement can be supervised with a very simple metric the Performance Index (PI). This metric is also the base for all internal goal adjustments. It is simply defined that a value of 1 means that the goal is achieved, if the value is smaller than one it is over achieved and if it is bigger than one the goal is missed. The deviation from one is also a measure for over or under achievement and thus a possibility to project how resource adjustments can influence the measured goal achievement. The definition is also pretty simple. For a response time goal the actual measured response time is divided by the goal value and for an execution velocity goal the goal value is divided by the actual value:

$$\text{Response Time Goal} \quad : \quad PI = \frac{\text{Actual Acieved Response Time}}{\text{Response Time Goal}}$$

$$\text{Execution Velocity Goal} \quad : \quad PI = \frac{\text{Execution Velocity Goal}}{\text{Actual Achieved Execution Velocity}}$$

The definition and calculation of the performance index is pretty simple and we only have to take a look how it is calculated for a percentile response time goal. When we introduced the percentile response time goal we already mentioned that we count all ended transactions for a certain time period up to the defined bucket at which we get the defined percentage value. In figure 5.10 the percentile response time goal for the service class is defined that 90% of all transactions should end within 1 second. In order to determine the actual average response time we must count all transactions until we meet the 90% value up to the 11th bucket. This bucket corresponds to a response time value of 1.175 to 1.25 seconds. Now we use 1.25 seconds as the actual achieved response time and because of the goal of 1 second the performance index results to 1.25, so the goal is not being achieved in this example.

Service Class Transactions

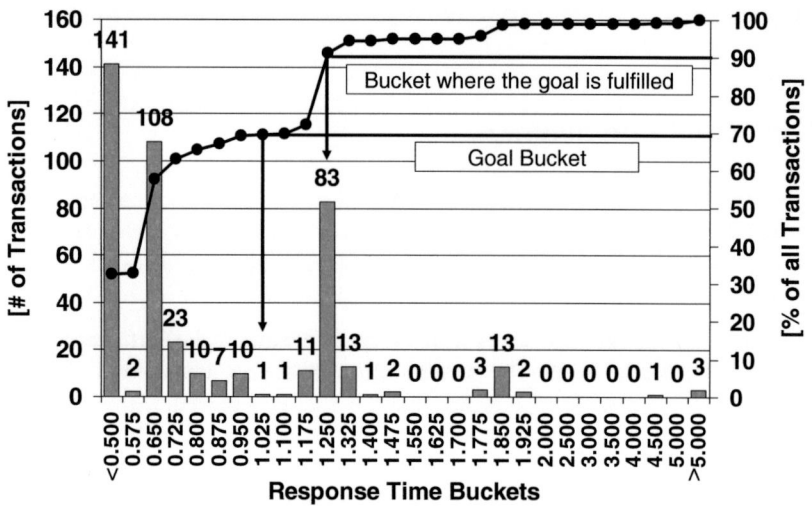

Figure 5.10.: Actual Response Time for a Percentile Response Time Goal

5.5. z/OS Workload Manager Algorithms

We will now take a closer look on how WLM calculates the access to resources for work running on the system. At this point the installation has the work classified into service classes and defined goals to tell WLM how the work should execute on z/OS. The steps for WLM are now to capture runtime statistics for the work, to assess whether the service classes meet their goals and if necessary to adjust the access to the system resources. A detailed description which is the base for the this section can be found in [13].

5.5.1. Data Sampling

WLM must collects state information about the work in the system which can then be used to assess and calculate the necessary resource access for the service classes. State data is the using and delay information for every execution unit in the system. The data is collected for every execution unit (TCB or SRB) and accumulated on a per address space or enclave basis which encapsulate the execution units. Because it is possible that multiple execution units execute for an address space or enclave it is also possible to obtain more than one state for them. The data is then further accumulated on a service class basis and used on this granularity for resource adjustment.

Table 5.2 shows the available state information. As already mentioned there are 4 state categories: Idle, Other, Using and Delay. An address space or enclave is considered idle if no execution units wants to use any kind of resource. So this is really a single state occurrence while multiple execution units which execute could be found in different states. z/OS Workload Manager actively manages 4 resources: CPU, I/O, Memory and Server Address Spaces. In addition it is able to take actions for lock contentions but this is on a per request basis and not dependent to the goal achievement of the work.

We can observe that even with *only* four resources we see multiple different states for each resource. For example three different CPU types and states exist. Using states for regular CPs, for zAAPs and for zIIPs and accordingly the same amount of delay states. For memory or storage many more delay situations can be observed. For example paging delays can be divided in multiple categories for private and common storage. In addition it is necessary to recognize whether an address space is being swapped out and either can't swap in (*Auxiliary Swap Delay* or is not allowed to swap in *Multi-Programming (MPL) Delay*. Another long list of delays exist for enclaves because enclaves may not be associated with an address space and then it is necessary to identify the address spaces from which enclaves require storage.

Two very special delays are *CPU Capping Delay* and *WLM Queue Delay:*.

- CPU capping delay occur if WLM sets execution units non dispatchable. This is done if the resource consumption of the work needs to be throttled.

- WLM queue delay relate to WLM managed work queues which are offered to middleware applications to control the server address spaces which process the work.

System State	Using	Delay	CPU	I/O	Storage	Other
IDLE						×
OTHER						×
CPU Using	×		×			
zAAP Using	×		×			
zIIP Using	×		×			
DASD I/O Using	×			×		
CPU Delay		×	×			
zAAP Delay		×	×			
zIIP Delay		×	×			
CPU Capping Delay		×	×			
DASD I/O Delay		×		×		
Auxiliary Private Paging Delay		×			×	
Auxiliary Common Paging Delay		×			×	
Auxiliary Virtual I/O Delay		×			×	
Auxiliary Hiper-Space (SCR) Delay		×			×	
Auxiliary Hiper-Space (CAC) Delay		×			×	
Auxiliary Swap Delay		×			×	
Auxiliary Cross Memory Delay		×			×	
Multi-Programming (MPL) Delay		×			×	
Shared Paging Delay		×			×	
Enclave Private Paging Delay		×			×	
Enclave Virtual I/O Delay		×			×	
Enclave Hiper-Space Delay		×			×	
Enclave MPL Delay		×			×	
Enclave Swap Delay		×			×	
Buffer-pool Delay		×			×	
WLM Queue Delay		×				×

Table 5.2.: WLM Data Sample Categories

Not all delay categories are still meaningful. Some were invented related to a newer technology in the past which is no longer really important, like Hiperspaces. Other delay categories are introduced just recently like buffer pool delay for DB2 buffer pools.

5.5.2. Histories

			Example 1		Example 2		Example 3	
		Time	Timer	6	Timer	16	Timer	64
Row	Timer	mm:ss	Data	After Roll	Data	After Roll	Data	After Roll
1	1	00:10	5	**0**	5	**0**	5	**0**
2	2	00:20	11	**16**	11	**5**	11	**5**
3	4	00:40	22	**22**	22	**11**	22	**11**
4	16	02:40	35	**35**	35	**22**	35	**22**
5	64	10:40	51	**51**	51	**86**	51	**35**
Last		21:20	77	**77**	77	**77**	77	**51**

Table 5.3.: Data Aging in WLM Histories

The state data needs to be accumulated on a service class basis. For each address space or enclave 28 counters for each state category exist which represent the occurrence of the state for a defined time period. The state information is collected every 250 milliseconds for address spaces and enclaves and accumulated on a service class every 10 seconds. At this point the state counters of the address spaces and enclaves are reset. For evaluating and assessing the resource access of the work a 10 second period might be too small. In order to decide a change a certain minimum number of states should be available. For many algorithms WLM tries to accumulate at least 500 state samples as a base for all comparisons. 500 state samples may or may not be accumulated during the last 10 seconds so it is necessary to create a longer history of state information. The history is created by accumulating the actual state information every second, fourth, 16th and 64th interval into a new bucket. Altogether 6 buckets of the 28 counters are kept for each service class with the first bucket representing the current expired 10 second interval, the second bucket the last 20 second, the third bucket up to last 40 seconds and the fifth bucket up to the last 10 minutes. The sixth bucket is an exception. The data is not rolled (accumulated) from the fifth to the sixth bucket. Instead the sixth bucket is cleared and the fifth bucket is copied to the sixth bucket. Table 5.3 shows three examples how data is rolled up in the buckets:

Example 1 At every second 10s interval the data which was just accumulated to the first bucket is added to the second bucket. The first bucket is cleared.

Example 2 At every 16th interval the data of the fourth bucket is added to the fifth bucket. The fourth bucket is cleared. Then the data of the third bucket is added to the fourth bucket and the third bucket is cleared and so forth.

Example 3 At the 64th interval the buckets 1 to 5 are moved up to the buckets 2 to 6 and the 6th row is deleted. At this point after 21 minutes the data is expired.

System State	Adjusted	Row1	Row2	Row3	**Row4**	Row5	Row6
IDLE	2734	0	110	130	**2384**	12302	10187
OTHER	20	0	0	0	**20**	20	157
CPU Using	72	0	0	1	**71**	411	266
DASD I/O Using	1097	0	0	0	**1097**	5581	3512
CPU Delay	43	0	0	0	**43**	178	135
DASD I/O Delay	165	0	0	0	**165**	815	577
... All other data is zero ...							

Table 5.4.: Service Class State Sample Matrix

Table 5.4 shows an example from a service class control block. The example only depicts the state data samples which are not zero. The first step is to roll the history as described before. Then WLM tries to find the row up to which at least 500 non idle state samples are available. The rows up to the row which meets the minimum 500 sample criteria are summed together and the result is placed in the *Adjusted* samples. All further decisions which require state samples use the adjusted samples. If 500 samples can already be found in the first row, the second row will also always be used. That means WLM bases its decision always on at least 20 seconds of state data.

Annotations

- Using the history approach allows to cover a long period of state information, up to 20 minutes in this case with minimal memory occupancy.

- Values of the first two rows are doubled when they are added to the adjusted state vector to give more emphasis on the recent events in the system.

- The base for all decisions are the non-idle samples. Idle samples are just tracked for reporting purposes.

- Using the history approach in this way also has the effect that decision for a service class X might be based on a 20 second time period while the decision for service class Y might be based on a 10 minute time period. It is also possible that these service classes are traded against each other. But this is meaningful because it is better to base decisions on a statistically meaningful number of state information than on a fixed intervals.

- Response Time Distributions are also captured in histories in the same way as the state data. Also an adjusted distribution is created every 10 seconds which is used to determine the goal achievement of the service class.

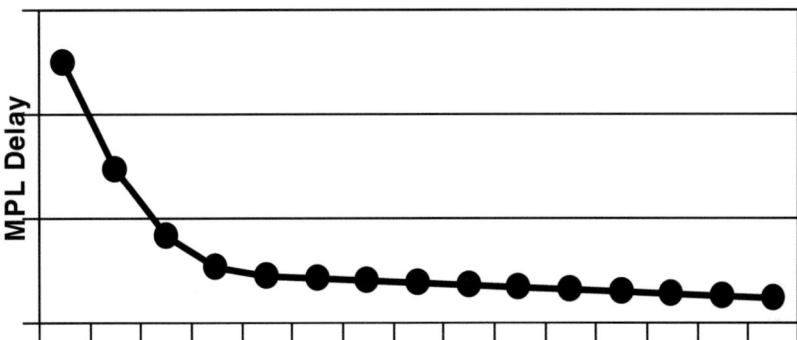

Rate MPL Slots (Address Spaces in Memory) to Ready Users

Figure 5.11.: Data Plots

5.5.3. Data Plots

Another possibility to track information exists if a relationship between the data exists. Such data can be saved in a plot. The idea of a plot is to learn about the relationship in the current system and then to identify the changing point when the relationship of the information causes a drastic change in system or work behavior. A simple example are the number of address spaces which are allowed to reside in storage (Multi Programming (MPL) Slots) in relation to the READY USERS of a service class. The quotient of MPL slots to READY USERS can be tracked versus the MPL delay. MPL delay is measured if an address space becomes READY but it is not in memory. If the address space can't be swapped because the the Multi Programming Targets of the system keep it out the number of available slots is too low. So a relation ship between the rate of MPL slots to Ready Users and MPL delay can be continuously tracked (see figure 5.11). At some point the MPL delay will become very small or even zero because enough slots are available. On the other side if too few slots exists the MPL delay is very high. The knee of the curve is now the interesting area where changes for few slots will make a big difference. For a situation when system resources become tight WLM will try to manage the work at the edge of the knee so that the MPL delays do not go up too drastically and on the other hand the work does not flood the system.

Annotation

One of the most effective macro controls of the system is to define how many address spaces are allowed to be swapped in (Multi Programming Level). This allows to restrict work which has a tendency to over utilize the memory but also restricts work which may over utilize the processors. Work which is swapped out can't use the processor and it's memory content is eligible to get paged out.

5.5.4. Policy Adjustment

The process of adjusting the resource access for work towards the user defined goals is named *Policy* or *Goal* adjustment. Figure 5.12 depicts the basic policy adjustment process. This process runs every 10 seconds. In between data is collected, for example the state sampling data and system utilization information. The collected data is accumulated by service class at the beginning of the policy adjustment process. At the same time the goal achievement of the service classes is calculated. The value of the goal achievement the performance index (PI) is used to trigger the goal adjustment process.

The goal adjustment starts whenever a service classes misses its goals meaning the PI is greater than 1. It can also already start when the PI of all service classes

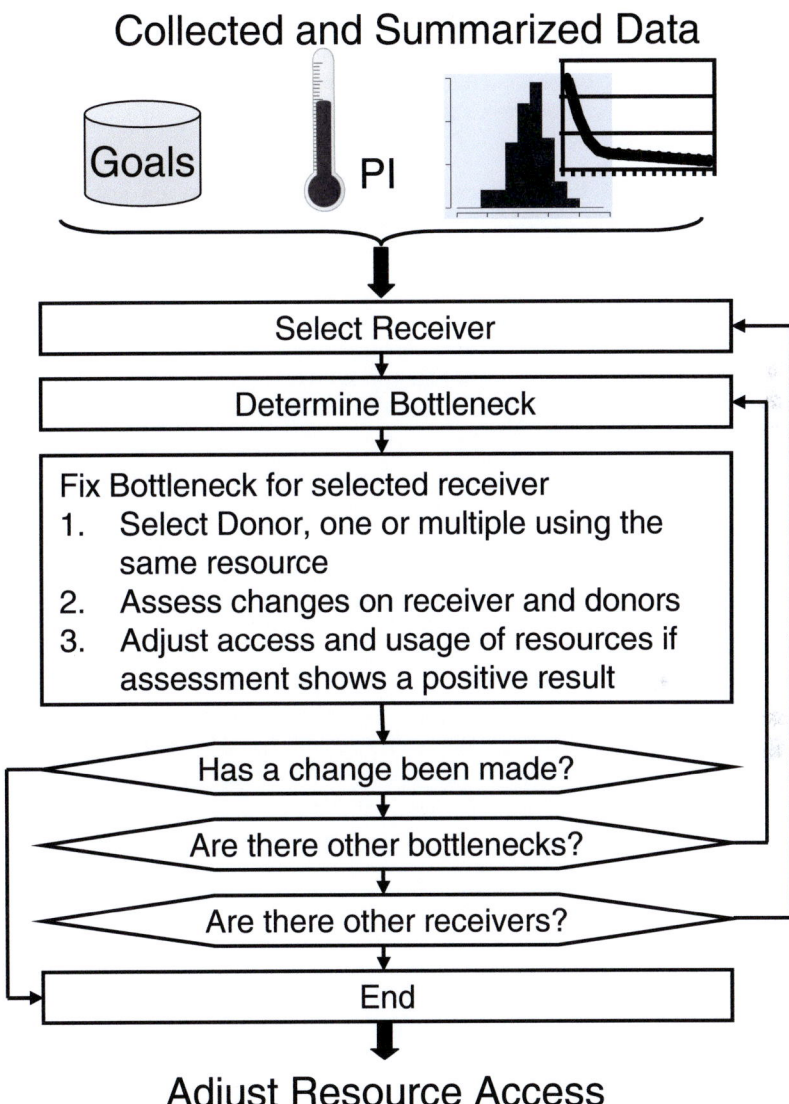

Figure 5.12.: Policy Adjustment Process

is better than 1. The trigger would then be to assess whether it is possible to help service classes which are close to a PI of 1 and thus balance the system resources better between the work of the system. Another factor are service classes which do not have a specific goal; discretionary service classes. It is also possible to help such work but we will ignore these cases for simplicity purposes.

We assume that some service classes do not meet their goals so it is necessary to assess whether changing the access to resources is possible and can help the work. First WLM selects a receiver for which the resource access needs to be changed. This is the service classes with the highest importance and the worst PI. The next step is to determine the bottleneck. For this reason WLM examines the adjusted sample set and identifies the delay category with the highest value. WLM tries to fix this bottleneck. It selects one or multiple donors which could help the service class in question. The first important selection criterion is that the service class which is selected also uses the same resource. For example a service class which shows I/O problems might use the device addresses between 100 and 200. So only service classes which also use device addresses of the same range are of possible help and service classes which use completely different devices can be ignored. Such overlapping conditions are calculated in the preparation steps of this algorithm.

The donors are selected in a way that service classes with the lowest importance meeting their goals are selected first. In addition it must be possible that the donors can give up access to resources for the requesting service class. For example a lower important service class which already has a lower dispatching priority is of no help for a service class which WLM wants to help with CPU resources. Finally two important checks have to be made:

1. Does the selected donor really help the service class? We already showed an example where this isn't the case but it is also possible that the donor might help but the help is not sufficient so the algorithm needs to look for additional donors.

2. Is it allowed to use the selected donor? The dominating factor here is how the performance index of the donor will change if the change will be made. We will discuss this in more detail but it is clear that a donor with lower importance can always be used. So the question really is of interest if donors with equal or higher importance than the receiver have been selected.

At the end of this assessment a set of questions is asked which determine how long the algorithm runs. The first most important is whether the change which

WLM just has assessed could be made? If that's the case the algorithm is completed. That means the algorithm is completed as soon as it is successful for one target receiver. We will later see that it is possible to end up with multiple service classes being helped but only one service class is selected as primary target. The idea behind this solution is to change the system only on behalf of one entity and then observe the change again before another change is done. If it wasn't possible to perform the change the algorithm checks whether it is possible to help the service class for the next delay category following the idea that the second or third best help might still accomplish something. If no other resource can be assessed for this service class then another receiver is chosen which is the next important service class with the second worst PI and so forth.

5.5.5. Policy Adjustment Example: Fix MPL Delay

We will describe the algorithm in more detail with assessing an MPL adjustment for a service class. The Multi Programming Level is adjusted by changing two thresholds which exist for each service class in the system, see figure 5.13.

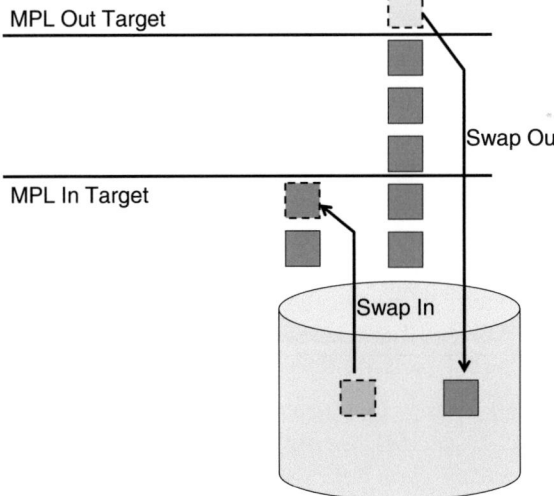

Figure 5.13.: Swapping Related to MPL In and Out Targets

The MPL OUT target is the high bound. If this value is set to a value of N below 999 it means that no more than N address spaces are allowed to reside in memory at the same time. Every additional address space is being swapped out. If a swapped out address space gets ready and wants to use the processors it needs to get swapped in but at the same time another address space of the same service class must be swapped out. This is called an Exchange Swap.

The low bound is the MPL In Target. If this value is set to a value of M below 999 it means that at least M address spaces must be swapped in. If the In Target is not satisfied an address space is swapped in even if this requires to swap out other work. The purpose of the Out target is to restrict work of a service class to avoid that the work dominates the system. The purpose of the In target is to guarantee a certain service for work of a service class and to avoid that it gets swapped out completely. It should be mentioned that the Out target can be set to zero. That is a kind of an emergency brake for the system to push work completely out in order to survive extreme over load situations. Also as already mentioned MPL is one of the most effective controls of the system.

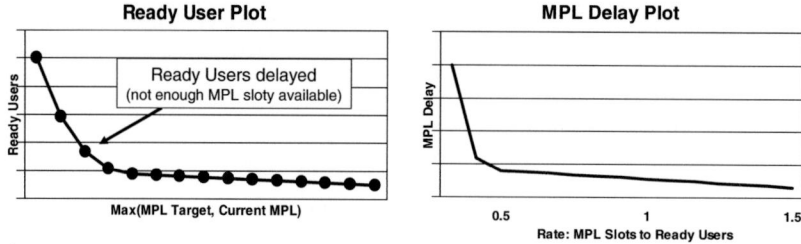

Figure 5.14.: Plots to Adjust MPL In and Out Targets

In order to adjust the targets two plots are maintained for each service class. The plots are updated every 10 seconds with a new plot point and the changes develop over time. The two plots are depicted in figure 5.14:

1. The Ready User Average Plot tracks the number of ready users against the current MPL or the MPL out target (assuming the out target is set below 999). If the ready users back up this is an indication that not enough MPL slots are available. If no out target is set this can mean that other work is dominating the system so a possible action might be to set an in target for the work. The plot is also used if an out target is changed in order to predict how the number of Ready Users might change. The plot is used in two ways:

- For the receiver to project at what point the number of ready users decrease. So for a receiver we will look to the right of the current entry and we will try to find the change when additional slots will not provide any significant help

- For the donor to assess how many more Ready Users can be expected if we lower the out target. For this purpose we will take a look to the left.

2. With the number of Ready Users found in this plot we will then try to find a corresponding or expected MPL delay. At this point we have to mention that we can't calculate a change of Performance Index based on the change in number of Ready Users. But we can do this calculation if we understand the change in delay. Therefore we will use the MPL delay Plot which we already used as an example in section 5.5.3. WLM calculates the rate of Ready Users to MPL slots and then obtains the expected MPL Delay from the MPL Delay Plot. This delay value is then used for all further projections.

5.5.6. Projecting a Change for Accessing a Resource

The example above gives the algorithm a projected delay either for a receiver or a donor of a change. This projected delay which was read from the MPL delay plot can also be obtained from a state history or it may be calculated for other cases. The value is used as the starting point to project how the performance index changes. The calculation differs whether an execution velocity or response time goal has been defined for the service class.

Execution Velocity Goal

For an execution velocity goal the projected delay can be immediately used to calculated a projected execution velocity and a projected local PI. The projected delay in formulas below is the changed delay for the state category which is assessed plus the sum of all other measured delay samples.

$$\text{Projected Exvel} = \frac{\text{Using Samples}}{\text{Using Samples} + \text{Projected Delay}}$$

$$\text{Local Projected PI} = \frac{\text{Execution Velocity Goal}}{\text{Projected ExVel}}$$

Response Time Goal

For a response time goal the response time change will be calculated from the actual response time multiplied with the proportion of the delay delta to all non idle samples. The projected response time delta is used to calculate the local.

$$\text{Delay}\Delta \quad = \quad \text{Current Delay} - \text{Projected Delay}$$

$$\text{Projected RT}\Delta \quad = \quad \frac{\text{Delay}\Delta}{\text{Non Idle Samples}} \times \text{Actual RT}$$

$$\text{Local Projected PI} \quad = \quad \frac{\text{Projected RT}\Delta}{\text{RT Goal}}$$

Local and Sysplex PI

In the calculations above we obtained a local PI as result. WLM is a sysplex-wide function. That means a goal assessment also assesses the change for the work within the cluster. Information is sent to all systems which include the local observations for a service class on a system in the cluster. These local observations are summarized by each system to sysplex-wide observations and they are used to calculate a sysplex-wide PI for each service class:

$$\text{Sysplex PI} = \frac{\text{Local Observations}}{\text{Sysplex Observations}} \times \text{Local PI}$$

For the projection the calculation is the same:

$$\text{Sysplex Projected PI} = \frac{\text{Local Observations}}{\text{Sysplex Observations}} \times \text{Local Projected PI}$$

5.5.7. Receiver Value Assessment

The next step is to assess whether the projected change helps the service class. The receiver value is basically the result of the previous calculations and whether the anticipated change really helps the receiver. For adjusting MPL it is possible to either find a number of new MPL slots for the receiver which reduces the MPL delays significantly or not. If such a number exists it is only necessary to find enough donors, so the following Net Value test is by far more interesting. For other resources like adjusting CPU dispatch priorities it might be very well possible to find donors which all show Net Value but they altogether do not provide enough Receiver Value.

5.5.8. Net Value Assessment

Donor Receiver	Meet Sysplex Meet Local	Meet Sysplex **Miss Local**	**Miss Sysplex** Meet Local	**Miss Sysplex** **Miss Local**
Meet Sysplex Meet Local	3	5		
Meet Sysplex **Miss Local**		1	2	
Miss Sysplex Meet Local	4			
Miss Sysplex **Miss Local**		2	1	

Table 5.5.: Net Value Decision Matrix

The Net Value test considers both performance indexes: Sysplex and Local. It also ranks the receiver and donors. The ranking is derived from the importance level. The terms *Meet Sysplex*, *Miss Sysplex*, *Meet Local* and *Miss Local* in the decision matrix shown in table 5.5 means whether the local or sysplex PI is above or below one.

The decision matrix in table 5.5 shows under which circumstances changes can be made and under which circumstances not. The first row for example shows that a change is never made for a high important service class which meets all goals and the selected donors whether they are of the same or lower importance miss their goals. Also the first column shows that a change will always be made if the receiver misses a goal and the donor does not. The inner part of the matrix covers the more interesting cases. To understand them properly we need to define three terms:

PI_GAIN   means that the performance index of the receiver is improved or the performance index of receiver and donor come closer together.

GS_GAIN   means that the service for a resource group of which the minimum is not fulfilled is improved.

PI_OR_GS_GAIN
means that either of the two conditions is fulfilled.

With these definitions we can explain the decisions in table 5.5:

1. Net Value exists if the receiver has higher rank, or receiver and donor have the same rank and a PI_OR_GS_GAIN exists

2. Net Value exists if the receiver has higher rank than the donors

3. Net Value exists if PI_OR_GS_GAIN exists

4. Net Value always exists

5. No Net Value ever

5.5.9. Policy Adjustment Example: Fix CPU Delay

The policy adjustment process is an iterative process. In order to show this we will discuss a possible scenario for adjusting dispatch priorities for service classes. For this example we do not care about the projections we will only focus on possible alternating adjustment steps.

Dispatch Priorities

Table 5.6 shows the dispatch priorities which are used in the system. The two highest priorities FF and FE are fixed for system work which is classified to the service classes SYSTEM and SYSSTC. The range between F9 and FD is not used and it is followed by the range of dispatch priorities which are dynamically adjusted for user defined service classes with a goal definition. At the top of this range a dispatch priority is reserved for small consumers. The idea is that it has not much value to exercise the adjustment algorithm for service classes which consumes very little CPU. Because they consume that little it is better to just give them access to CPU and to no longer worry about them. The decision which service classes fall into this category is made every 10 seconds and the number of service classes is also restricted which can run at this dispatch priority level.

The dynamically managed dispatch priorities are the range in which the adjustment algorithm attempts to optimally place the service classes to ensure their goal achievement and the best possible system throughput. Another small range of unused dispatch priorities is followed by the range for discretionary work. Discretionary work always runs at the bottom of the dispatch priority ranges. An algorithm called Mean-Time-to-Wait adjustment is used to differentiate the work units of this category based on their CPU and I/O intensiveness. CPU

| Dispatch priority | | Service |
decimal	hexadecimal	Class
255	FF	SYSTEM
254	FE	SYSSTC
253	FD	
...	...	Not used
249	F9	
248	F8	Small consumer
247	F7	Installation defined Service Classes
...	...	Dynamically managed
204	CC	dispatch priorities
203	CB	Not used
202	CA	
201	C9	Discretionary
...	...	Mean Time to Wait
192	C0	Algorithm
191	BF	Quiesced work

Table 5.6.: Dispatch Priorities in z/OS

intensive work will always have the lowest DP of the range. If work units are transferring I/O and have to wait their dispatch priority is being raised so that they can get faster access to the CPU once the I/O transfer has been completed.

Work which is quiesced is placed at the bottom of the range. This seems a little strange because the work can still process. But there are other possibilities from really preventing it to make any progress.

Evaluating Dispatch Priorities

The example in figure 5.15 shows a typical situation of 9 service classes with a service class named I which misses its goals and the evaluation steps to adjust the dispatch priorities for I. The algorithm has also already detected that CPU delay is the primary reason and the next step is to fix the CPU bottleneck. It is assumed that service class I is at dispatch priority 241 together with 2 other service classes G and H and 6 other service classes at a higher dispatch priority. WLM always gives out the dispatch priorities in steps of 2 therefore the next higher DP is 243.

The CPU algorithm first attempts to raise the DP of service class I. Then it calculates the net and receiver values and if this is not successful it attempts in the next step to lower the DP of service classes with higher dispatch priorities. This alternating technique of raising and lowering dispatch priorities is used until either all possibilities have been evaluated or a possible and feasible change couldn't be found.

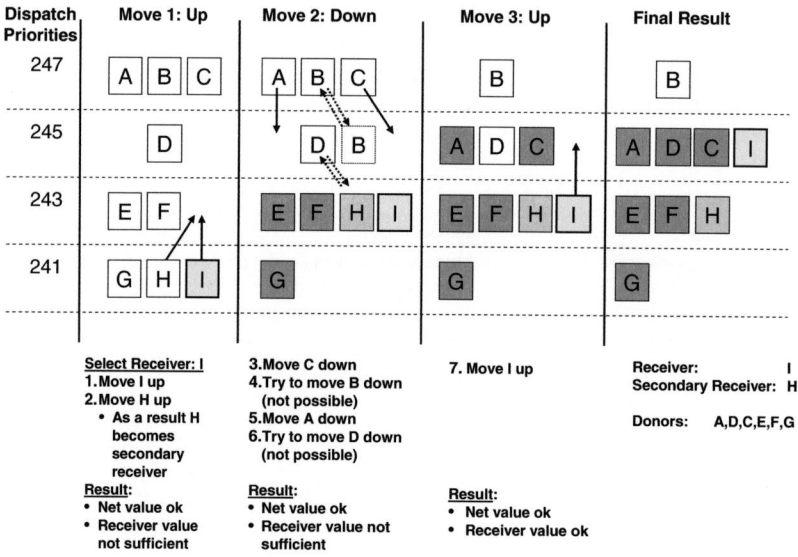

Figure 5.15.: Example for Adjusting Dispatch Priorities

The first step is to assess what it means to raise the DP of service class I to 243. This change will effect the service classes G, H, E, and F. G and H are affected because their work units can't compete equally with service class I anymore and E, and F are affected because they have to compete with this work now. WLM will deduct the CPU consumption of I from DP level 241 and adds it to DP level 243. In addition it projects how many CPU delays can be reduced by this change. The receiver value test projects the result for the receiver service class I. The net value test assesses whether the change is allowed for all potential donors.

We will assume that the change for I from 241 to 243 is possible for the service classes G, E, and F but not for service class H. The next test is what it would mean to also raise the DP for H from 241 to 243. This allows H to compete with E, and F and still with I. After assessing this second change we assume that it is possible for the goal achievement of E, F, and G. At this point we have the situation that we helped a service class which was not our primary target. We need to help it in order to continue with the assessment for service class I. So service class H is a secondary receiver, a service class which is being helped in order to help another service class.

We further assume that first set of changes is possible but not sufficient to help service class I. The next step is to evaluate whether the DP of other work can be lowered. This may or may not help but if it doesn't it can be a good preparation for another attempt to raise the DP of service class I. In this step we examine all service classes with higher dispatch priorities and calculate various possibilities how the DP of the service classes can be lowered. We assume as a result that it is not possible to lower the DP of B and that it is also not possible to lower the DP of D to the same level as E, F, H, and I. But we assume that A and C can move to the lower DP level. After this step we accomplished to have more work at DP 245 but we haven't helped service class I.

The next step again is to raise the DP of I to 245. In this case we assume that the DP can be raised. Now we have to calculate the receiver value and the impact on all donors again: A, D, C, E, F, H, and G. We assume that the impact on the donors is acceptable and that raising the DP of I to 245 now provides sufficient receiver value. At this point the algorithm terminates and the change can be carried out. As a result of this change we end up with a very different situation from where we started. We lowered the DP of 2 service classes A, and C and we increased the competition for four service classes: D, E, F, and G.

Such complex changes take place very often. Many installations have 15 to 25 service classes which quiet often require complex assessments. It also possible that the DP of the service classes either move to the high or low end of the managed dispatch priority range. In that case the DPs are spread across the DP range. This process is named *unbunch*. It is also possible to restrict certain changes by marking service classes as critical. We will discuss such restrictions in the next section.

5.5.10. Policy Adjustment Example: Time-line for Changes

The examples above analyzed the individual assessment steps. For a typical load change on a system a set of adjustments might be necessary to get the system back to a stable state. The following example is a controlled test scenario for a system with 4 major workloads: CICS, IMS, TSO and Batch. CICS, IMS, and TSO process a constant flow of work. At some point a set of batch jobs is submitted which change the load utilization of the system and which change the existing stable situation of the system. We will observe how the system reacts and how long it takes to get back to a stable situation again.

Service Class Definition

Service Class	Period	Goal Type	Goal Value	Importance
CICS	1	Avg. RT	0.1s	2
IMS	1	Avg. RT	10s	3
TSO	1	Avg. RT	0.1s	3
	2	Avg. RT	1.0s	3
	3	Avg. RT	3.0s	4
Batch	1	ExVel	10	5

Table 5.7.: Sample Service Class Definition

Table 5.7 depicts the service class definitions. CICS is the most important work in the system which also has pretty stringent goal[4]. IMS has a lower importance and a very relaxed goal definition. TSO is defined with three periods to age out longer running requests. For the test we will only follow the first period which covers the short running requests and the majority of the TSO load. Finally BATCH is the lowest important work in the system.

The scenario starts with a balanced system, see figure 5.16. At this point the system is only utilized to around 90%[5]. The CPU consumption of the service classes is measured in CPU Service Units. In the beginning we can observe very constant service rates for CICS, IMS and TSO, and nearly no service consumption for Batch. Then at a certain point we submit a lot of Batch jobs and observe how the service rates and also the performance achievement of the work changes.

Before we start the batch work we can observe that CICS is just meeting its goals, see figure 5.17. The PI for CICS is very constant around 0.9, so just below 1. For TSO first period and IMS the goal is highly overachieved and the PI is well below 0.5. When the batch work is started we can observe the following aspects:

---

[4]The test was performed on a very small test system
[5]This is not explicitly shown in the graphic

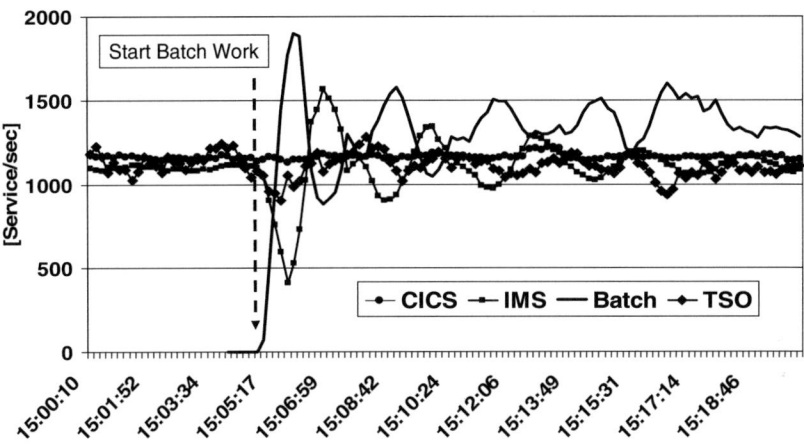

Figure 5.16.: Sample Work Execution

- The system utilization goes up to 100% (not shown)
- The service rate for batch is initially much higher than the service rate of the other work
- The service rate for IMS drops. This is an indication that batch initially has an equal DP to IMS. If it would have a higher DP the service rate for IMS would go to 0.
- The PI of Batch is initially low but then goes way up. The PI of TSO and IMS also raise. The raise of the PI for TSO is also an indication that DP of TSO was equal to IMS and Batch.
- CICS seems to be unaffected. The PI does not change and the service rate remains constant. So the DP for CICS is initially higher than for the other work and also remains higher throughout the whole test scenario.

When WLM starts to change the DP for TSO, IMS and BATCH we can recognize that the service rate for IMS comes back. At the same time the PI drops below one. The PI drops to a very low value again because of the relaxed goal definition for IMS. We can also observe that the service rate after the first changes goes above its original value. From that time on we can observe that the DP for IMS, TSO and BATCH are constantly changed because the ser-

Performance Index of the Work

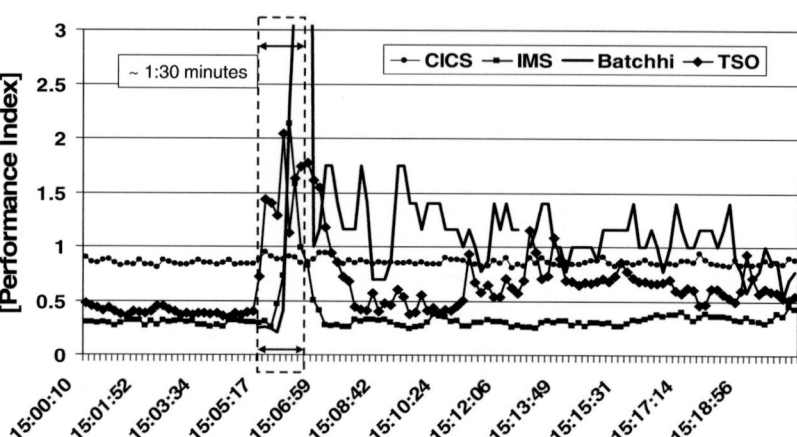

Figure 5.17.: Sample Goal Achievement

vice rate for these service classes do not remain constant. The question comes up why these changes occur? the answer is simple. IMS has a higher importance than Batch but also very relaxed goals. When it meets its goals it also overachieves the goals to a high extent. This can't really be avoided because as soon as IMS has a higher DP than Batch it runs so good that it is selected as a donor in one of the following adjustment cycles. It must also be understood that this is not wrong because the goal was defined so easy. On the other hand CICS is a very good example how a stringent goal protects work. The system has no other possibility than to give CICS the highest DP in the system based on importance level and goal definition. As a result we can nicely observe the influence and effects of setting stringent and relaxed goals.

Altogether it takes around one and a half minute, so basically six to 9 adjustment cycles to resolve the workload spike. After that the system is stable again but now with competing workloads as discussed.

5.5.11. Test Scenario versus Real Environment

The example above is easy to understand. In a real environment the decisions are much more complex and an analysis also requires much more understand-

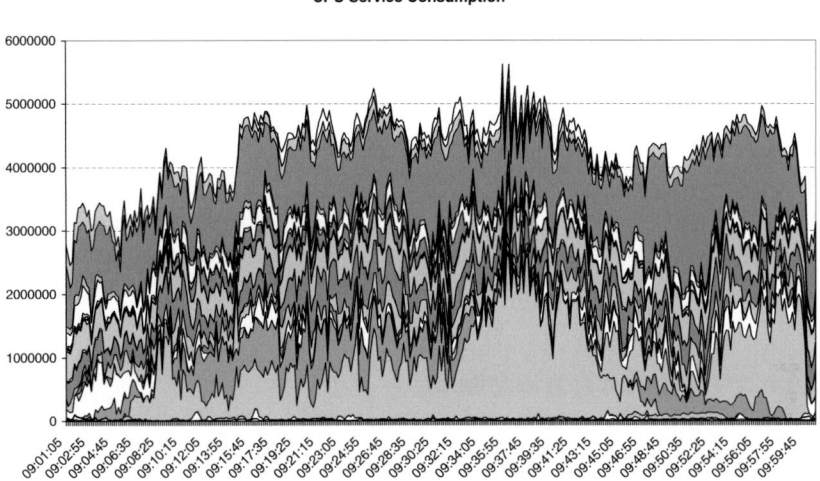

Figure 5.18.: CPU Service consumption in a real system

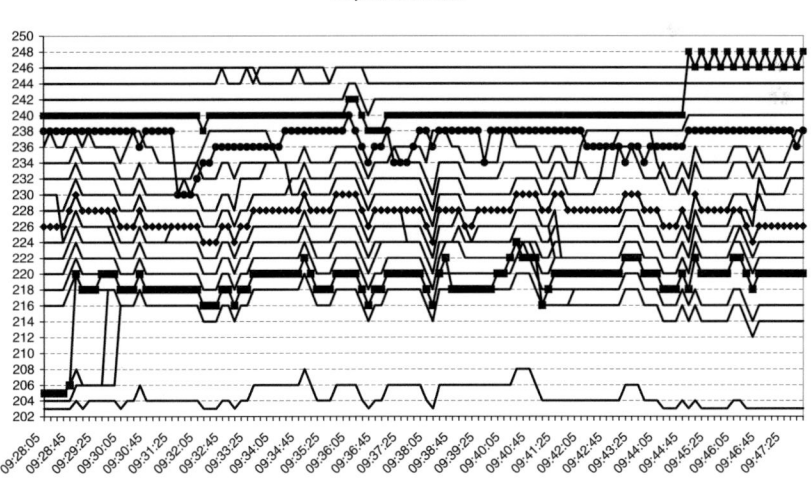

Figure 5.19.: Dispatch Priorities in a real system

ing of the workload situation. Figure 5.18 shows the CPU service consumption for service classes in a real production system. We can observe many more more service classes which also show very different consumption values. Figure 5.19 shows the dispatch priorities. Each line represents the dispatch priority change for a service class. We can observe that adjustments take place periodically. This is driven by the goal achievement as described in the previous section but many more service classes are involved in such decision.

This should only show that a real system analysis is more difficult than the examples described before and it should demonstrate that WLM continuously tunes the environment.

5.5.12. Resource Adjustment

As we learned for policy adjustment a change is possibly done on on behalf of one selected receiver. Policy adjustment always requires to compare service classes against each other and simply speaking take something from someone to give it somebody else. Also policy adjustment only runs every 10 seconds.

For more simplistic adjustments the cycle of 10 seconds is too long and the effort of trading work against each other might also not always be necessary. Especially if the system is underutilized it may not be required to consider all aspects of policy adjustment. Some resource changes can be made much simpler. In order to address such concerns another algorithm runs every 2 seconds in the system. This algorithm is named "Resource Adjustment" and it deals situations where the system over or under utilized. The full decision tree is depicted in figure 5.20.

If an over load situation is recognized the most effective reaction of the system is to swap address spaces out of the system. We already discussed the efficiency of this control. Such an over load situation occurs if too many work units can't be dispatched or if the available storage thresholds exceed all high watermarks. The system now uses an emergency break and tries to free up as much resources as possible in order to mitigate the situation. Policy adjustment can later adjust the MPL targets based on goal assessment but at this time the system starts to swap out work from bottom to top. The first work which is eligible for being swapped out is discretionary work and then followed by the lowest import service classes meeting their goals and so forth. Typically this will resolve critical contention situations and allows the high important work to complete within their objectives. The action might be too drastic but policy adjustment can correct it at a later point in time.

The other situation is when the system is lowly utilized. Low utilization is typically given if the system is less than 90% utilized from a CPU perspective and if sufficient unused memory is available. It is possible that work wants to get into the system but the MPL targets might prevent this absed on previous contention situations which have been resolved meanwhile. WLM will make a projection whether raising the MPL target will not lead to a contention situation and then adjust the MPL target by 1 every 2 seconds as long as these conditions are met.

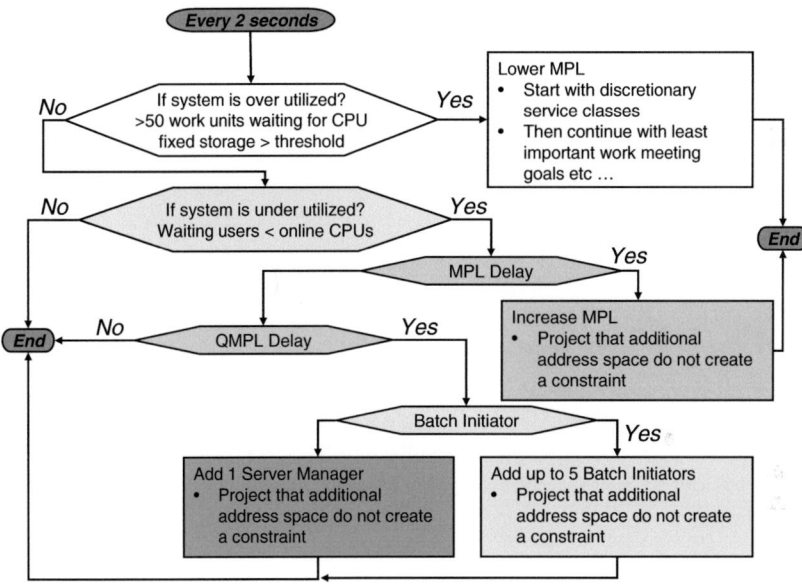

Figure 5.20.: Resource Adjustment

Related to MPL adjustment is WLM queue management. WLM queue management provides work queues for application programs and starts server address space which are able to consume the work requests. The delay of the work queues are measured as Queue MPL (QMPL) delay and the adjustment is very much like MPL adjustment. One special case of queue management is WLM batch management where WLM manages the number of batch initiators for service classes in a sysplex environment. Policy adjustment routines exist to address such adjustment but also if the system is lowly utilized there is no point to wait until policy adjustment runs. In such cases it is possible to start

1 server address space or up to 5 batch initiators. We will discuss queue management a little deeper in chapter 5.6 because it is a very good example for scalability and availability management of WLM.

5.5.13. Timed Algorithms

Policy adjustment, resource adjustment, and the Hiperdispatch balancer are 3 re-occurring timed algorithms of the system. Altogether 20 timed algorithms exist which run between 1 millisecond and some also only on a per minute basis. For some of these algorithms the scheduling time is dependent on the system speed while other algorithms always run at a fixed time period. For example we discussed briefly the transaction management for CICS and IMS. CICS and IMS use WLM services to associate a Performance Block to each transaction and book keep when the transaction has been started plus transaction execution states. Now when the transaction ends the ending time and the completion must be book kept as well. The middleware components achieve this by just adding a small control block to a queue which is examined by WLM on current systems around every millisecond. Then the completion time is transferred to the service class structures in the system.

Many timed algorithms collect information which is used by the three major algorithms. For example the CPU utilization and the Ready User numbers are very frequently updated. Also swap analysis and taking actions for swapping work in and out of the system based on adjusted targets is done on a very frequent basis.

5.5.14. Management Approach and Restrictions

So far we discussed the WLM management approach in its full flexible form but this might not always be desired. There are situations for an installation where it wants to restrict certain flexibility and wants to assign more fixed rules, for example:

- Some work has a very high urgency and when it runs it needs to complete as fast as possible. In such cases dispatch priority management might not be desirable and just assuring a high dispatch priority is sufficient.

- Especially online work runs best when it finds all required data in memory. If an installation runs OLTP during day time and very memory intensive batch during night time it is possible that the memory for the OLTP regions is migrated to page data sets. This can result in a significant delay time at the beginning of the day time shift because many pages need to be paged in again. In order to avoid such situations it might be desirable to set targets which prevent that the OLTP storage is migrated to page data sets at least not within one night shift.

- Some work has a tendency to dominate the CPU especially some batch work. Even if it may have low dispatch priorities this may have some unwanted side effects which still may incur some delay on higher important work. Also some applications might be dangerous and even if they require high access to the CPU it might be desirable to restrict its overall consumption.

These are three examples which lead to the development of restrictions for the management algorithms. It is also clear that using such restrictive knobs too extensive will result in a system with very fixed resource assignments and very little flexibility. A complete other set of reasons related to pricing exist which may require to impose restrictions especially on CPU consumption. We will briefly touch this at the end without going into too much detail.

5.5.15. Resource Groups

Resource Groups are mechanisms which allow to restrict CPU resource consumption and they allow to guarantee a minimum amount of CPU service for service classes. The functionality is provided by two limits:

- A maximum limit which ensures that over a longer period the CPU consumption will always stay below the definition.

- A minimum limit which ensures that the specified amount of CPU can be consumed as long as the CPU demand exists.

Both limits are defined in service units, as a multiple of logical processors or as a multiple of fraction of the partition share.

A service class can only be associated with one resource group but a resource group can encompass multiple service classes. Resource groups can be managed across the systems in a sysplex or just on the individual systems.

The minimum limit is guaranteed by the policy adjustment algorithm. When we discussed the policy adjustment algorithm we saw the term PI_AND_GS_GAIN. GS_GAIN refers to an adjustment for a resource group minimum limit. Work which is protected by a resource group minimum receives the minimum service regardless of its importance. That means even higher importance work which even may not meet its goals may become a donor for a resource group minimum. Within a resource group the importance and goal of service classes determines the relative priority of the work. This applies to both limits.

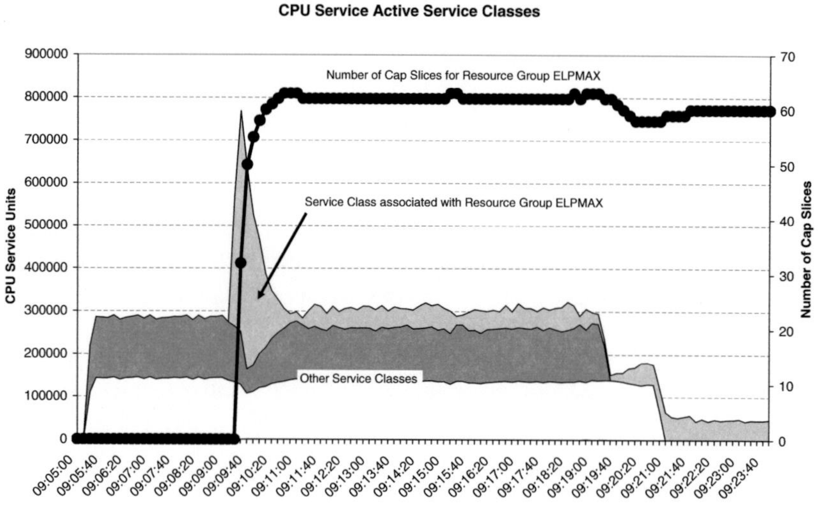

CPU Service Active Service Classes

Figure 5.21.: Example for a Resource Group with Maximum Limit

Figure 5.21 shows the function of a resource group on a single system. The used resource group type derives the limits from the weight or share of the partition on the CEC. There is no minimum defined and the maximum for resource group ELPMAX is set to 60% of the LPAR share of the partition. Based on its share which is pretty small for this partition it can consume roughly 8700 SU/s. The resource group definition entitles the resource group to use 60% of the share or up to 5200 SU/s.

The scenario shows 3 service classes running on the partition. One of the service classes is associated with resource group ELPMAX. The CEC is not highly used so the service classes and the partition can consume much more than the 8700 SU/s. When the work for the service class which is associated with ELPMAX is started we can observe a big spike of CPU consumption which is capped down to roughly 5000 SU/s after around 2 minutes. WLM creates a cap pattern which sets the units of work within the service class(es) non dispatchable to cap the work.

A resource group is usually always below the maximum possible consumption. The reason is that the cap pattern is defined in slices and the consumption is approximated in number of slices when the work is dispatchable. This algorithms always ensures that the number of slices stay below the defined capping limit. The red curve in the graph shows the number of cap slices. At the time when the graph was created 64 cap slices could be defined. Meanwhile the number is increased to 256 cap slices in order to support a higher precision. The small graph shows nicely how the consumption of resource group ELPMAX remains capped even after the work of the other 2 service classes has completed.

5.5.16. CPU Critical

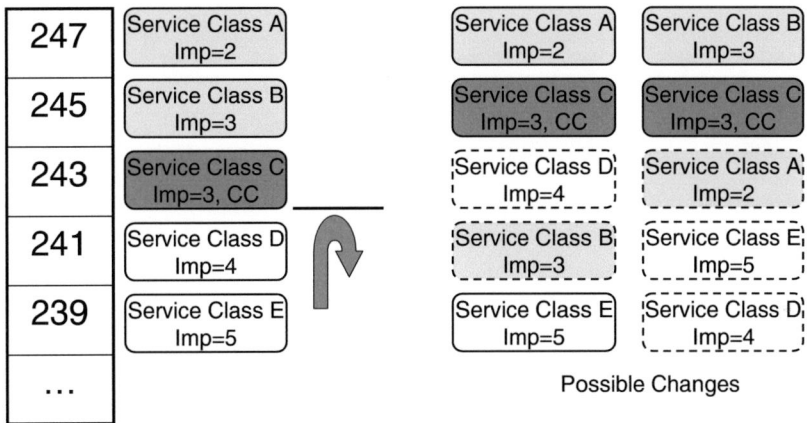

Figure 5.22.: Example for a Service Class with CPU Critical Definition

CPU Critical is a service class attribute which ensures that lower important work can never get a dispatch priority equal or higher than the service class for which this attribute is specified. Figure 5.22 illustrates a service class C at importance 3 which is defined as CPU Critical and the two service classes D and E with lower importances. Service Classes E and D will always have a lower dispatch priority than C. C can still compete with A and B for CPU access. D, and E can also still compete with A, and B but this requires that A, or B get a lower DP than C. On the right hand side two possible changes are depicted.

5.5.17. Storage Critical

Storage Frames

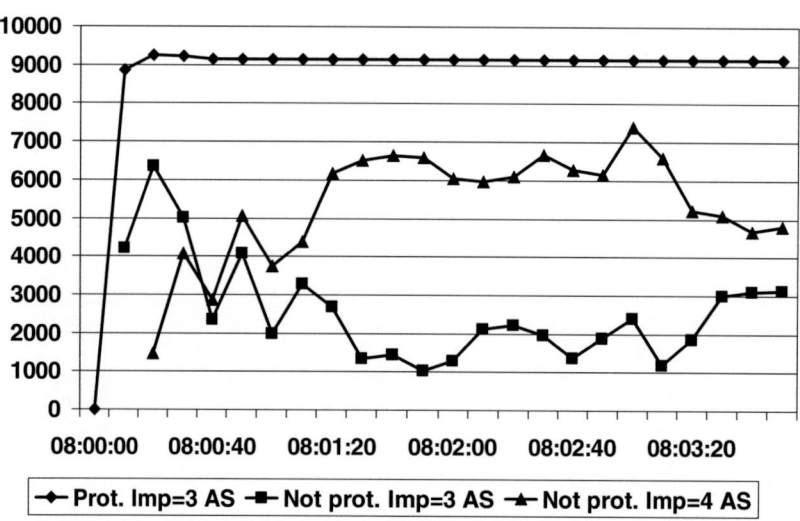

Figure 5.23.: Storage Frames of Service Classes

Storage Critical is important if memory is a limited resource. On a system with 2 GB main memory it was easy that OLTP work lost its storage frames during a night shift with heavy batch workload. Meanwhile the urgency for this control has diminished because the memory sizes of systems is drastically higher. This is very different from CPU Critical or Resource Groups which are still often used.

Figure 5.23 and 5.24 show the effect of storage Critical. The test scenarios consists of 3 service classes:

- Service Class with Importance 3, Execution Velocity Goal of 1 and Storage Critical

- Service Class with Importance 3, Execution Velocity of 1 and no storage protection

- Service Class with Importance 4, Execution Velocity of 20 and also no storage protection

The effect can easily be observed. The two unprotected service classes compete with each other for storage while the protected service class maintains its storage unchanged and also doesn't show any paging activity.

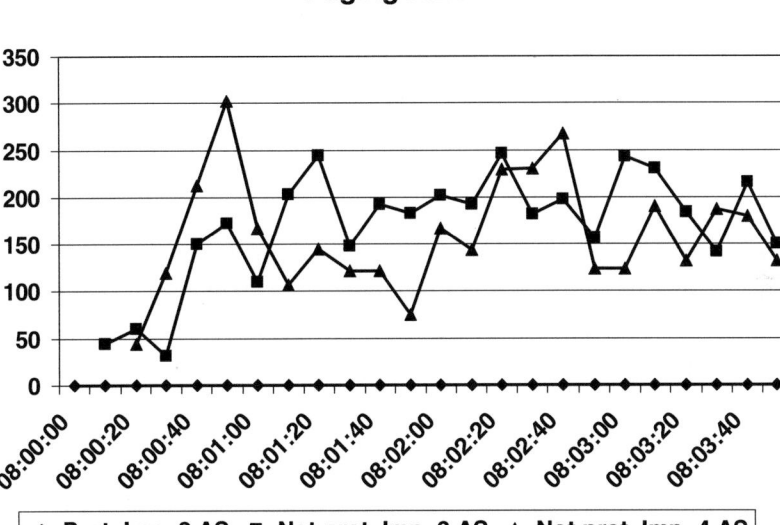

Figure 5.24.: Paging Rate of Service Classes

5.5.18. Discretionary Goal Management

Discretionary Goal Management follows the philosophy that only so much resources should be given to work which is required to meet its goals. The difficulty for work which is defined as discretionary is that it always has lower resource access to resources than work with goal definitions. This is also the case if the work with goal definitions highly over achieves its goal. In that case Discretionary Goal Management takes a little of the system resources from the highly overachieving work and gives it to the discretionary work. This should especially avoid situations that discretionary work can't get access to system resources while over achieving work dominates the system.

The mechanism used to take some of the CPU resources from over achieving

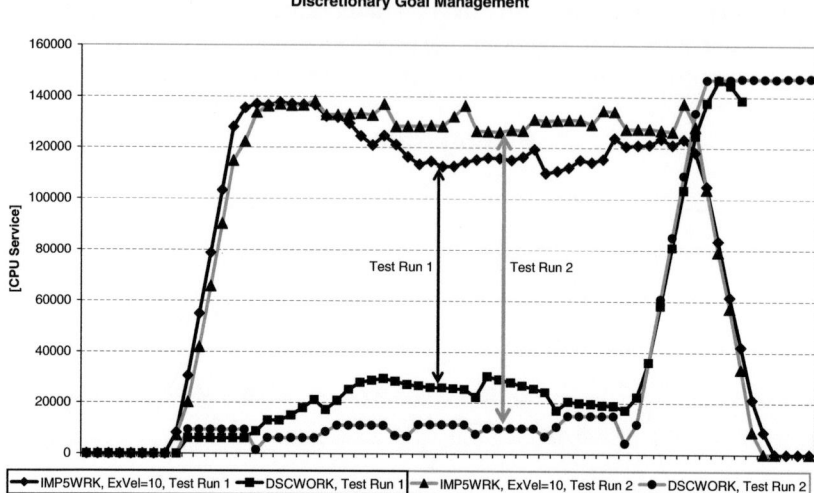

Figure 5.25.: Discretionary Goal Management

work is by defining an internal resource group and by associating the over achieving work with this internal resource group. This is only possible if no resource group was already defined for the service class which could donate for discretionary work. WLM will take a little of the CPU resources by defining a dynamic maximum limit for the internal resource group. WLM also always assures that this limit never causes the service class with a goal definition to miss its goal.

Figure 5.25 shows a test scenario of two service classes one with a goal definition and one being defined as discretionary. The two test runs were performed at different times but because the elapse time and behavior the curves were placed in the same chart to depict the difference:

Test Run 1 Discretionary Goal Management takes some of the resources from the service class with goal definition and gives it to the service class defined as discretionary.

Test Run 2 Discretionary Goal Management is turned off. This can be achieved by associating an external resource group to the service class with goal definition without a maximum and minimum limit[6].

---

[6]Because only a service class can only be associated with one resource group

We can observe that the CPU consumption of the Discretionary work is higher but not extreme when discretionary goal management caps the work with goal definition. It is also necessary that some additional conditions are met by the service class with goal definition:

- The PI is less than 0.7 and remains below this level even if the service class is capped

- The goal is an execution velocity goal with a value less or equal 30 or a response time goal with more than 1 minute

The first condition ensures that only really over achieving work is eligible for discretionary goal management. The second condition ensures that only work with "long" response time goals or quiet relaxed throughput goals are eligible.

5.6. z/OS Workload Manager Advanced Functions

The z/OS Workload Manager is a systems management function which is integrated into the operating system. Up to this point we discussed its primary objective to optimize the resource access for workloads towards end user defined goals. But WLM does more. It provides a set of additional functions which primarily support subsystems and middleware with the specific focus on scalability and high availability. We already discussed Hiperdispatch and the algorithmic part of parking and unparking logical processors as well as distributing the work across the nodes is integrated in WLM. In this section we will briefly discuss other functions which build on top of the basic goal and resource algorithms, such as:

- Routing support

- Contention management

- Scalable Server and Batch Environments

- Workload Scheduling Support

- Adjusting CEC wide resources

- Supporting software licensing

5.6.1. Routing Support

One of the strength of z/OS is the integrated sysplex technology (see chapter 6). A sysplex is a cluster of z/OS systems and most middleware components exploit the cluster by providing distributed implementations. The sysplex-wide implementations allow the middleware to spread the work across the system and instances of the middleware in the sysplex. At a minimum a round robin based routing methodology is usually supported but for scalability and availability concerns this is not sufficient. Intelligent routing means that the system utilization, system constraints like storage shortages and goal achievement of the workload needs to be considered. Also it is required to consider higher important work running on the systems as well as under certain considerations lower important work too. This all requires that the routing component require information from WLM on how work can be best distributed in the cluster.

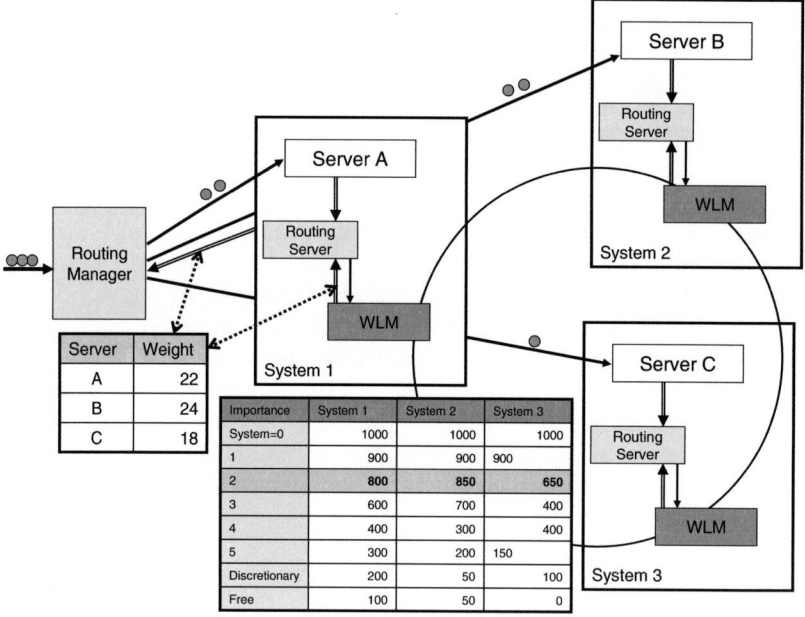

Server	Weight
A	22
B	24
C	18

Importance	System 1	System 2	System 3
System=0	1000	1000	1000
1	900	900	900
2	800	850	650
3	600	700	400
4	400	300	400
5	300	200	150
Discretionary	200	50	100
Free	100	50	0

Figure 5.26.: Routing Support

WLM has developed a quiet complex set of routing services which can be used by routing components. The most important routing components are Sysplex

Distributor (SD) which assist middleware. CICS uses SD as well as Websphere Application Server (WAS) but WAS also supports its own routing function. For WAS the usage of the router depends on the connection type (IIOP, IOR or HTTP). DB2 has a gateway routing mechanism which requests information from WLM to place distributed requests on the system. Another set of placement decision is for permanent session logins which create a permanent connection of the client to a host. TSO but also IMS uses such session placement functions which are integrated in Virtual Terminal Access Method (VTAM). Finally CICS which uses SD for incoming work requests also supports its own distribution mechanism for routing work between Terminal Owning and Application Owning regions. All of these routing functions depend on information and guidance from WLM as the central component which overlooks the actual systems and workload states.

WLM provides interfaces which allow the routing components to obtain recommendations. In many cases the placement recommendation which is returned to the router is a table which either contains the systems or registered routing instances plus a weighting factor which indicates which instances are best suited to receive work. The weighting factors are calculated based on the following factors or at least a subset of them:

- The service consumption of the work on systems in the sysplex. The service consumption is passed around in the sysplex so that each system has a picture of how the other systems are utilized and especially how the different importance levels of the workloads are utilized.

- System constraints like SQA and CSA overflows are very hard conditions because nodes which have serious storage constraints are not suited to receive additional work.

- Internal queuing for some middleware components or abnormal request termination can be considered too. This requires that the middleware components pass such information to WLM.

- The goal achievement of the work is considered and systems where the work achieves the goals more easily are typically preferred routing candidates.

- The middleware or middleware monitors have the ability to set a health indicator to prevent routing or to reduce routing to certain systems. This again requires a communication between the middleware and WLM

Routing is a very important aspect not only for scalability but also for availability in a cluster environment. The possibility to move work away from a system which becomes sick is a guarantee that the workload and this the stability of the business survives during contention situations.

5.6.2. Contention Management

Contention for resource locks are one of the most critical factors which can reduce the throughput of large applications. The typical situation is that a lower important unit of work was able to obtain a resource lock but than looses its ability to get to a processor. Work with higher dispatch priorities which also wants to access the resource now backs up. Such a situation can occur quiet often on highly utilized systems with on-line work and lower important Batch work all using the same database.

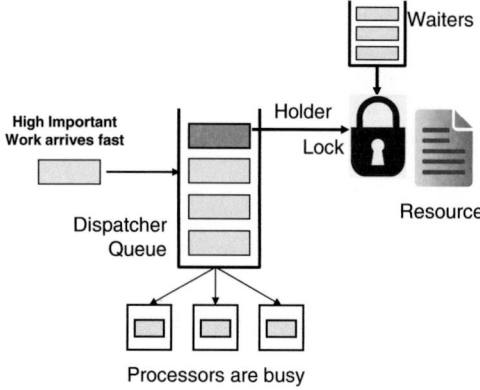

Figure 5.27.: Contention Situation

It is impossible to monitor all locks something which is typically done by middleware resource monitors. Lock monitors usually exist for hot-spots. Such monitors observe the queue length of waiting elements for the resource. In most cases resource locks within subsystems are implemented as suspend locks unlikely than operating system locks which are more typically implemented as spin locks. But it is also necessary to solve high suspend lock contention situations.

WLM now offers a set of subsystem interfaces which allow the monitors to signal lock contention to WLM which then takes some actions:

- The most typical action is to promote the holder of the lock to a dispatch priority which ensures that the work gets access to the CPU. WLM maintains a dispatch priority which is dynamically adjusted and which guarantees that 40% of the work in the system can execute above or equal to it. This ensures that lock promotion requests cannot take out other important work from executing but it also ensures that lock promotion requests get access to the CPU.

- Sometimes a more chronic contention situation is recognized. This may be the case if long running updates require to hold a lock for a quiet substantial period of time. For such cases WLM offers an interface which will not simply promote the holder of the lock. Instead the highest important waiter is determined and the holder is managed towards the goals of the highest important waiter.

As already mentioned it is not always possible for the middleware to instrument all of their locks or latches. The possibility that contention occurs for not instrumented latches can't be eliminated. This is certainly a rare case but there are also precautions to help such cases. WLM is able to determine how long work has to wait for the processor. If it is recognized that work must wait for a very long period it is possible to just give it some access to the processor without really knowing whether a problem exists or not. This function has been implemented as a last security valve. On very highly utilized systems it is very well possible that especially low important batch work must wait for the processors for multiple seconds. If such a situation is recognized WLM gives this work one major time slice to execute. The underlying idea is that this is hopefully enough in case the work holds a latch or lock to release it.

Contention management is a crucial part for the stability and availability of the system. Fats lock resolution is required for an application to scale up and to support high incoming traffic. Contention management has evolved over the last years and with adding more and more support in WLM as well as the middleware components critical lock contention situations have nearly completely diminished.

5.6.3. Scalable Server Environments

We introduced enclaves in section 5.4.7 to encapsulate work requests on z/OS. It is the preferred possibility to manage units of work across multiple server address spaces. When an enclave is created the request start time is book kept. Whenever an execution unit joins the enclave the execution time is recognized.

Thus it is easy to determine enclave wait time which is simply the time when no execution unit runs under the enclave.

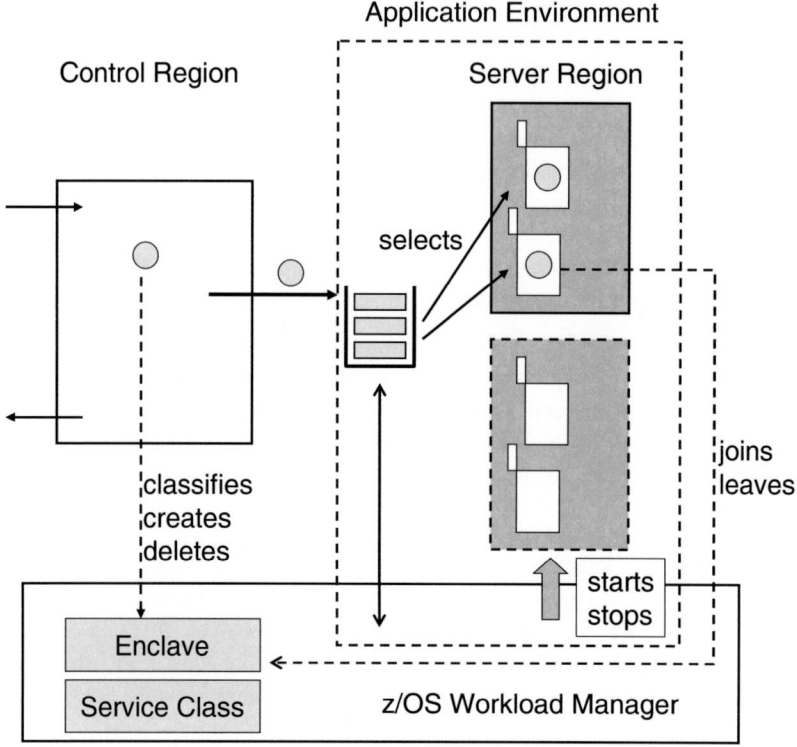

Figure 5.28.: WLM Queue Management

Middleware applications are typically structure in one or multiple control regions and multiple application regions which start the programs to process the end user requests. Middleware monitors or system programmers have to maintain, start, and stop the application regions. The difficulty of this approach is that the number of application regions is not associated with the actual system throughput nor the goal achievement of the work or any other relevant performance metric. Therefore scalability depends on planning or specialized functions of the middleware. This deficiency can be addressed with the help of enclaves if it is possible to queue enclaves or work requests, measure their retention time on the queue and react on the retention time and its influence of the goal achievement accordingly.

WLM Queue Management fills this gap. It allows an installation to define application environments for middleware as part of the service definition, see section 5.4.9. An application environment is a named entity which is used to tell WLM how an application region can be started. WLM requires basically two pieces of information:

- The name of start procedure which is used to start the application region

- The start parameters which have to be passed to the procedure and which are required to execute the application region

Both can be defined in the service definition. An application region typically a control region can connect as a work manager to WLM. Then it can use the WLM application environments. The application environment defines a logical queue. The control region receives requests from outside the system, classifies them, creates enclaves and puts the work request on the application environment queue. Based on the service class which is associated with the enclave WLM creates one queue per service class within the application environment. Then WLM is able to monitor the retention time of the work requests on the queue and start server address spaces according to the goal achievement, system utilization and considering system constraints. Figure 5.28 depicts the interaction between control region, WLM and the server regions. In the section 5.5.12 we introduced the resource adjustment algorithm which allows to quickly start server address spaces on a 2 second basis. This is possible if the system is under-utilized. Otherwise policy adjustment can adjust the number of server address spaces. This adjustment is very similar to the algorithm which we discussed for MPL management.

Queue Management is a very popular advanced function of WLM. The main users are DB2 for DB2 Stored Procedures and Websphere Application Server (WAS). There are many additions to the basic algorithm which we just briefly discussed. For example WAS does not require a definition of the application environment in the service definition rather it defines it when the control region connects to WLM. DB2 for example uses a sub function which also allows to start and stop the server tasks which are able to process work in a stored procedure address space and there are many more additions.

Queue Server Management supports both, scalability which is much better adjusted to system resource usage and availability because WLM restarts server address spaces immediately when an address space abnormally terminates.

5.6.4. WLM Batch Management

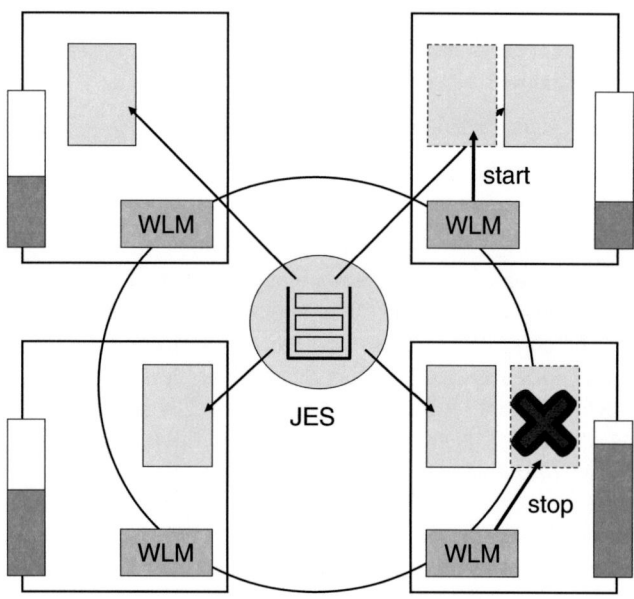

Figure 5.29.: WLM Batch Management

WLM Batch Queue Management is based on Queue Server Management. The difference is that WLM does not actively maintain the queue but it receives periodically information about the queues from the JES subsystem. A WLM managed Batch queue is defined by setting an indication in a JES configuration file that a "Batch Execution Class" is now associated with a WLM queue. The main difference or enhancement to Queue Server Management is that Batch Queue Management works sysplex-wide. JES puts a converted batch job which is ready for execution on its spool dataset and WLM starts the initiators which are eligible to process the batch job on the best suited system. Again this function also has many additions for example it is possible to move an initiator from a very busy system to a system which has much more available capacity (see figure 5.29).

5.6.5. Workload Scheduling Support

Workload Scheduling is an important function especially for a z/OS cluster which has a long lasting Batch heritage. Workload scheduler provide functionality for installations to send batch work suites into the system. Such batch workloads might need to be scheduled at certain times of the day or night but also if resource dependencies are fulfilled. Such resource dependencies in a z/OS sysplex environment can be the availability of a certain database system or database version, the availability of a JES subsystem[7].

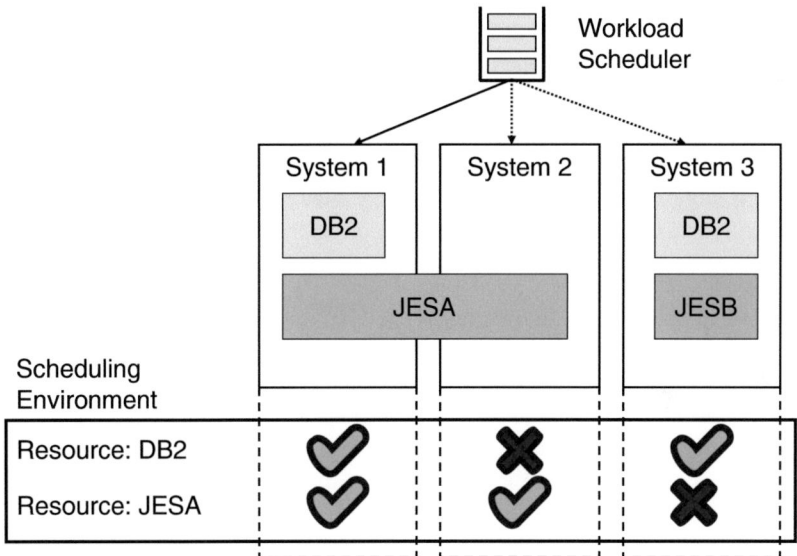

Figure 5.30.: WLM Supported Workload Scheduling

WLM provides a construct named "Scheduling Environment" which allows the specification of named resource states. Such resource states can beset to ON meaning that the resource is available or OFF. The states can be set by programs or via operator commands. The resource states are combined to scheduling environments which are defined in the WLM Service Definition (see **??**). A workload scheduling product can now test the scheduling environments to

---

[7]It hasn't been mentioned but in a sysplex environment multiple JES environments can coexist with each other

identify systems which meet the requirements to submit jobs too. Also the scheduling environments can be defined in the Job Control of Batch Jobs and JES will then ensure that the job will only run on a system which meets all the resource requirements.

Figure 5.30 shows an example of a three way sysplex environment, a workload scheduler which needs to submit jobs into the sysplex and two resources which are needed by the jobs: Subsystem DB2 and the JES subsystem JESA. The scheduling environment defined in WLM now reflects the availability states of the resources. System 1 is the only system on which the DB2 subsystem and JESA are available. The workload scheduler can now submit the jobs directly to System 1. But it is also possible to submit the jobs on System 2 because the Multi Access Spool of JESA allows it to execute the jobs either on System 1 or 2. In this case JESA ensures that only System 1 selects the jobs with the scheduling environment from the JES SPOOL data set.

Scheduling Environments are a good example to directly support availability states on a large sysplex. This makes it pretty easy for workload scheduling and job entry systems to execute jobs on the correct systems.

5.6.6. Adjusting Resources in a CEC

We discussed an example of very high CPU contention between two z/OS systems in section 4.3.3. In such cases the local management within a z/OS system is not sufficient to help the mission critical work. If we assume that the production system SYP1 in the example is by far more important than the test system it would be wise to give SYP1 a higher share of the CPU resources. But doing this for all times might also not useful. Especially during night shifts it is possible that the work in the development environment is more important than the batch work running in the production system. What would be needed is a workload dependent adjustment of the CPU share.

This requirement can be accomplished within a sysplex environment on the same CEC. By definition the systems of the same sysplex on the same CEC form an "LPAR Cluster". Within this cluster it is possible to shift CPU weight and channel paths between the systems in a way that no partition outside of the cluster is effected. Both functions depend on the service classes which execute on the z/OS systems. The weight shift function is for example an extension to the adjustment function for dispatch priorities.

Figure 5.31 illustrates the decision process which first assesses whether a local adjustment of CPU dispatch priorities is possible (Steps 1 to 4). If this gives enough improvement then dispatch priorities are adjusted (Steps 5) and the adjustment is completed. But if this is not possible a test is performed whether the systems runs in an LPAR Cluster (Step 6). The LPAR Cluster requires that a coupling facility structure is created through which the systems exchange specific information for these adjustments[8]. WLM starts the weight adjustment process when the LPAR cluster exists and CPU Weight Management is enabled. First it gets information from the cluster and projects possible weight changes. This can easily be done because on all systems in the sysplex the same service definition is active and all systems run the same service classes. So all what is required is that the information about the service classes on other systems plus consumption data from PR/SMis collected (Step 7). The receiver donor logic is the same as described in section 5.5 (Step 7). The system initiates the weight change if the projections show that the change is beneficial (Step 8). A weight change will always ensure that the sum of all weights of the systems in the LPAR cluster do not change (Step 9).

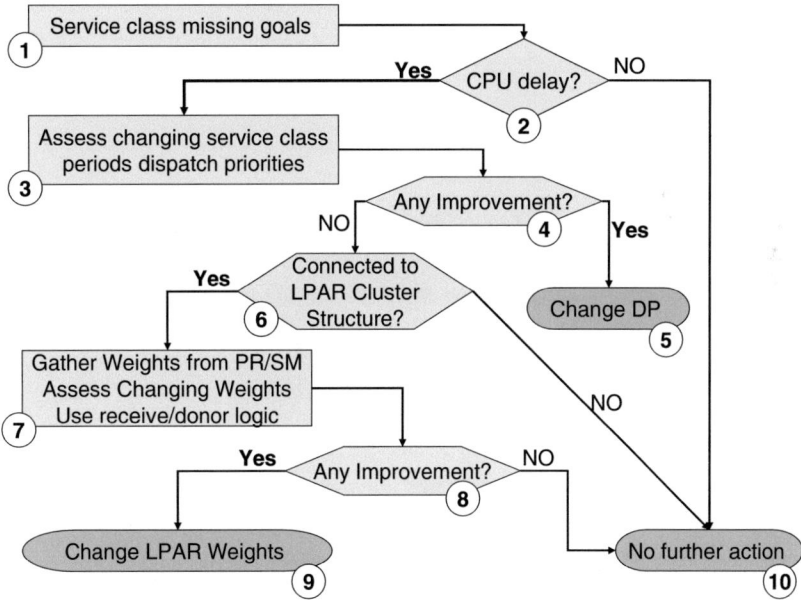

Figure 5.31.: WLM Policy Adjustment for Weight Changes

---

[8]Other information is exchanged directly between the WLM instances in the same sysplex

The functionality for CEC wide resource adjustment is named "Intelligent Resource Director (IRD)". It is another example how different components work together to establish a higher level functionality.

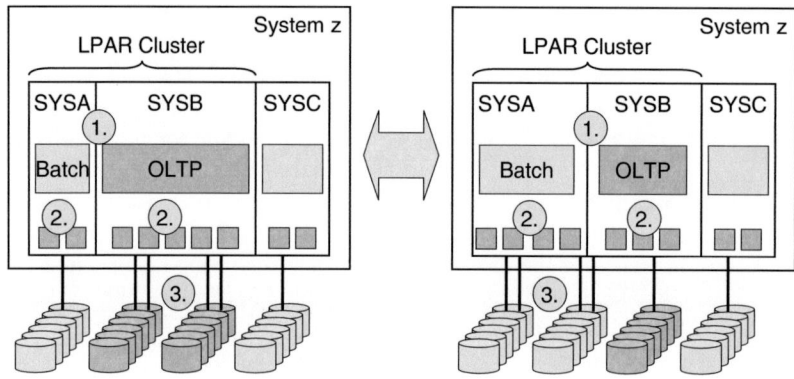

Figure 5.32.: Intelligent Resource Director Functions

Figure 5.32 depicts the functions. The numbers in the graphic correspond to the numbers below. IRD contains 4 functions:

1. CPU Weight Management as described above. This is a function between WLM, PR/SM and it exploits parallel sysplex functionality.

2. Vary CPU On/Off Management is an optimization function which attempts to do something similar like Hiperdispatch. If too many logical processors are defined for a partition the time a logical processor can be dispatched can be too small especially if the CEC shows CPU contention. In such cases CPU vary On/Off management allows to vary logical processors offline and bring them back online if the CECE utilization drops. Meanwhile this function has been superseded by Hiperdispatch which is by far more efficient, see section 4.7.

3. Dynamic Channel Path management allows to switch channels between partitions very similar to shifting weights between partitions. This function is established between WLM and the I/O Supervisor. The function was very important when the channel speed was limited. meanwhile with bi-directional FICON channels it is not really important from a scalability point. But it is still important as a high availability feature which allows to replace a channel immediately in case a channel path fails.

4. Channel Path Priority Queuing offers a function which prioritized work requests in the channel subsystem either based on workload importance or based on fixed definitions by the installation. This function is not depicted in figure 5.32.

5.6.7. Support for Software Licensing

Another comprehensive area which is supported by WLM is software licensing. The question how expensive it is to execute certain software products on z/OS is a very huge area of considerations. Offload processors which have been discussed in section 4.4 are one important factor. They allow to switch processor types so that the software license bill becomes smaller. There are many different software licensing models on z/OS, a System z and with a parallel sysplex and this is not subject to this write up. Besides offloading work another possibility to control software license is by controlling the CPU consumption of z/OS partitions on System z. IBM offers a function named "Defined Capacity Limit" which allows an installation to define a licensing cap for a z/OS partition. The cap is enforced on the basis of a *4 Hour Rolling Average* (4HRAvg). This allows the partition to run above the defined capping limit as long as the 4HRAvg is below the defined limit. A very interesting extension is named "Group Capacity Limit" which allows to combine multiple partitions under one limit and ensure that the sum of the CPU consumption of these partitions stays below the group limit. the interesting feature of this function is that a partition can borrow CPU from partitions which are in the same group and which do not exploit their share while the group as a whole is already being capped.

Partition	Limit	Weight	Target MSU
IRD3	None	52	≈ 8.5
IRD4	None	102	≈ 16.7
IRD5	None	152	≈ 24.8
Group	50	306	50

Table 5.8.: Group Capping Definitions

Table 5.8shows an example of 3 partitions on a CEC which run in the same

capacity group. The group capacity limit is set to 50 MSU[9]. Figure 5.33 shows
how the partitions request capacity and how much they are able to get. In the
beginning after starting the partitions the 4HRAvg of the group allows the partitions to use more capacity than the group limit permits. Two partitions IRD3
and IRD4 use around 63 MSU each so that the 4HRAvg reaches 50 MSU after
1.5 hours. Partition IRD5 does not run any workload at this time. When the
group limit is reached the group is being capped. That means the partitions are
reduced to the amount of MSU which they are entitled to based on their weight
definitions, see table at the top of figure 5.33. Because IRD5 still doesn't run
any meaningful work the MSU which are not used by this partition can be given
to the two other partitions which request CPU. IRD uses only 3 of the 25 MSU
it is entitled to. So based on the shares of partition IRD3 and IRD4, IRD3 can
use 8 MSU more and IRD4 around 14 MSU more than they are entitled to.

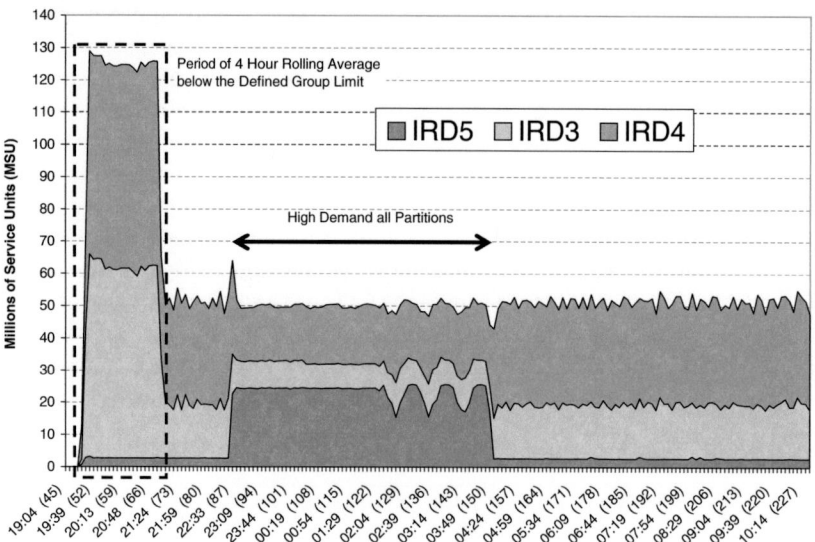

Figure 5.33.: Group Capping Example

When work is started on IRD5 it requests the CPU back from the other partitions. IRD3 and IRD4 are now pushed back to their entitlements and all partitions are now capped until the work is stopped again on IRD5. At that point
IRD3 and IRD4 can expand and use the unused capacity of IRD5 again.

---

[9]MSU = Million of Service Units

It is clear that this is a powerful function and that it needs to be used with care. Running production partitions under such high contention as shown in the example is certainly not a good idea but the example shows how the function works.

5.6.8. Subsystem Participation

Middleware, Subsystem	Classification	Monitoring Services	Enclaves	Queue Mngmt.	Routing Services	Special Functions
CICS	X	X				
IMS	X	X				
DB2	X	(1) (2)	X	X	X	(3)
WAS	X	(2)	X	X	X	
SAP R/3	X		X			
JES2/3	X			(4)		(5)
VTAM TCP/IP					X	
NetView	X		X			
LDAP	X		X			
Oracle 9i	X		X			
(6)	X					

1. as extension to CICS and IMS
2. for reporting purposes
3. Bufferpool and contention management
4. Batch Server Management
5. Scheduling environments
6. TSO, APPC, OMVS, STC, LSFM

Table 5.9.: Subsystem Participation with z/OS Workload Management

Throughout the whole chapter we discussed how WLM interacts with the subsystems and middleware running on the operating system. In fact this is the real success story of this management function. Algorithms are only useful if they are exploited. The subsystem participation starts with using the classification capabilities of work to the exploitation of sophisticated functions like queue management services. All major subsystems and middleware products support the Workload Management concept on z/OS which also provide a lot of benefit to them. For example a scalable server environment as it is exploited by

Websphere and DB2 only requires very little coding effort within the middleware. Table 5.9 lists middleware and subsystems and how they exploit WLM functions.

5.7. Summary

z/OS Workload manager ensures that many different workloads can share a z/OS system, a parallel sysplex and a System z CEC. The base functions ensure that the work gets access to system resources based on the installation defined goals, their demand and the workload mix on the system. The algorithms not only try to simply give the most important work the highest access to CPU they rather optimize the access to system resources by giving them the resources they need to fulfill the goal definitions.

In addition WLM includes many technologies to support the scalability of the work and the environment, such as:

- Starts and stops server spaces to help scale-out of middleware on z/OS
- Starts and stops initiators for batch work across systems to ensure that work finds the best place to execute
- Shifts weights between partitions of the same CEC
- Balances work across processor nodes to run work efficiently on few processors to avoid cache misses
- Gives routing recommendations to load balancing functions
- Promotes work to resolve lock contentions and allow to run high workload demands

The list above is not complete and should just give some examples. Interestingly we can use nearly the same examples to understand how high availability is support by WLM:

- Starting, stopping and re-starting server address spaces and batch initiators improve the availability of the managed applications.
- Shifting weights between partitions of the same CEC to ensure that important work is not being harmed by lower important work.
- Giving out routing recommendations ensure that work is not routed to systems which have severely constraints or on which the application is not working properly.

- Promoting work ensures that work can continuously operate and does not timeout

In can be understood that Workload Management is not just a feature but a very important function which differentiates the operating system from other operating systems.

6. Parallel Sysplex

In the beginning of the 90s the development of bipolar or TTL technology became too expensive. This affected the future development of the technology as well as its usage because of the enormous electricity consumption for cooling. The size of the systems were immense compared to today's mainframes and also required from customers to build very large and complex data centers. In the beginning of the '90s IBM made the decision to stop all future enhancements of bipolar technology and rather put all emphasis on CMOS technology. The difficulty at that time was that CMOS technology didn't provide neither the single processor speed nor the total system capacity of existing bipolar technology. The first generation of CMOS processors only provide 28% of the single processor speed and only 16% of the total system capacity. Consequently CMOS technology was not able to replace bipolar technology immediately.

As a result IBM introduced a cluster technology which allowed to couple multiple z/OS systems together which then at least achieved the same and even more total system capacity. It took four generations of CMOS systems until they reached the total capacity of the last IBM bipolar system. Therefore sysplex technology was an important factor for scalability at that time.

Figure 6.1 illustrates the total system capacity of CMOS systems from the first generation to the zEC12. The last IBM bipolar processor was named H5. Its capacity is set to one and the capacity of the other systems is shown relative to it. Meanwhile the capacity of the last generations is far above the capacity of the systems of the early '90s. The zEC12 provides more than 152 times the capacity of the IBM H5 system. The capacity of today's systems is sufficient for many installations. The motivation for cluster technology has changed. It is nowadays more important with respect to high availability and continuous operations than scalability.

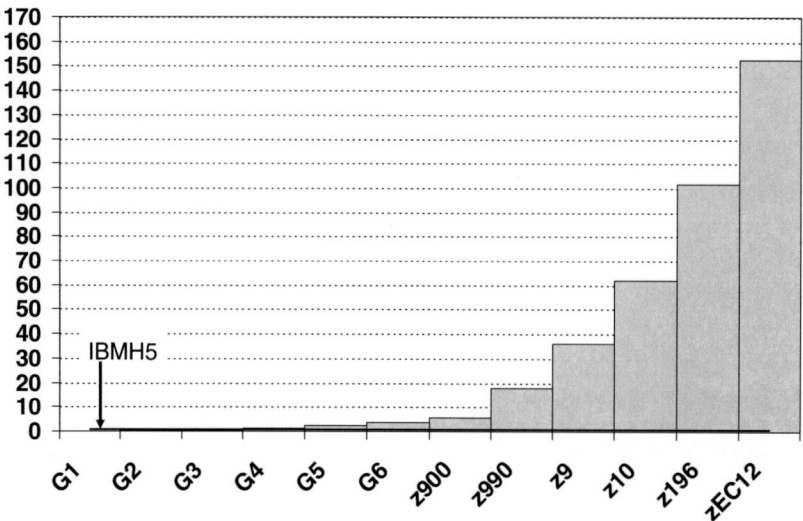

Figure 6.1.: Total System Capacity of System z compared to IBM H5

6.1. High Availability Aspects

We defined High Availability in the beginning in section 1.2. There are various aspects of High Availability which need clarification when look from a higher on the system and the complete IT infrastructure:

Reliability   is the ability of a system or component to perform its required functions under stated conditions for a specified period of time. This aspect is especially important when we look at the hardware which defines the reliability of its components.

Availability   is the ability of an environment to mask individual errors or individual component failures.

Disaster Recovery
                  is the ability of an infrastructure to recover from unplanned outages.

Continuous Operations
                  is the ability of an infrastructure to maintain continuous access to applications when everything is working properly. This in-

cludes that the applications can be used properly even during period of planned backups or scheduled maintenance.

We use the terminology High Availability to cover all these aspects. Other terms are Business Resilience which can also be used for Disaster Recovery or Business Continuity for Continuous Operations. The following sections about cluster technology and the parallel sysplex are based on documentation in [8], [9], [10], and [11].

6.2. Cluster Technologies

Before we start to look at the components of the parallel sysplex we will take a brief look at the cluster technologies which have been evolved in information technology.

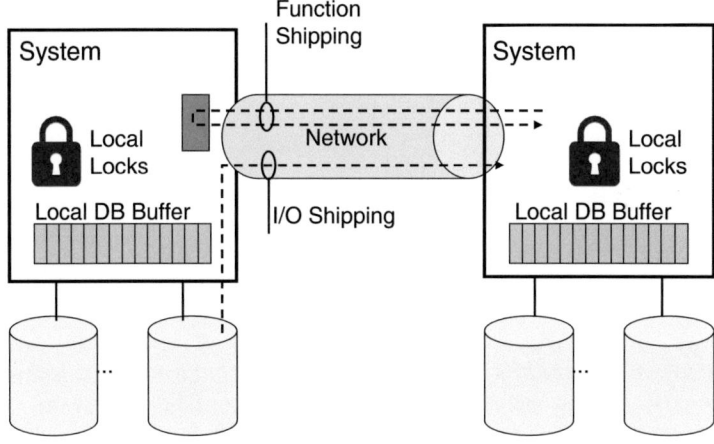

Figure 6.2.: Shared-Nothing Cluster

6.2.1. Shared-Nothing Cluster

A shared nothing cluster or also known as data partitioning technology is a collection of systems which are connected by a network. Each system has I/O devices attached to it but nothing is shared between these systems. The data is distributed across the systems or partitioned. In order to implement a distributed application software methods must be used to access the data or function on remote nodes. The two typical methods are I/O shipping or function shipping. For I/O shipping the system which requires a data item asks a remote system where it is stored to obtain it and send it to the requesting system. Function shipping sends a request to a remote system where the application and data is located. The request is executed on the remote system and only the result is returned to the requesting system.

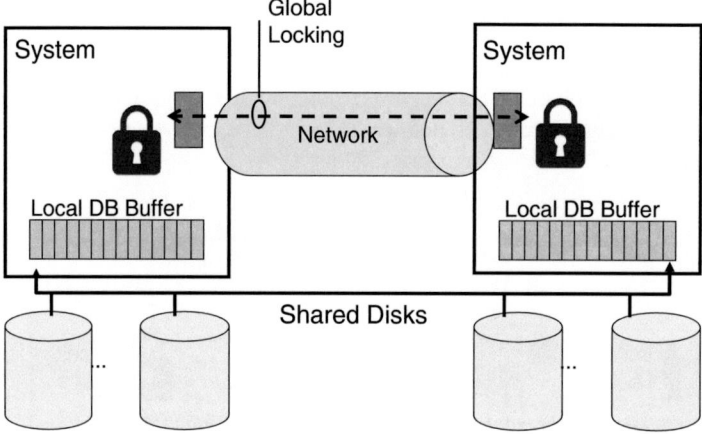

Figure 6.3.: Shared-Disk Cluster

The advantage of this method is that no cache coherency and no global locking problems exist. But the methodology requires high coordination between the involved system and network latency is also a very visible issue. Such methods are typically effective on a small scale but show performance limitations on large scale environments. Another difficulty is the availability of the data and the access to it. If a system which hosts certain data is down the data is typically not accessible anymore.

6.2.2. Shared-Disk Cluster

The first step to overcome some of the limitations of a shared nothing environment is an environment with shared disk architecture. The advantage of this environment is that the data can be accessed from all systems in the environment. The challenge for distributed applications is now to ensure that the access to the data is coordinated. This challenge lead to the development of global lock managers which coordinate the access to data bases. A distributed application for example a distributed data base which wants to modify a data item must first obtain a lock to the data page or data table where the item resides. It sends a request to the global lock manager and eventually obtains the lock. The lock manager sends lock requests to all involved systems to inform the local instances of the data base. If a local instance already buffers the data page or table it must invalidate it. The requesting instance then modifies the data item and writes it back to the I/O system so that it can be obtained from other instances again. Finally the lock is released.

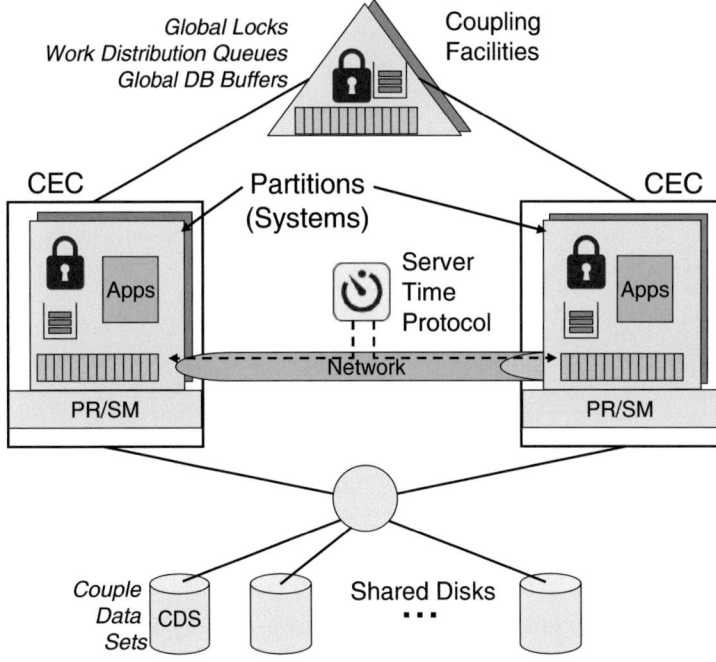

Figure 6.4.: Parallel Sysplex

This data sharing method is very efficient but still requires a lot of network access for global lock requests. Also for high availability concerns the technology is suited to back up the important I/O devices so that in case of failures back up copies of the data exist. Very interesting in this context are methods which ensure that locks which are obtained from a failing node can be released so that a failure of one system does not drag down the whole environment.

Shared disk cluster are the most common data sharing methods. One of the first and very efficient technology was introduced by Digital Equipment with their VAX cluster which also provided a single system image for users which want to login to the environment. IBM /370 systems, IBM HACMP solution and Oracle 9i also use shared disk architectures.

6.2.3. Shared-Disk and Shared-Memory Cluster

The next logical step is to provide also a shared memory component for the systems of the cluster and to ensure that all systems in the cluster use the same time reference. The Parallel Sysplex architecture uses this shared memory component which is named coupling facility, a common time reference and it is built on the shared disk architecture of System /370.

6.3. Parallel Sysplex Overview

The parallel sysplex introduces two more components, the coupling facility and a common time reference. The coupling facility is either a separate system or a partition of a CEC. At least all production sysplex environments use 2 coupling facilities and deploy methods to synchronize its data. The purpose of the coupling facility is to share storage in the sysplex. Theoretically it is also possible to define a sysplex environment without a coupling facility but this is not really be used anymore. The terminology parallel sysplex refers to the fact that a coupling facility is used to share data in the sysplex environment.

The operating system of the coupling facility is named Coupling Facility Control Code (CFCC). This operating system is very basic. Its main function consists of maintaining data structures which are used to share information between z/OS and middleware components in the parallel sysplex and it provides signaling functions to inform connected systems about state changes of the data structures. The coupling facility supports 3 different structure types: Lock, cache and List structures of which the list structures can be serialized or un-serialized. All structures need to be defined in the couple data sets of the parallel sysplex. The Couple Data Sets (CDS) define also the sysplex communication groups and policies which are sysplex-wide in use.

The other important piece of the parallel sysplex is time synchronization. Originally an external time reference (ETR) was used. Due to the signaling time a distance of up to 40 km was possible for a parallel sysplex. By placing the ETR into a different site 40km away from the systems and by using two ETRs which is required for redundancy it was possible to spread a parallel sysplex across 100km. Meanwhile ETRs are no longer state of the art and replaced by the Server Time Protocol (STP) which is based on Network Time Protocol (NTP) and which allows to synchronize the systems over the network.

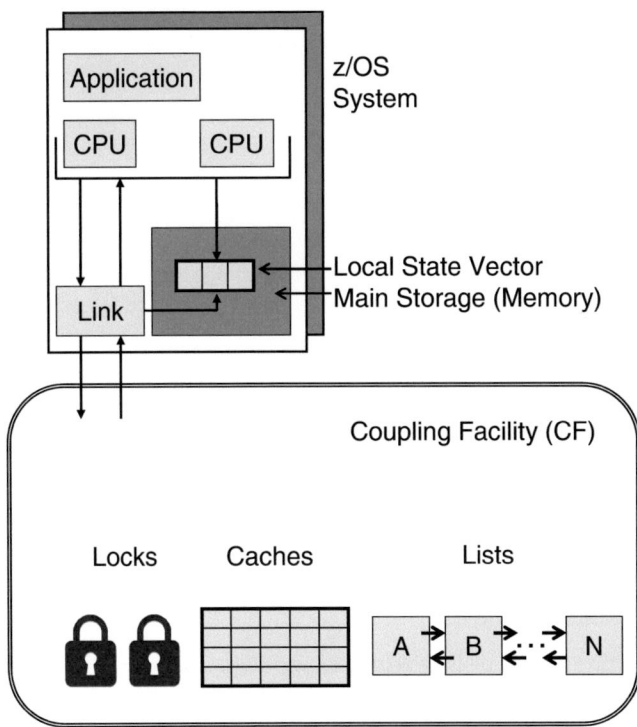

Figure 6.5.: Coupling Facility Components

6.4. Sysplex Couple Data Sets

CDS	Description
Sysplex	Sysplex Status XCF groups Which CDS exist
ARM	Policy which started tasks and batch jobs can be restarted
BPXMCDS	Shared HFS and zFS
CFRM	CFs and structure attributes
LOGR	Logger structures and streams
SFM	How to manage System, Signalling and CF failures
WLM	Service Definition

Volume 1 / Volume 2 / Volume 3:

CDS	Volume 1	Volume 2	Volume 3
Sysplex	Primary	Alternate	Spare
ARM	Primary	Alternate	Spare
BPXMCDS	Spare	Primary	Alternate
CFRM	Alternate	Spare	Primary
LOGR	Spare	Primary	Alternate
SFM	Primary	Alternate	Spare
WLM	Alternate	Spare	Primary

Figure 6.6.: Sysplex Couple Data Sets

Couple Data Sets (CDS) are data sets that contain status and policy information for the sysplex. They provide a way for the systems in the sysplex to share this information so that they can manage the sysplex environment cooperatively. There are seven different types of Couple Data Sets that could be used in a sysplex. Each type is associated with a different system component, such as WLM, System Logger, or XCF. These components use the the Couple Data Sets as a repository of information. For example:

- Transient control information, such as the time of the latest status update for each system in the sysplex (Sysplex CDS).

- More permanent control information, such as information about System Logger offload data sets.

- Policy information, such as WLM service class definitions in the sysplex.

The information held in the CDS is critical for continuous operations of the sysplex. If one of the system components loses access to its CDS, that component may fail. The impact on either a single system or the entire sysplex depends on which component loses access to it, for example:

- If a system loses access to all the sysplex CDS, it is unable to update its system status. As a result the system is partitioned out of the sysplex.

- If a system loses access to a WLM CDS, it can remain in the sysplex but its service policy is from this time unsynchronized to the other systems.

- If a system loses access to all Sysplex Failure Management (SFM) CDS, SFM is disabled across the entire sysplex.

When the first system is IPLed into the sysplex it reads its CDS definitions from the COUPLExx parmlib member. This system makes sure that the CDS are available for use in the sysplex, and then it adds them to the sysplex. All systems that subsequently join the sysplex must use the same CDS. After the systemn are active in a sysplex, it is possible to change the CDS configuration of a sysplex dynamically.

Figure 6.6 shows the couple data sets which can be defined in a sysplex and a possible design how CDS can be spread across multiple logical devices in the sysplex. For each component there should be at least a primary and alternate CDS. It is possible to switch the alternate and primary CDS during runtime. A primary CDS is used for all read and write operations. The alternate CDS only for write operations. That ensures that both CDS always reflect the same component status throughout the sysplex. The spare CDS ensures that the installation can add a second CDS whenever it is necessary to take the primary CDS out of the sysplex. That ensures that the components have never to rely on a single CDS. The distribution of primary and alternate CDS shown above also attempts to avoid contention on specific volumes in the sysplex. For example the primary Sysplex CDS and primary Coupling Facility Recovery Management (CFRM) CDS should be placed on different volumes. They are not busy during normal operations but especially the CFRM CDS can become very busy during recovery situations.

6.5. Coupling Facility

The coupling facility is the shared memory component of the parallel sysplex. It supports three structures allowing system components and middleware to maintain common data structures in the cluster.

6.5.1. Lock Structure

The lock model is implemented with lock structures in the coupling facilities and lock managers on the systems. The model grants exclusive or shared access to a resource or denies it depending on the state of the resource (see figure

6.7). In the coupling facility the lock structure is a vector which maintains two information: Which system if any holds the lock exclusively and which systems if any access the lock shared. The shared state is indicated by a bit which exists for each system. The vector does not represent each lock but a hash table to the locks. Therefore it is possible to observe one of two states if the has table entry is being used:

1. The application on the system which is marked as holder of the lock really holds the lock. This is a real lock contention situation. In this case the lock request is either denied or the lock manager implements a mechanism to suspend the holder and inform it once the lock is freed.

2. The application on the indicated system holds a different lock but both locks have the same hash table index. In this case a false contention situation exists. The lock request can be permitted but only if the systems exchange information between each other.

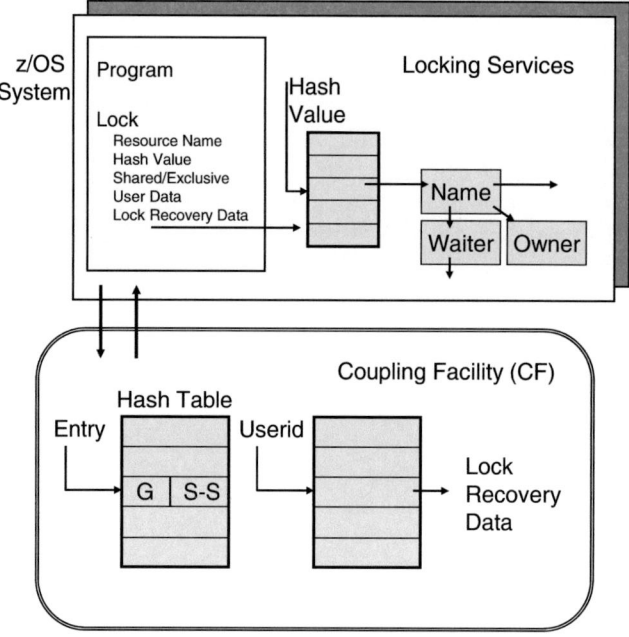

Figure 6.7.: Lock Structure

The maintenance of the lock is implemented by lock managers. An application requests a global lock by asking its local lock manager instance. The local lock manager resolves all local conflicts and then sends a lock request to the coupling facility structure. This is a synchronous request that means the lock manager waits for the completion. If the entry is free the lock request can be granted and the application can start to use the resource. The lock manager also transfers information about the application to the coupling facility into a second related structure. This ensures that other lock manager instances can recover the lock in case the system goes unexpected down.

The situation is more complex if the hash index indicates that the lock might be occupied on another system. The lock manager now tests which locks are kept on the system in its local structure. If the requested lock is the same as the held lock the lock request can be denied or the caller can be suspended to wait for the lock. If the requested lock is different the lock manager uses the information from the local lock structure to inform the other systems that a false contention exists and that the lock request can be granted. This requires additional data exchange to the other systems and it is required to build a structure which depicts the usage of the hash index.

6.5.2. List Structure

List structures are intended to exchange messages between applications or operating system components. List structures can be used with or without a lock. The lock table allows to serialize the add and remove of list entries. List structures can be maintained in various access methods: LIFO, FIFO or by key.

Two state information exist for list structures in each system: The Local State (LS) vector exists for each list on each system. It is set when an entry in the list is modified. The Global State (GS) vector exists once per system and it is changed whenever a list structure is modified. Figure 6.8 illustrates the flow between systems and a list structure.

1. The application which wants to use a list structure initializes the connection to it. The application registers and establishes a listener on the local state vector of the list.

2. It is now possible to add one or multiple entries to a list entry.

3. As a result of this change all global state vectors are changed and also the entry of the local state vectors which reflect the changed list entry.

4. The change of the global state vector causes that the dispatcher receives

control on the interested system and that it can schedule the listener immediately to a processor.

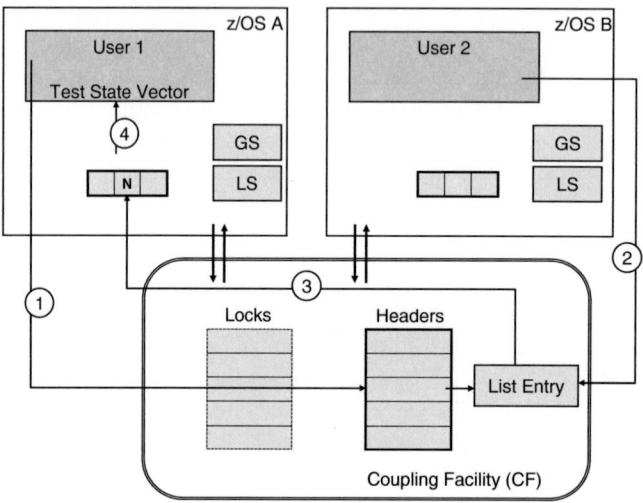

Figure 6.8.: List Structure

6.5.3. Cache Structure

Cache Structures of the coupling facility are being used to either synchronize the update to data items or to exchange data. In the first case the cache structure is used as a directory. In this case the cache data entry only tells the system whether an item is being updated or not. The data itself is always obtained directly from disk and also written back to disk. In the second case the data item also resides in the coupling facility and can be obtained from it.

The Cache structure always consists of two parts a registration or directory entry and optionally a data entry. The directory entry consists of a name and a registration field in which each system signals whether it is interested in the data item. The storage class allows to define how the storage of the cache structure is managed and the Castout Class defines the policy how the data is written to disk. The Castout Lock provides a lock for writing out the data and the Change Bit indicates whether the data has been changed. Finally the Cache data is connected to the directory entry. There are two main methods how data can be managed in the coupling facility and on disk:

- For a "Store-In" Cache Structure the data is written to the coupling facility and not immediately on disk. The Castout Class now defines the rules how the data is written to disk and the Castout Lock ensures that the data is not modified while it is written out to disk.

- For a "Store-Through" Cache Structure the data is always written in parallel to disk when it is also written to the coupling facility. This ensures that never data can get lost and the coupling facility is primarily used to speed up the read process to the data.

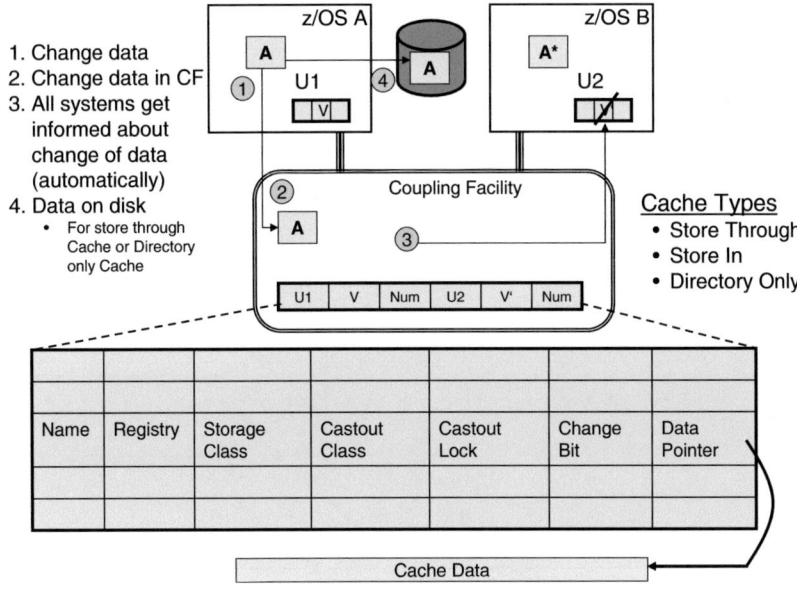

Figure 6.9.: Cache Structure

Each system maintains a state vector which contains a change bit for each cache entry. Figure 6.9 illustrates the flow between systems and a cache structure.

1. Application A wants to change a data item.

2. It calls to the coupling facility and provides the name of the cache structure and the data entry.

3. Within the coupling facility the change bit of the data entry is set and all systems which are registered to the data entry are informed automatically. On the systems the state vector of the cache structure and the data item is changed. Each system establishes a listener which is invoked and which now allows to invalidate local copies of the data item.

4. In this example the serialization to the data is not shown. It is possible that the application first requests a lock which could also be maintained in a lock structure of the coupling facility. Typically this also involves a lock manager which is separate component. Finally the data item can also be written in parallel to disk. This is typically used for mission critical data. Another option is to write the data in parallel to a second coupling facility.

6.6. Sysplex Setup

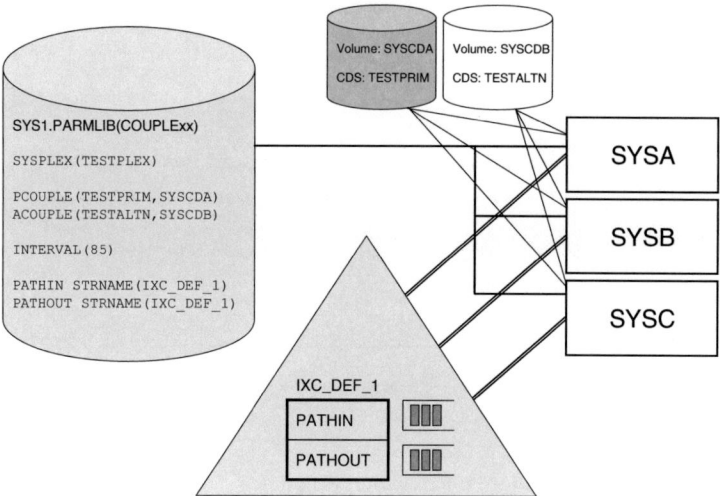

Figure 6.10.: Sysplex Setup

The sysplex setup is defined during IPL of the systems. The main parmlib member is COUPLExx. Figure 6.10 shows some of the definitions from the COUPLExx member:

- The name of the sysplex: TESTPLEX

- The name of the primary and alternate Sysplex Couple Data Sets and the volumes on which they should reside

- The time out interval for systems which leads to actions to partition a system off the sysplex if it doesnt up date the its sysplex state within this time frame.

- The PATHIN and PATHOUT definition of a XCF[1] signaling structure.

In this example we assume that a sysplex always contains coupling facilities. This wasn't required when sysplex technology was introduced and it is still possible to set up a sysplex without coupling facility. In this case the XCF signaling structures will use Channel to Channel (CTC) connections to set up the signaling paths. This is not commonly used anymore, especially because the number of CTC connections grows quadratic with the number of system in the sysplex:

$$\text{Required CTC Connections} = \frac{n(n-1)}{2} \text{ for n systems}$$

With coupling facilities a new system requires only the connectivity to them.

6.6.1. XCF Groups

The main cluster communication takes place via sysplex signaling. The information is exchanged with the help of list structures. These list structures are named XCF Groups. nearly every operating system component and all major subsystems, like CICS, IMS, or Websphere use XCF groups for data exchange in a parallel sysplex cluster. The operating system component WLM, which we discussed in the previous chapter uses XCF groups to exchange performance information between the WLM members in a sysplex. In addition many operating system components as well as the middleware components use other coupling facility structures to exchange information for special functions. A more detailed discussion follows.

6.6.2. Coupling Facility Duplexing

Not all CF exploiters provide the ability to recover from a structure failure. For those that do, certain types of structure failures require disruptive recovery

---

[1]Cross System Coupling Services

processing. Recovery from a structure failure can be time consuming, even for exploiters that provide recovery support. One possibility to avoid this is to use CF structure duplexing. Two types of structure duplexing exist: User-managed duplexing, that means the component provides it own duplexing support and system-managed duplexing which is the duplexing support which is optionally available for all types of structures.

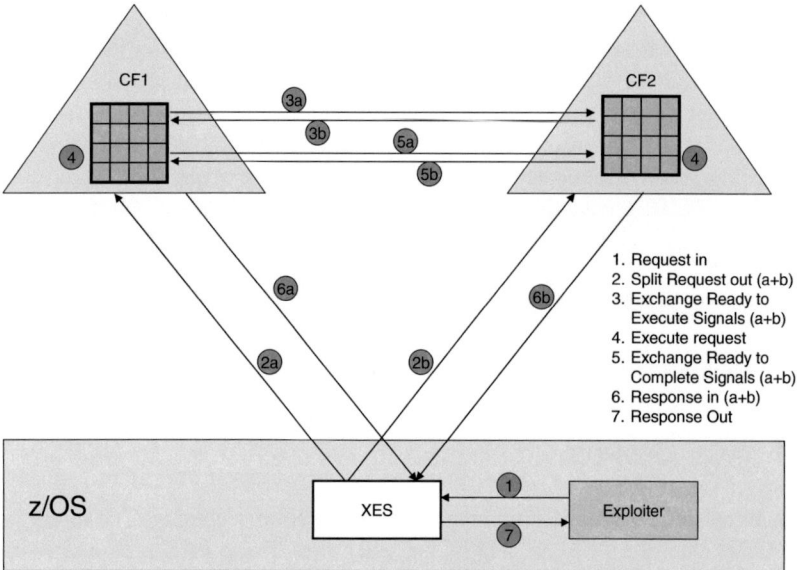

Figure 6.11.: Coupling Facility Duplexing

System-managed CF structure duplexing is designed to provide a general purpose, hardware assisted mechanism for duplexing CF structures. Figure 6.11 shows the way system managed structure duplexing is implemented.

1. The CF write request is split at the XES (Cross System Extended Services) driver on the z/OS system.

2. It is sent synchronously out to both coupling facilities in the parallel sysplex.

3. First the coupling facilities exchange information that they both received the structure update request.

4. They execute the update request.

5. And exchange information that the request was executed.

6. When all CF handshakes are completed they send the response back to the z/OS system.

7. XES sends the response back to the caller (7).

The two synchronization points at (3) and (5) allow to reset the request whenever necessary.

It is obvious that this type of processing requires more time than just simply updating a coupling facility structure. Therefore it is not used for all type of structures. Structures which can fail without impacting the overall operation of the business are typically not duplexed. Also it should be remembered at this point that the other option to securely maintain an application state is to use a coupling facility structure in Store Through mode which updates the data on hard disk synchronously. It simply shows different possibilities to achieve high availability and resilience.

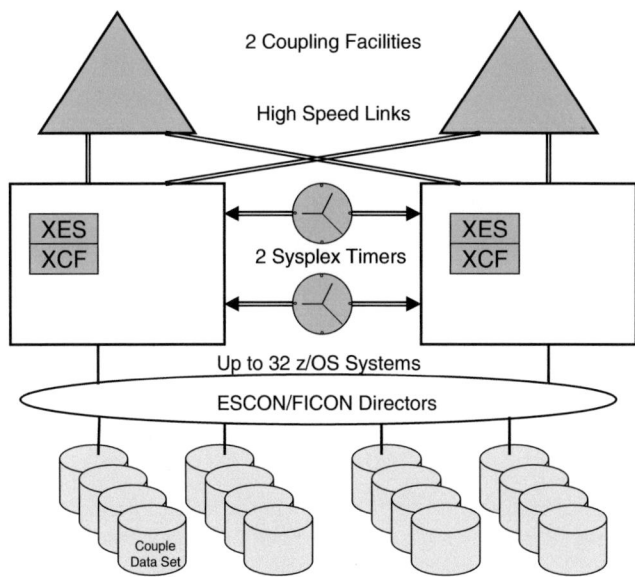

Figure 6.12.: Original Parallel Sysplex Configuration

6.7. Parallel Sysplex Configuration

The configuration of a parallel sysplex has changed significantly since its introduction in 1993. Originally a parallel sysplex encompassed up to 32 CECs with each CEC running a single partition, 2 separate coupling facilities and 2 external sysplex timer, see figure 6.12. The sysplex timerhave been replaced by the server time protocol and CECs typically run multiple partitions. Nevertheless it is still possible that a CEC is dominated by one big partition which participates in a production syplex. But it is also possible that multiple partitions on the same CEC are members of the same syplex.

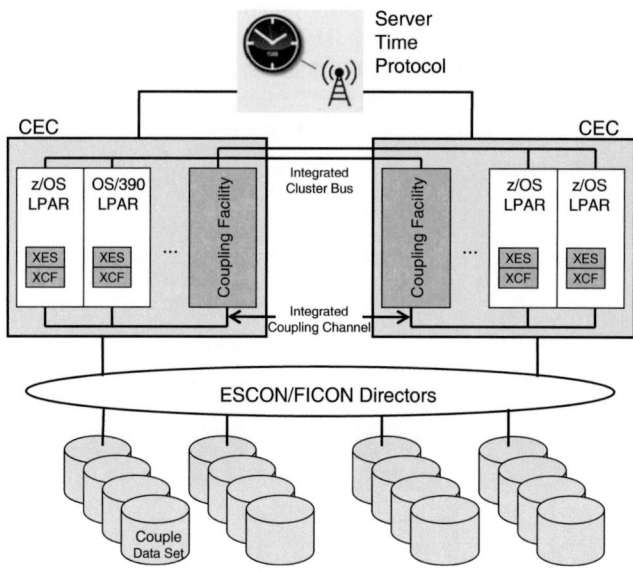

Figure 6.13.: Modern Parallel Sysplex Configuration

Coupling facilities can be either partitions of the CEC or still be on separate hardware systems. Many installations like to have the coupling facilities still separated because this enhances their resiliency against CEC outages and enhance their flexibility in locating the hardware systems in different data centers. Figure 6.13 depicts a more modern parallel sysplex configuration. The graphic implies that a parallel sysplex consists of multiple hardware systems which are all located at the same site. This is not really the case anymore. For high availability reasons most installations operate at least 2 sites and spread their system across these sites. A parallel sysplex has meanwhile evolved to a "Global Dispersed Parallel Sysplex (GDPS)" and we will discuss in detail what this really means and what levels of availability can be achieved with dispersing the systems.

6.8. Using IMS as an Example how a Parallel Sysplex is exploited

The next question is what it takes to exploit the coupling facility and with it the parallel sysplex technology. Large middleware components like Customer Information Control System (CICS) and Information Management System (IMS) already supported multi system environments. Introducing the parallel sysplex technology does not immediately mean that these middleware application were able to use all possibilities of the coupling facility. As an example we will take a look at IMS.

IMS was introduced in 1968 for the Apollo space program. It consists of two components a database and a transaction monitor. The original IMS database is named DL/1 (Data Language 1) and it is a hierarchical database system. The database was named after its query language. IMS also supports another database implementation named Fast Path Data Entry Database (DEDB). DEDB was created to support customers which have lower resilience requirements for the database. In addition IMS supports DB2 which is a relational database and which was introduced on MVS in 1983. IMS uses the IBM Resource Lock Manager (IRLM) for multi system locking. IRLM was also originally designed for IMS but it became a common component for shared DB2 and IMS database environments.

IMS supports short living requests and permanent sessions like TSO sessions. They exist from logon to logout of end users connected to the IMS control region. The requirement for sessions is that they should be distributed in a multi system environment in order to avoid load imbalances. It is also needed to distributed the short living client requests (messages) to the systems which can best process them. For accessing the databases IMS keeps local data buffers which need to be synchronized and locking needs to be supported between the IMS instances which is performed by IRLM. Figure 6.14 depicts the structure on an IMS environment.

The IMS transaction monitor controls flow of end user requests which are

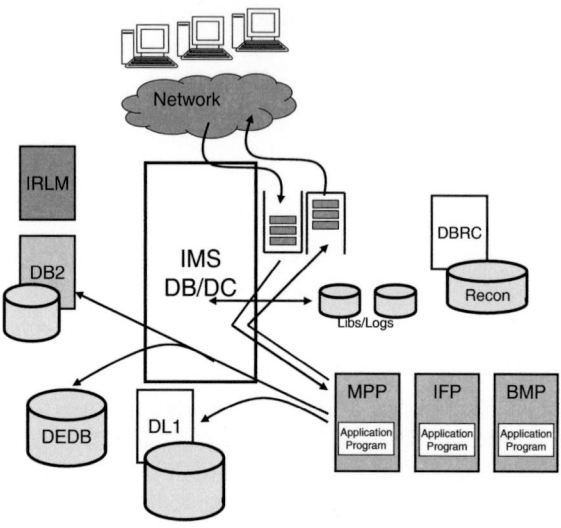

Figure 6.14.: Information Management System Structure

named messages. Messages are received either from the network or other programs like Batch. The control region verifies the message and then passes it to a processing region which is named Message Processing Region (MPP or MPR). The MPP starts the application program to process the request which may access the data base and returns the result in an output queue which is passed back to the client. Besides MPPs there are two other type of message processing regions:

BMP (Batch Message Processing) regions run programs which typically don't pass the output back to a waiting client.

IFP (IMS Fats Path) regions access the DEDB data bases.

Like all middleware transaction monitors IMS supports LOG writers which are required to protocol synchronization points for failure recovery. The failure recovery is performed by Database Recovery Control (DBRC) which runs in a separate address space.

Supporting everything at once is nearly impossible. When parallel sysplex technology was released only XCF was able to use list structures to support the communication for the XCF groups in the coupling facility. Components

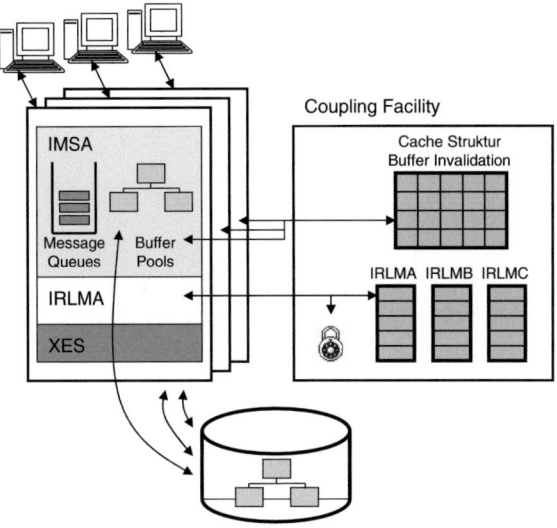

Figure 6.15.: IMS Parallel Sysplex Exploitation Step 1

like IRLM supported multi system locking but initially they were only able to use parallel sysplex technology indirectly by using XCF message flow.

The support for parallel sysplex technology of IMS can be seen in two phases. The first phase which is illustrated in figure 6.15, enabled sysplex wide locking anf buffer invalidation for local buffer pools. IRLM uses lock structures for global locking and buffer invalidation uses a coupling facility cache structure.

The IRLM lock structure is used to manage the hash indexes of locks between the systems and a list structure in which the IRLM instances maintain additional information to their locks. In case of a system outage the IRLM instances on still running systems are able to take over the responsibility of the failing instance and either free the locks or ensure that the processes can complete their processing.

The IMS cache structure is used as a directory to maintain the validity state of the local data buffers. This reduces the traffic between the systems but data access always requires to go directly to disk.

The second step of parallel sysplex exploitation tries to address the open items. One open item is session placement. In this case IMS is able to profit from

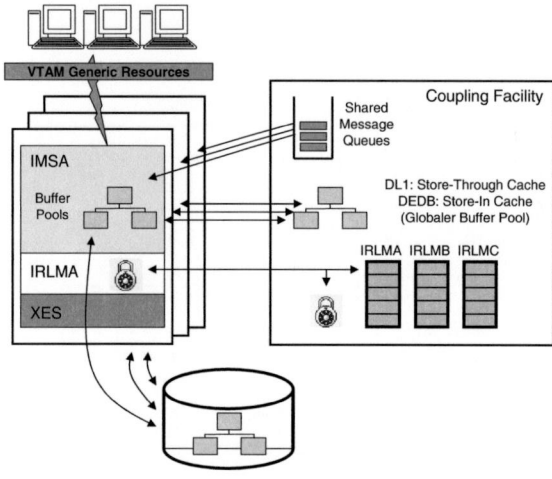

Figure 6.16.: IMS Parallel Sysplex Exploitation Step 2

VTAM Generic Resources. This is a technique which is used by TSO to place a new session to the system which is the best fit for it. The idea is to spread the sessions between systems to avoid over-utilization and to ensure that systems which show problems or run other high important work are not selected. VTAM generic Resources is based on WLM routing recommendations as discussed in section 5.6.1.

The second item is the placement of short running requests. WLM developed sysplex routing services to assist routing functions to place user requests on the systems which are best suited to process them and also to distribute the requests in a sysplex environment. But IMS uses a different technology which is based on its in and output processing. Every incoming IMS message is placed in an Input queue and every out going message into an Output queue. IMS now places these Input and Output queues in the coupling facility and uses a list structure for them. If a system receives a new message this message is always placed on the shared message queue in the coupling facility. The next system which has available capacity and on which the IMS control region runs selects the message from the coupling facility and processes it. This guarantees that the messages which are typically short lived are distributed automatically to the system which can most easily process them. Also if load shifts in the sysplex environment the load also shifts for the IMS processing automatically. Figure

6.16 summarizes the sysplex exploitation of IMS.

Finally data buffers can be held globally in the coupling facility. IMS databases offer two options for maintaining global buffer pools in the coupling facility: For DL/1 the global buffer pool is implemented as a store-through cache. That means all data items are also written automatically to disk when they are updated and the copy is written to the coupling facility. This always ensures that the data is consistent. It is easy to understand that this is not the best performing way to share data in a parallel sysplex but for installations using DL/1 data bases it is more interesting to always maintain consistent data then to optimize on performance. For DEDB databases a Store-In cache structure or technology is used. DEDB databases typically do not have the same high availability concerns than DL/1 data bases and therefore optimizing on performance is a desired functionality. This example and the exploitation of parallel sysplex technology shows that it is often more important for installations to optimize on availability and ensuring consistency than to optimize on performance. This should be clearly noted for all types of exploitation on System z.

6.9. Parallel Sysplex Exploitation Summary

Middleware Subsystem	Lock Structure	List Structure	Cache Structure
CICS		Shared Memory	VSM/RLS Buffers
IMS		Shared Message Queues	Global Buffer Pools
DB2		Data Sharing Groups	Global Buffer Pools
IRLM	Global Lock Tables		
z/OS Logger		Log Streams	
GRS	Lock Contention		
Tape Allocation		Multi System Tape Usage	
RACF			Frequently Used Data
VTAM		Multi-node persistant sessions Generic Resources	
JES		Checkpoint and Spool data sets	
WLM		Multi-System Enclaves[2]	LPAR Cluster
XCF		Signaling	

Table 6.1.: Parallel Sysplex Exploitation

Table 6.1 summarizes the exploitation of Coupling Facility Structures for major IBM middleware and z/OS operating system components. Together with the exploitation of XCF groups which we discussed before we can see a high degree of parallel sysplex exploitation. Nevertheless we have to notice that the full exploitation by a middleware component like IMS took 6 years and the deployment of the functionality by customer installations even longer.

6.10. Business resilience

Business Resilience is the ability of a system or company to adapt itself to unplanned situations. Ideally the system or company can survive any kind of unplanned incident as well as to plan for continuous operations for planned events. Meanwhile information technology is so critical for companies that the necessity to protect itself for unplanned events is one of the most critical and most highly valued features of an enterprise wide IT infrastructure.

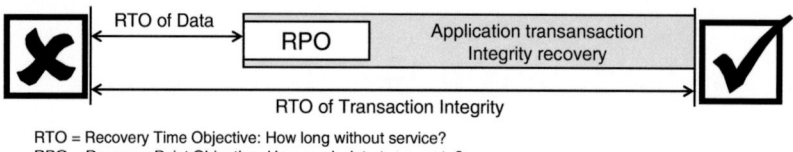

RTO = Recovery Time Objective: How long without service?
RPO = Recovery Point Objective: How much data to recreate?

Figure 6.17.: Recovery Objectives

There are two metrics which describe high availability and business resilience solutions (see figure 6.17:

Recovery Time Objective (RTO) This value tells how long a business remains out of service for a disaster incident.

Recovery Point Objective (RPO) Tells how much data has been lost and how much data needs to be recovered or recreated. RPO is also described as a time value.

After a disaster incident, RTO of data tells how long it takes until the system is up and data can be accessed again. The next step is to recover the lost data or to reset the system to a saved recovery point. RTO of transaction integrity tells how long it takes until the system is again fully operational after a disaster incident.

The recovery objectives as well as the availability objectives have dramatically changed during the last 50 years, see figure 6.18. In the beginning of computer infrastructure as part of companies the loss of systems was not a critical situation to the business. In the beginning mostly internal booking ran on computer systems. A loss of the computer infrastructure had no immediate effect on the business. Restart times of more than 1 day were not unusual also data loss of more than 1 day was still consumable. With the technology becoming more and more part of the daily business the objectives for availability became more and more stringent. In fact today financial institutions must provide a 24 hour availability for all days in the week. Global processes do not allow to take the whole environment down.

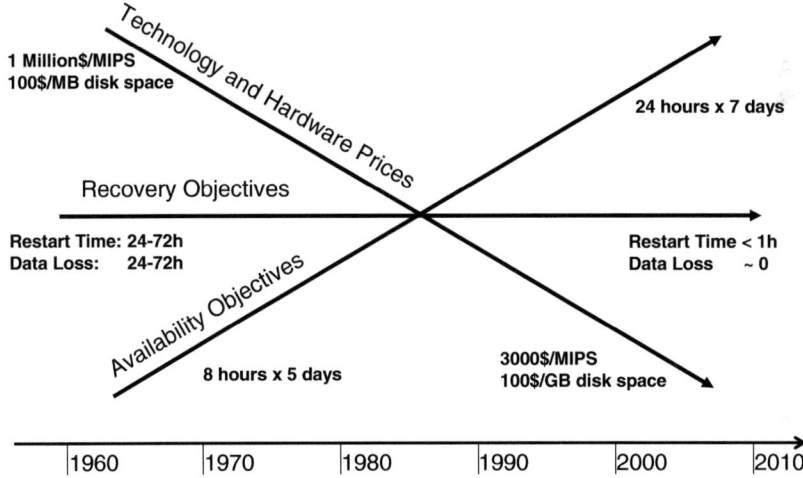

Figure 6.18.: Requirements on Recovery Objectives

6.10.1. Continuous Operations

One important factor to reach a high available environment as well as to enable an environment to reach a state of continuous operations is the ability to upgrade the environment without shutting it down. A cluster of systems, like the parallel sysplex is ideal to achieve this goal. The cluster consists of multiple systems which cooperate to provide the service to the end users. At least this is the ideal situation. Cooperation means that the middleware and applications on the cluster provide a common service to the end users and not that the cluster is just a loosely coupled set of systems which all provide different services. In reality both type of clusters can be found. From a high availability and continuous operations point of view we will primarily take a look at clusters in which the middleware is distributed across the systems in the cluster providing a single system image to the end user. That doesn't mean that certain systems can't special workloads. This is also often the case and does not interfere with the general concept as long as the main purpose of the cluster preserved.

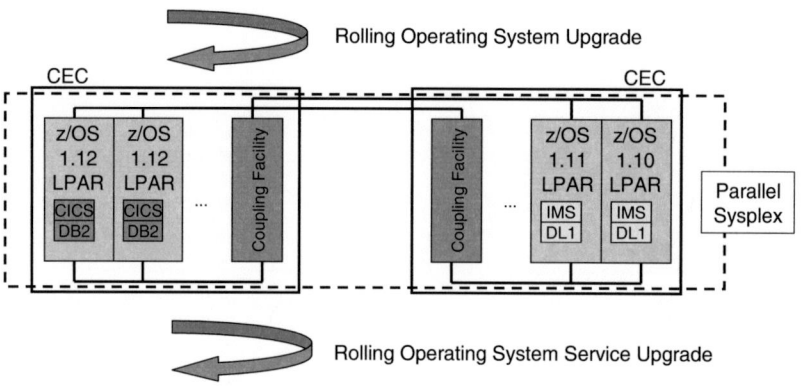

Figure 6.19.: Rolling Upgrades and Service

It is necessary in such an environment is to provide a technique to upgrade the systems without shutting down the cluster and without interrupting the service to the end users. The same applies for upgrading the major middleware components as well as bringing up service on the systems. For upgrading a system, the system needs to be re-ipled. This is also often the case if a major middleware component is upgraded as well as if new service is brought on the system especially if parts of the system nucleus is changed. The idea is to shut down only a single system, upgrade the system and to re-ipl it. The service to the end user is taken over by the remaining systems in the sysplex. Sometimes this may require to increase the capacity of a CEC and/or to move middleware applications to other systems in the cluster. It also requires that different versions of the operating system can work together. For z/OS this means that an operating system version can always work together with a defined number of lower versions as well as higher versions.

6.11. Disaster Recovery Prevention

After introducing the parallel sysplex we will now further explore what it means to enable this environment to survive site disasters. One important factor is redundancy, for example using two coupling facilities and coupling facility duplexing (see section 6.6.2) is one item to it. The reliability build into System z another factor. But what else is needed to prepare for disaster recovery events. At least two factors need to be discussed:

1. How to add CPU Capacity if a system or a site fails to take over the work?

2. How and to what extent is it possible to mirror permanent and temporary data?

6.11.1. Capacity Backup

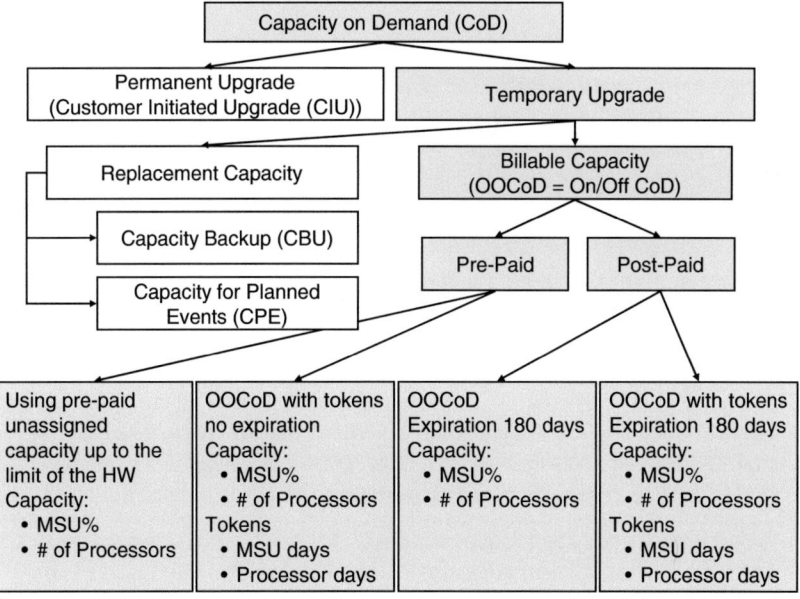

Figure 6.20.: Capacity Upgrade Options

Figure 6.20 summarizes the various capacity upgrade options on System z. Capacity Upgrade can be divided in the following categories:

- Permanent upgrades which allows an installation to increase the capacity permanently because simply more capacity is required

- Temporary upgrades which are thought to either survive a disaster scenario, which can be used for a planned event or which is required to provide the capacity for high business scenarios like the end of a month or a quarter which shows a much higher number of business transactions than normal operation hours.

We are mainly interested in the Capacity Backup (CBU) and Capacity increase for planned events (CPE) option because these are specifically designed for High Availability reasons. CBU and CPE allow to increase the number of physical processors for a pre-defined time period in order to survive a down incident or a planned upgrade or test scenario.

6.11.2. Data Mirror Techniques

While the parallel sysplex provides the capability to maintain redundant processing capacity for continuous operations we have to take a look how the data can be kept available across system failures. The standard technique is data replication. Now replicating data at pre-defined time intervals is not effective therefore it is necessary to copy the data at the time when it is generated or modified. Such techniques are mirror techniques. The difference is that the data which is contained on a hard drive is not copied at once but each modification is copied when it is modified or created. A flash copy of the hard drive might still be necessary to create an initial copy of the drive and to create a synchronization point.

Basically two mirror techniques exist:

- Synchronous copy techniques which require that the data is written simultaneously at both sites and the final acknowledgment to the application is returned when the data exists at sites.

- Asynchronous copy techniques which copy the data also instantaneously but the acknowledgment is returned when the first copy at the local site is created.

We will discuss bot copy techniques together with data mirroring for tape devices and swap techniques in the next sections. This discussion also includes latency considerations.

6.12. Peer-to-Peer Remote Copy

Synchronous copy techniques exist today for different large system environment. This is not a feature of the system hardware but of the I/O hardware. A synchronous copy is created by a handshake mechanism of the physical control units at the two sites. The idea is to have an identical copy at the remote site and a physical control unit which is just a redundant instance of the local physical control unit. The IBM implementation on System z and z/OS is named Peer-to-Peer Remote Copy (PPRC). Other vendors name their techniques for example Truecopy from Hitachi Data Systems.

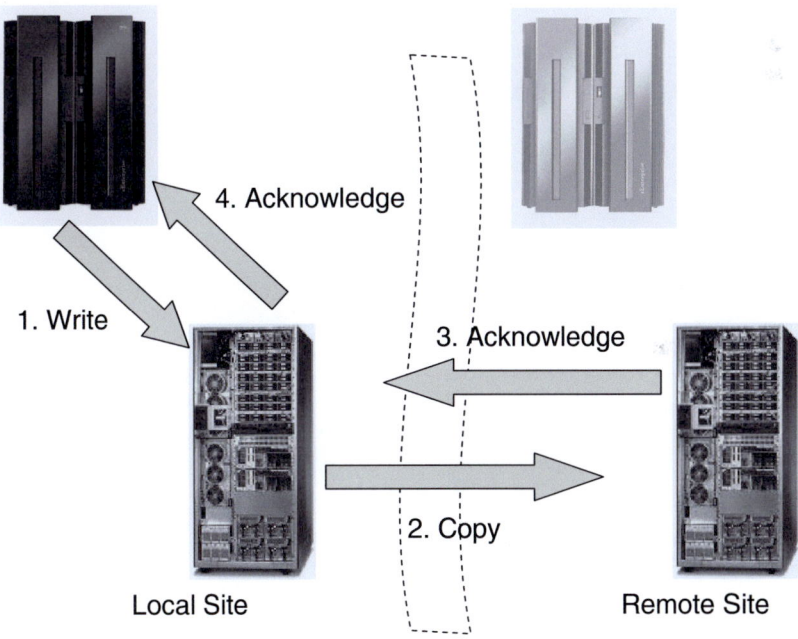

Figure 6.21.: Peer-to-Peer Remote Copy

Synchronous copy guarantees "zero data loss" by the means of atomic write operation. This means the write either completes on both sides or not at all.

Write is not considered complete until acknowledgment by both local and remote storage. Most applications wait for a write transaction to complete before proceeding with further work, hence overall performance will be impacted by the distance of the sites between the copy occurs. An often-overlooked aspect of synchronous copy is the fact that failure of remote replica, or even just the interconnection, stops by definition any and all writes (freezing the local storage system). This is the behavior that guarantees zero data loss. However, this also requires that a commercial system must also freeze at this point and it does not continue to proceed with local writes and thus loosing the desired zero recovery point objective. We will emphasis this fact and the additional technique which has been implemented on System z and z/OS to support the freeze and a take over with minimal overall system impact.

6.12.1. Latency of Synchronous Copy

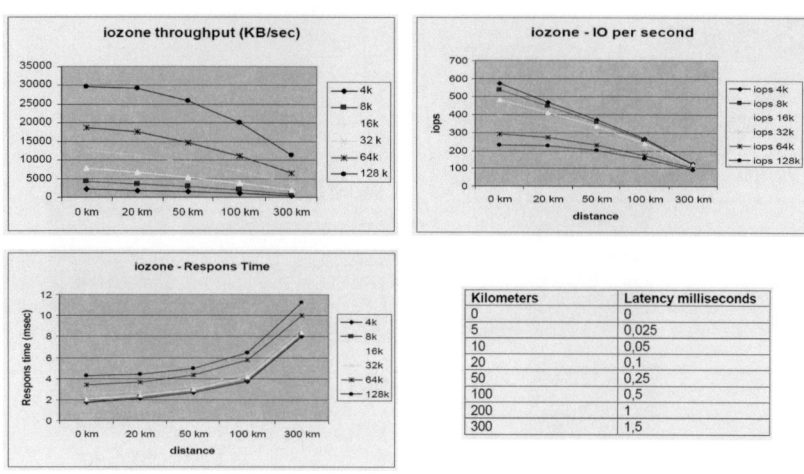

Figure 6.22.: I/O Benchmark for Synchronous Copy

In order to evaluate the impact of synchronous copy during runtime we will take a look at a common benchmark (iozone) for synchronous copy operations[3]. Iozone is an I/O performance benchmark executed on AIX and DS8000. DS8000 control units are also connected to z/OS and System z systems and the

---

[3]This section is based on an evaluation of the PSSC Montpellier, published at GSE 2008 in [12]

benchmark results can be used to evaluate the impact for z/OS applications as well. First of all the maximal possible speed in a fiber channel is two third of the speed of light which is around 200000 km/s. So the maximal possible round trip for a 10 km distance between two physical control units is 100 microseconds which is twice the signal latency of 50 microseconds. In some newer measurements and calculations it can be seen that 67 microseconds are possible for a 10km round trip distance but this is just a theoretical value.

Figure 6.22 illustrates the relationship between block size and distance to throughput, I/Os per second and I/O response time. It can be seen that a 4 block size is most advantageous from a performance point. Nevertheless the response time impact for a 100km distance is already very significant with 4 milliseconds because it must be seen together with the fact that a local write to a DASD can complete in much less than 4 milliseconds. Also the limiting factors to I/O throughput and the number I/O per seconds which can be issued to the I/O subsystem show that from a practical point of view a distance of more than 100km is not efficient. In fact most installations separate their disaster recovery sites by less than 50km. We will discuss the impact of a "relative short" distance between disaster recovery sites too.

6.12.2. Hyperswap

PPRC enables an installation to create just in time copies of the current write operations with an acceptable latency as long as the distance is within a 100 km range of the two sites and the ability to achieve a recovery point objective of zero. We have to discuss what can be done if a problem is recognized and how is it possible to switch over to the remote site with minimal recovery time. In order to achieve a recovery time with minimal impact and which is nearly transparent to the running applications a technique has been implemented on z/OS which is named Hyperswap. Hyperswap is enabled to keep a second set of unit control blocks (UCBs) for each device in the system. The mirror UCBs can be placed in a secondary sub-channel set for example. In this example a device with the number 123 might have a mirror 523 which is connected to the sub-channel of the secondary device. This means that all primary and all secondary devices are configured on z/OS and that a mirror (or secondary) UCB is defined for each primary device UCB. If now an error occurs the following processing starts:

- Errors recognized

- Running I/Os are terminated. They are returned to the application and the application can restart them. This is necessary because it is not possible to evaluate the state of each individual I/O already not for performance reasons.

- Waiting I/Os are elongated. For waiting I7Os it is possible to keep them alive because the Start Sub-channel hasn't been issued yet. Therefore it is possible to just leave them in the wait until the secondary I/O devices can take over.

- Primary devices drain and will be set to an error state

- UCB status switched to secondary UCB. This means the UCB now connects to the sub-channel of the secondary device and the mirror UCB to the sub-channel of the primary device.

- Secondary devices take over and the waiting I/Os can be started

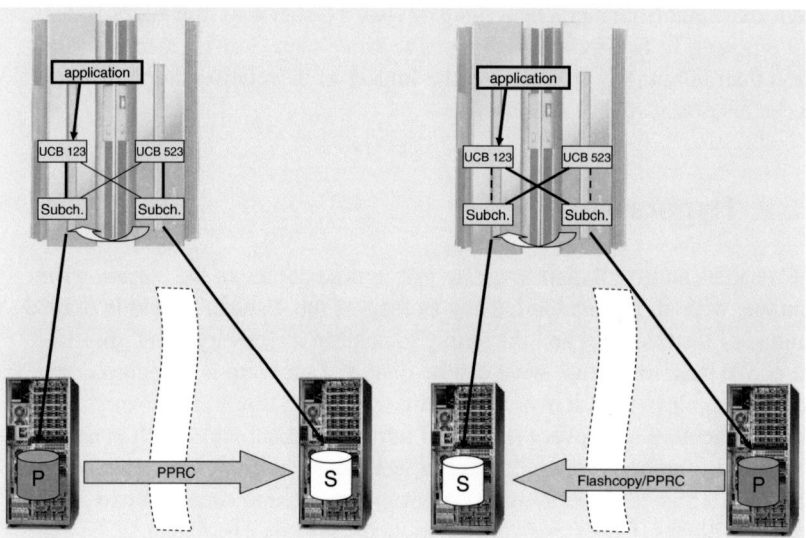

Figure 6.23.: Hyperswap

This procedure can complete within seconds even for a very large number of I/O devices and thus works nearly transparently to the applications. The old primary devices which are now the secondary devices are in an error state until the error has been fixed. After taking the secondary devices on-line again it is necessary to copy the content from the primary devices back to the primary set and then start to continue with PPRC for each single write operation.

Hyperswap is possible on an I/O subsystem level. Nevertheless for data consistency reason all primary devices are switched to all secondary devices so that the primary set always resides on the same site. The advantage of this procedure is that data integrity can always be achieved. If only a single I/O subsystem would be copied it is possible that the primary content of the data is spread across sites and a consecutive error can cause loss of parts of the data.

6.13. Extended Remote Copy

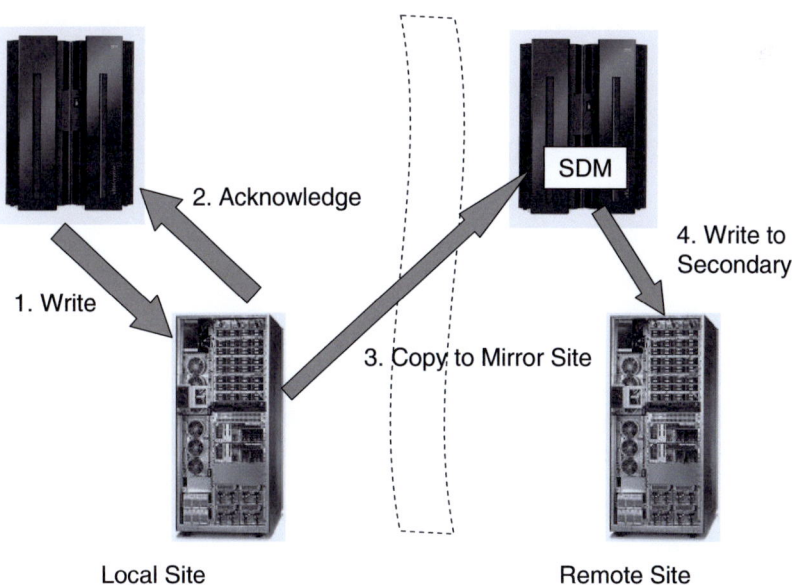

Figure 6.24.: Extended Remote Copy

Extended Remote Copy (XRC) is the IBM implementation for asynchronous copy operations on System z and z/OS. There are basically two versions of asynchronous copy operations:

- Full asynchronous copy is complete as soon as the storage acknowledges the write operation. This can also be already the case if the write is just buffered and not even issued.

- Semi-synchronous copy completes if a local copy is written to disk and the asynchronous copy operation has been initiated. XRC is a semi synchronous copy operation because the local copy always completes.

XRC requires a software component named System Data Mover (SDM). The System data Mover resides on the remote system and ensures that no dependent write operations are mode out of sequence and the data residing on the secondary volumes provide a time consistent copy of the primary volumes being mirrored.

XRC allows to copy data of long distance thus knowing that a recovery point objective of 0 cant be achieved. We will discuss how it is possible to combine PPRC and XRC technologies to achieve a global environment for disaster recovery and continuous operations. XRC as a z/OS copy services solution can be compared to Global Mirror for ESS, which is a controller-based solution for either the open systems or System z environments. Both Global Mirror for ESS (Asynchronous PPRC) and XRC (Global Mirror for z/Series) are asynchronous replication technologies, although their implementations are somewhat different.

6.14. Peer-to-Peer Virtual tape Support

The Peer-to-Peer Virtual Tape Support (VTS) automatically creates a copy of any newly created or updated tape volume in both Virtual Tape Servers, unless the assigned Management Class does not request a copy. This process is performed transparently to the customer application and with no host processor resources required. Either volume copy can then be used to satisfy a specific customer mount. This copy of all new or updated virtual volumes can be created using one of two possible modes of operation:

Immediate copy Creates a copy of the logical volume in the companion connected Virtual Tape Server prior to completion of a rewind/unload command. This mode provides the highest level of data protection.

Deferred copy Creates a copy of the logical volume in the companion connected Virtual Tape Server as activity permits after receiving a rewind/unload command.

The Virtual Tape Controllers provide the connection to the hosts and to two virtual tape servers. Each VTC provides synchronization of the copy of logical volumes, creates logical volume copies using large block transfers of compressed logical volumes, balances workload between the two Virtual Tape Servers, directs specific volume mounts to the Virtual Tape Server with a cached copy of the requested virtual volume, and displays the status and current configuration of the Peer-to-Peer VTS.

6.15. Disaster Recovery Scenarios

6.15.1. Single Site Workload (Active/Standby)

Figure 6.25 shows a GDPS layout which primarily uses one site for production systems and the second site purely for recovery purposes. The sysplex with active production systems is always completly located in only one site. The second site primarily consists only of standby capacity and an I/O subsystem with mirrored devices. Usually PPRC is used to copy the device activity synchronously to the second site. Such a layout only requires full access of the systems to its local I/O subsystem plus additional cabling effort for mirroring the coupling facility and the PPRC devices. The second site is a standby and disaster recovery test site. Typically only one system is running on the second site, the K-system which controls the interoperability of the primary site and the takeover to the secondary site in case of a malfunction. In addition Capacity Backup (CBU) is in place to enable processors required for the systems of the secondary site in case of a failure.

6.15.2. Single Site Failure Scenario

A single site failure will always cause a takeover to the second site. The first step is to restart systems on the second site and to restart the middleware and applications. Typically the restart of of middleware and rebuilding their states takes most of the recovery time. Therefore such a layout does not guarantee continuous operations. Recovery times can exceed 1 hour. The recovery point is determined by the amount of data mirrored and write policies of the coupling facility structures. But a recovery point objective of 0 is achievable for such a configuration. Besides the difficulty that this configuration always implies to live with a downtime it also implies that that after a failure the secondary site is completely stand alone until the problem of the primary site has been fixed.

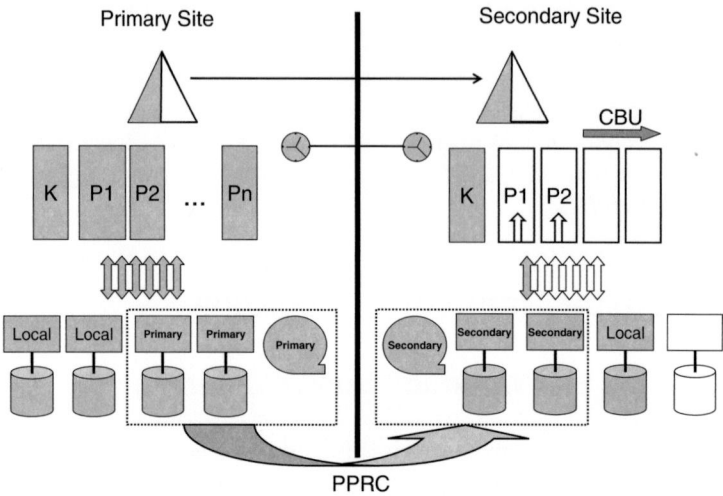

Figure 6.25.: Single Site Workload (Active/Standby)

Therefore it is also possible to gradually enhance this configuration by using Hyperswap and additional cabling for the I/O subsystem. Then it is possible to survive only an I/O subsystem failure and also to use the original primary site as PPRC backup site while the secondary site has taken over the data processing.

6.15.3. Multi Site Workload (Active/Active)

A better but also more cost intensive solution is an active/active configuration. For this configuration the workload is spread across the two sites. Typically half of the systems run on site 1 and the other half on site 2. The I/O subsystem is again fully located in one site and Hyperswap is typically used to protect the environment against an I/O subsystem failure. Another option is to use Coupling facility duplexing depending on the urgency to how fast the systems need to be back on-line again and how much latency is acceptable for the installation. The standby capacity is now also spread across the sites. Because this environment provides full access from each site to each I/O subsystem much more cabling and connectivity is required. Nevertheless this environment is the choice for most installations today.

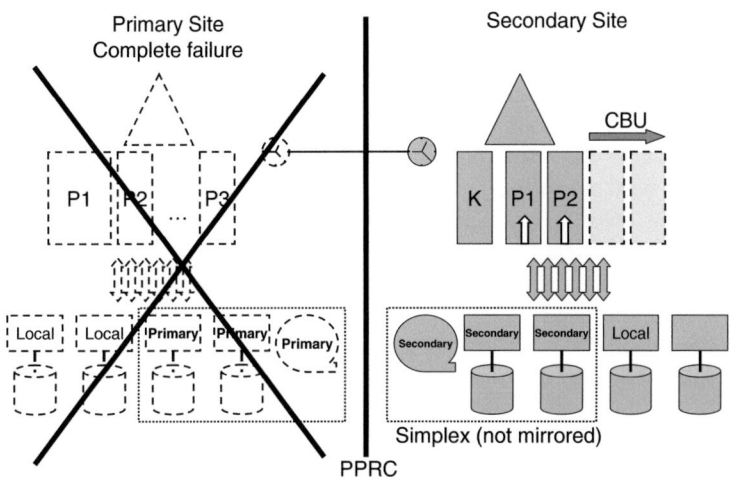

Figure 6.26.: Single Site Failure Scenario

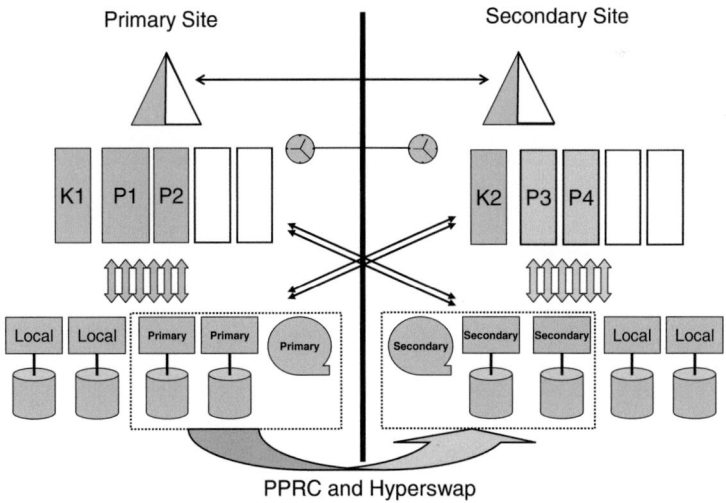

Figure 6.27.: Multi Site Workload (Active/Active)

6.15.4. Multi Site Failure Scenario

There are two error scenarios: The first is an I/O subsystem only failure, see figure 6.28. Hyperswap will then switch the UCBs in all systems from the primary I/O subsystem to the secondary site. Typically such a failure can be solved between 10 and 60 seconds depending on the size of the number of devices which need to be swapped. The secondary scenario is a system failure. Now the backup capacity needs to be activated and the failing systems need to be restarted on the still active site. It is theoretical possible that this situation can be handled while the overall environment is still operational to the end users. On the other hand this also depends from the system load when the failure occurred and the white space capacity which is available on all running systems. In any case this configuration has the highest potential for continuous operations.

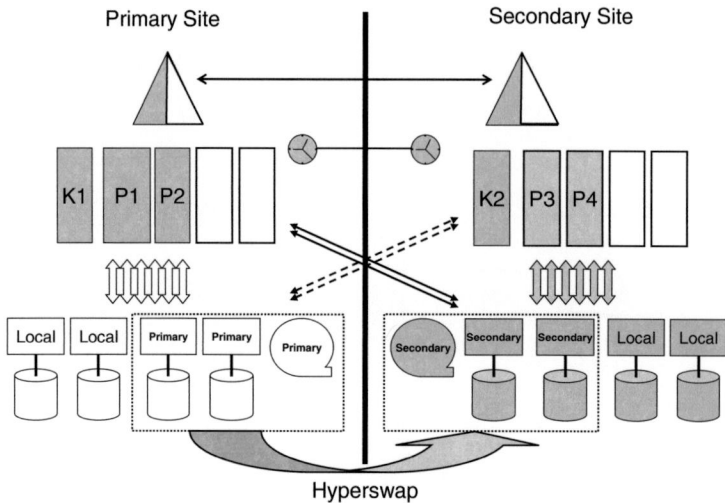

Figure 6.28.: Multi Site Workload: I/O Subsystem Failure

Figure 6.29 shows a complete failure of the primary site with a full takeover of the secondary site. After using the I/O devices of site 2 as primary devices systems P3 and P4 can continue to run. Sometimes it is possible that it is not necessary to restart the partitions P1 and P2 and just to provide standby capacity which can then be used by system P3 and P4. This is the case if all applications run across all sites. In this case a minimal recovery time can be as-

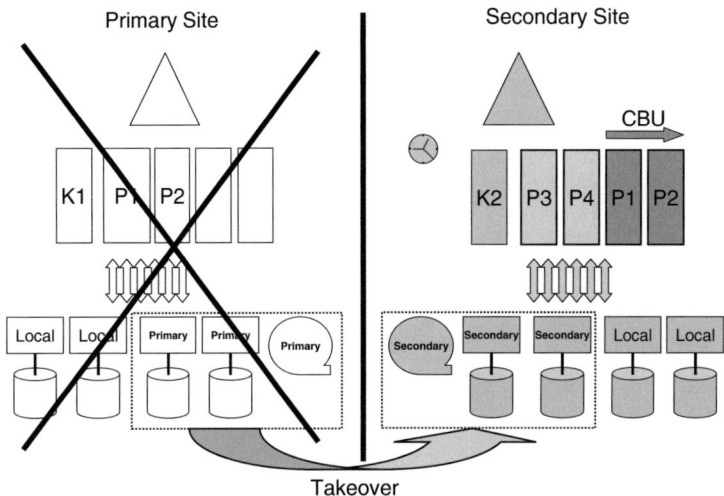

Figure 6.29.: Multi Site Workload: Complete Site Failure

sumed and the environment remains operational. If coupling facility duplexing is also active all cross system states are immediately available on the secondary site as well.

6.16. Summary of Business Resilience Concepts

Business resilience or high availability strategies which are implemented at customer sites can be classified into 4 categories:

1. Continuous Availability of data within a data center provides access to data without interruption. The data is synchronized between different disk volumes and in case of a disk failure the system can use the secondary devices nearly immediately. But this solution doesn't provide any protection against a data center failure because the environment is not spread across different sites.

2. The next step is to create two data centers and to use PPRC for mirroring the data between the sites within a metropolitan area. It is also assumed

that workload either runs across the two data centers or that it primarily uses one data center and the second provides only standby capability. This solution provides continuous availability and full disaster recovery within a region of up to 100km. The issue is the signal latency. Within a range of 20 to 50km the signal latency is very small and doesn't provide to much impact to OLTP workloads but for further separation this solution is limited. By using synchronous data copying the RPO is still zero and the RTO depends on the layout and strategy for the parallel sysplex but it can be kept below 1 hour. The issue of this solution is the low data separation which still requires the data centers to remain in the same metropolitan region which is not sufficient for all customers.

3. The third solution uses asynchronous data mirroring XRC on System z or Global Mirror (GM) on other platforms to separate the data centers at extended differences. The site separation is now given but typically the RTO is already much higher than for the metropolitan solution. Also this solution does not achieve an RPO of seconds.

4. Finally the solutions two and three are merged together. The three site concept uses a metropolitan solution for continuous availability and the third data center at an extended distance for additional disaster recovery to protect against failures which impact the metropolitan area. The local solution provides RPO and RTO like the second solution and the extension to the third site the qualities like the third solution. Typically the XRC solution is initiated by the secondary site which copies the data to the third site after it has acknowledged the write.

6.17. Summary

A metropolitan disaster happens more often than expected. Very typical are power failures which can affect millions of people. The most popular was the North East Coast power blackout in 2003. Since then the wikipedia lists 68 power outages world-wide which means 6 to 7 per year.

Data centers take precautions against power failures by installing emergency power supplies but also emergency power supplies can only survive a data center for a limited period of time. Parallel sysplex technology and the possibility to spread data centers across different locations are today the state-of-the-art way to protect the environment against disasters. Mechanisms like rolling system and service updates allow installations to continuously operate their environment. Altogether System z together with the techniques discussed in this chapter are currently the most secure and highest available computer platform.

7. Summary

This overview describes some important aspects for mainframe environment: Scalability and High availability. For Scalability we saw that simply increasing the number of processors on a system and just developing processing with higher frequencies does not automatically lead to better performance. Higher processor frequency increases the speed difference between processors and memory and as result we found out that additional cache levels are required to mitigate this difference. because not all processors can share the same caches a quiet sophisticated hierarchy of caches and book structures is required to add up to 96 processors on a system.

But that wasn't all. We found out that higher processor speed also increases the processing pipeline. In order to use the high speed efficiently a super-scalar design which finally requires techniques to crack and re-order instructions is required to make the best use of the technology. Many processors create another set of problems. Especially when we took a close look at the layout of a modern mainframe system we found out that at least always two work dispatching processes are involved. This creates difficulties for accessing data across the cache hierarchies and in chapter 4 we discussed this problem in great detail.

Finally scalability can even be limited by the second subject: High Availability. High Availability requires to separate data centers as much as possible but this is not so easy especially with respect on throughput and performance. But we also found other ways to improve performance on the system. In chapter 2 we saw that complex instructions which are designed for specialized purposes can help performance to a large extent.

For High Availability we started with the reliability concepts of the architecture. We discussed function like z/OS Workload Manager which not only add to manageability and scalability but also provide significant support to keep the system and applications running. Finally on a large scale the parallel sysplex and the design for GDPS emphasize what is needed to achieve a highly resilient environment and to achieve continuous operations.

This book only highlights some of the aspects to give an understanding on which levels design, functions and work is needed to achieve environments as they are required by large business institutions which depend heavily on Information Technology. System z and z/OS are the perfect example for it because this product and its ancestors set the industry standards for RAS and Quality of Services. No world-wide operating company is able to live without this infrastructure and it is also part of our daily business, for example in our own money transactions.

A. Glossary

A

ABIST   *Array Built-In Self-Test* - Built in self test machine for integrated circuits including memory arrays

AES   *Advanced Encryption Standard* - Specification for encryption of electronic data based on the design principle known as substitution permutation network.

AMD   *Air-Moving Device* - Fan

APPC   *Advanced Program to Program Communication* - Protocol for program to program communication between multiple systems

ARL   *Authority Revocation List* - List of revoked certificates which should not be relied on.

ASCB   *Address Space Control Block* - z/OS control block which represents a virtual storage entity tight to an end user or set of programs to execute

B

BCP   *Basic Control Program* - z/OS or MVS kernel routines

C

CA   *Certification Authority* - An entity that issues digital certificates

CBA   *Concurrent Book Add* - Add a book while the system is running

CBC   *Cipher Block Chaining* - Modes of operation that enable the repeated and secures use of block cipher under a single key

CBR   *Concurrent Book Replacement* - Unplug and exchange a book while the system is running

CC   *Cage Controller* - Controller for an entity of a System z frame which either contains processors (CEC cage) or I/O cards (I/O cage)

CCA   *IBM Common Cryptographic Architecture* - Architecture of cryptographic features and cards for IBM systems

CCW   *Channel Command Word* - Defines an I/O operation (read, write, control) to be performed on an I/O device

CDS   *Couple Dataset* - Dataset which contains control information to setup a parallel sysplex environment

CDSA   *Common Data Security Architecture* - Set of layered security services and cryptographic framework that provide an infrastructure for creating cross-platform, inter-operable, security-enabled applications for client-server environments

CE   *Correctable Error* - Error which can be detected and corrected for example memory bit errors

CEC   *Central Electronic Complex* - The system (processors, memory, I/O adapters), not including I/O devices

CECSIM   *Central Electronic Complex Simulation* - Firmware simulator for System z CEC

CFCC   *Coupling Facility Control Code* - Operating System of the coupling facility

CHPID   *Channel Path Identifier* - Identification of the channel path, typically a number

CICS   *Customer Information Control Server* - A transaction monitor that runs primarily on z/OS

CISC   *Complex Instruction Set Computing* - Processing architecture which contains many complex instructions which perform functions like small programs

CKD   *Count Key Data* - System z disk architecture

CKDS   *Cryptographic Key Data Set* - Keys that are protected under DES or AES are stored ina VSAM data set that is called CKDS

CP   *Central Processor* - Standard processor of a System z

CP	*Control Program* - Main component (hypervisor) of z/VM
CPACF	*CP Assist for Crypto Function* - Assist processor for cryptographic functions
CPU	*Central Processing Unit* - see CP
CRL	*Certificate Revocation List* - see ARL
CRT	*Chinese Remainder Theorem* - About congruences in number theory and abstract algebra
CSS	*Channel Subsystem* - The heart of moving data in and out of of a mainframe
CSSID	*Channel Subsystem Identifier* - Number which identifies the Channel Subsystem in case multiple exist
CVC	*Card Verification Code* - Security feature for credit cards
CVV	*Card Verification Value* - see CVC

D

DAE	*Data Analysis and Elimination* - z/OS RAS function which ensures that only data is captured which is needed to analyze system problems
DASD	*Direct Access Storage Device* - A storage device which supports direct access (typically a disk)
DB2	*Database* - Relational database based on E. F. Codd's theory of relational databases
DCA	*Distribution Converter Assembly* -
DCS	*Dynamic CPU Sparing* - Feature that allows inactive CPUs to act as dynamic spares
DDF	*Distributed Data Facility* - Component of DB2 to exchange information with external clients
DEDB	*Data Entry Database* - Fast path database for IMS
DES	*Data Encryption Standard* - Block cipher that uses shared secret encryption
DL/I	*Data Language Interface* - Database of IMS

DRAM   *Dynamic Random-Access Memory* - Memory which can be accessed byte wise and randomly

DRDA   *Distributed Relational Database Architecture* - Distributed database architecture of the open group standard

DSA   *Digital Signature Algorithm* - Algorithm which allows to verify the correctness of data exchanged on an unsecured network

DSS   *Digital Signature Standard* - DSA standard

E

EBC   *Electronic Code Book* - Simple block cipher method

ECC   *Error-Correction Codes* - Redundant data added to a data item for error detection and checking

ECKD   *Extended Count Key Data* - incorporates fixed-block and CKD architecture

EMIF   *ESCON Multiple Image Facility* - Feature which allows to use ESCON channels from multiple partitions

ESA/390   *Enterprise Systems Architecture/390* - 32-bit predecessor of System z architecture

ESCON   *Enterprise System Connection* - Half-duplex optical fiber serial channel

ESPIE   *Extended Specify Program Interruption Exit* - Interrupt exit routine

ESTAE   *Extended Specified Task Abnormal Exit* - Recovery routine for z/OS user or problem state programs

ESTI   *Enhanced Self-Timed Interface* -

ETR   *External Time Reference* - Device to synchronize all TOD (time-of-day) clocks in a cluster environment (Parallel Sysplex)

EXCP   *Execute Channel Program* - z/OS macro to execute an I/O operation

F

FCP   *Fibre Channel Protocol* - Transport protocol for transporting SCSI commands on Fibre Channel networks

FEDC   *First Error Data Capture* - Concept to collect all data required to analyze and fix a problem on its first occurrence

FICON   *Fibre Channel Connection* - Full-duplex fibre optical serial channel

FIFO   *First In, First Out* - Queuing mechanism

FIPS   *Federal Information Processing Standards* - Publicly announed standard developed by the US government for use in computer systems by all non military government agencies and government contractors

FLIH   *First Level Interrupt Handler* - Interrupt handler that gets immediate control when the interrupt occurs (where the new Program Status Word points to)

FRR   *Functional Recovery Routine* - Recovery routine for z/OS system programs

FRU   *Field-Replaceable Unit* - Circuit board, part or assembly that can be quickly removed from an electronic equipment

FSP   *Flexible Service Processor* - Firmware for diagnostic which connects the managed system to the HMC

G

GDPS   *Global Dispersed Parallel Sysplex* - Parallel Sysplex which is spatially distributed to ensure high availability

GRS   *Global Resource Serialization* - z/OS subsystem which supports global lock management

H

HCA   *Host Communication Adapter* - Infiniband I/O Adapter

HCD	*Hardware Configuration Dialog* - z/OS component to define I/O devices to the system
HFS	*Hierarchical File System* - UNIX file system on z/OS
HMC	*Hardware Management Console* - Console to access and manage hardware components of System z
HOM	*Hardware Object Module* -
HWA	*Hardware Address* -

I

I/O	*Input/Output* - Abbreviation for all parts which send data to and from an electronic complex
IBF	*Integrated Battery Facility* -
ICB	*Integrated Cluster Bus* - Bus for connecting system in a parallel sysplex for short distance. The bus relies on few parts and provides very high speed and reliable connectivity
ICF	*Integrated Coupling Facility* - Processor on system z which allows to run coupling facility control code
ICSF	*Integrated Cryptographic Service Facility* - Set of services on z/OS that manages security encryption keys
IETF	*Internet Engineering Task Force* - Open task force to improve the internet
IFL	*Integrated Facility for Linux* - Processor on system z which allows to execute z/VM and Linux operating systems
IML	*Initial Microcode Load* - Initialization process of System z hardware. At its completion, operating systems can be booted (IPLed).
IMS	*Information Management System* - A transaction monitor and database for z/OS (introduced 1968 for the Apollo space program)
IOCDS	*Input/Output Configuration Data Set* - Data set which contains hardware I/O definitions (related to IODF; also should be consistent with IODF)
IODF	*I/O Definition File* - Data file which contains the I/O definitions for System z (created by HCD)

IPC   *Inter Process Communication* - Protocol for system processes to interact which each other

IPKI   *Internet Public Key Infrastructure* - IETF standard for public keys

IPL   *Initial Program Load* - Process to start the z/OS operating system

IRB   *Interrupt Request Block* - z/OS Control Structure to start an I/O routine

IRD   *Intelligent Resource Director* - A combination of multiple z technologies to enhance the autonomic capabilities of PR/SM, z/OS and the I/O subsystem

IRLM   *IBM Resource Lock Manager* - Lock manager for DB2 and IMS

ISPF   *Interactive System Productivity Facility* - End user interface for TSO users

J

JES   *Job Entry System* - z/OS subsystems which support the execution of scheduled programs

K

KGUP   *Key Generation Utility Program* - The key generator utility program generates data, data-translation, MAC, PIN, and key-encrypting keys, and enciphers each type of key under a specific master key variant

L

LBIST   *Logic Built-In Self-Test* - Hardware or software built into integrated circuits which allows them to test their own function

LCP   *Logical Processor* - Representation of a processor to the virtual system or logical partition

LCSS   *Logical Channel Subsystem* - A system may use multiple logical channel subsystems (currently up to 4) to increase connectivity

LDAP   *Lightweight Directory Access Protocol* - Application protocol for accessing and maintaining distributed directory information services over an IP network

LED   *Light-Emitting Diode* - Semiconductor light source

LGA   *Land Grid Array* - Surface mount packaging technology which has the pins on the socket rather than on the integrated circuit. Opposite is pin grid array (PGA).

LIC   *Licensed Internal Code* - System z microcode or firmware

LICCC   *Licensed Internal Code Configuration Control* -

Ln   *Level n Cache* - L1 is closest to the processor, the highest number is used to describe memory ("storage" in System z terminology)

LPAR   *Logical Partition* - Container which hosts an operating system to execute on System z virtualization layer. Up to 60 LPARs are supported

M

MBA   *Memory Bus Adapter* - I/O hub chip used on z10 and earlier machines. No longer used on z196.

MCF   *Microcode Fix* - Corrected code for firmware layer

MCM   *Multi-Chip Module* - contains processor and storage controller chips

MCSS   *Multiple-logical-Channel Subsystem* - Restructuring of the physical CSS into multiple logical instances in order to enable more external devices to be attached to the CEC

MD5   *Message Authentication Code* - Widely used cryptographic hash function that produces 128-bit has value

MLCS   *Multiple Logical Channel Subsystems* - see MCSS

MMU   *Memory Management Unit* - Hardware component which handles virtual memory

MPL   *Multi Programming Level* - Term which expresses the ability of workload to access system resources

MRU   *Modular Refrigeration Unit* - Cooling unit

MSU   *Million of Service Units per Hour* - Unit to measure CPU capacity on System z

MTTW	*Mean Time To Wait* - Algorithm which gives access to units of work based on their deliberate wait time
MVS	*Multiple Virtual Storage* - Original name of z/OS based on the ability to support multiple applications in virtual storage

O

OAEP	*Optimal Asymmetric Encryption Padding* - Padding scheme for encryption
OCSP	*Online Certificate Status Protocol* -
OLTP	*Online Transaction Processing* - Umbrella term for transaction processing
OSA	*Open System Adapter* - Networking adapter

P

PAF	*Processor Availability Facility* -
PAV	*Parallel Access Volume* - Protocol which supports parallel access to the same I/O device
PCHID	*Physical Channel Identifier* - identifies the plug position of a channel adapter
PCP	*Physical Processor* - see CP
PKA	*Public Key Architecture* - Encryption architecture with 2 keys: one to encrypt the data and one to decrypt the cypher-text
PKDS	*Public Key Data Set* - VSAM data set that stores public and private keys
PKI	*Public Key Infrastructure* - see PKA
PPRC	*Peer to Peer Remote Copy* - A protocol to replicate a storage volume to a remote site
PR/SM	*Process Resource and System Manager* - Management component of the logical partition technology of System z (alias for LPAR hypervisor)

PSW   *Program Status Word* - Central register to control all program execution

PU   *Processing Unit* - Physical processor

Q

QDIO   *Queued Direct I/O* - memory to Memory I/O mechanism between LPARs on System z

R

RACF   *Resource Access Control Facility* - z/OS subsystem which supports access control

RAS   *Reliability, Availability, Serviceability* - Terminology to depict the robustness of information technology systems (originated from IBM mainframe)

RETAIN   *Remote Technical Assistance Information Network* - IBM network to handle service requests for end users

REXX   *Restructured Extended Executor* - Interpretive Execution Language from IBM

RISC   *Reduced Instruction Set Computing* - Processing architecture which only contains elementary instructions like LOAD, STORE, and register-to-register operations

RLS   *Record Level Sharing* - VSAM access method which introduces record sharing and serialization

RMF   *Resource Measurement Facility* - z/OS Performance Monitor

RRMS   *Resource Recovery Management Services* - z/OS component to synchronize the activities of various syncpoint managers

RSA   *Rivest-Shamir-Adleman* - Algorithm for public key cryptography

RSF   *Remote Support Facility* - Part of HMC to report and repair hardware and firmware components

S

S/360	*IBM System/360* - Is a mainframe computer system family announced by IBM on April 7, 1964. It is the computer architecture of which System z is the current incarnation.
SAP	*System Assist Processor* - System z I/O processor
SCC	*Storage Controller Control* - Storage controller chip
SCD	*Storage Controller Data* - Cache chip
SCE	*Storage Control Element* - Controls access to main storage data by processor unit
SDWA	*System Diagnostic Work Area* - Control structure to capture information in case of an abnormal program termination
SE	*Support Element* - Laptop that acts as user interface to System z machine
SEC/DED	*Single-Error Correction/Double-Error Detection* - Error correction codes
SIE	*Start Interpretive Execution* - Instruction to drive a processor in a logical partition (LPAR) or virtual machine (z/VM)
SIGP	*Signal Processor* - Instruction to inform a processor about status change
SLE	*Session Level Encryption* - Encryption between originator and receiver of data across all network elements
SLIH	*Second Level Interrupt Handler* - Term which encompasses a set of specialized interrupt handling routines
SMF	*Systems Management Facility* - z/OS component which supports performance and status logging
SMP	*Symmetric Multiprocessing* - A computer system with all physical processors accessing the same storage and I/O subsystems
SRB	*Service Request Block* - Control structure to execute a z/OS system program
SRC	*System Reference Code* - Sequence of data words to identify a unit that is reporting an error
SRM	*System Resource Manager* - Component of z/OS for resource man-

agement (introduced 1974, now part of WLM)

SSL *Secure Sockets Layer* - Cryptographic protocol that provides communication security over the internet

STP *Server Time Protocol* - Follow-on to ETR

SU/sec *Service Unit per second* - Capability of a System z processor to execute instructions

SVC *Supervisor Call* - Interface to invoke a z/OS system program

Sysplex *System Complex* - A single logical system running on one or more physical systems

System z *IBM mainframe computer brand* - Current 64-bit incarnation of the S/360 architecture

System z10 BC
System z10 Business Class - Mid-range model of System z processor family (2009)

System z10 EC
System z10 Enterprise Class - High end model of System z processor family (2008)

T

TCB *Task Control Block* - Control Structure to execute user or problem state programs on z/OS

TLS *Transport Layer Security* - see SSL

TSO *Time Sharing Option* - z/OS component which supports the parallel execution of multiple end users on MVS

U

UCB *Unit Control Block* - z/OS control structure which represents an I/O device

UoW *Unit of Work* - An execution unit on z/OS

USS *Unix System Services* - z/OS component which supports a full functioning UNIX environment on z/OS

V

VCPU *Virtual CPU* - see LCP

VMM *Virtual Machine Monitor* - Hypervisor or control program to run multiple virtual machines

VPD *Vital Product Data* - Collection of configuration and informational data associated with a particular set of hardware or software

VPN *Virtual Private Network* - Method of computer networking that allows users to share information (privately) between remote locations

VSAM *Virtual Storage Access Method* - A set of access methods for System z I/O devices

VTAM *Virtual Terminal Access Method* - Access method for communications devices (now part of z/OS TCPIP subsystem)

VTOC *Volume Table of Content* - Index of a DASD device

W

WLM *Workload Manager* - Central z/OS component for resource management (introduced 1995)

X

XCF *Cross System Coupling Services* - z/OS Services which support the exploitation of a z/OS sysplex

XES *Cross System Extended Services* - z/OS services which support the access to the coupling facility

XRC *Extended Remote Copy* - System z protocol for data replication

Z

z114 *zEnterprise 114* - Mid-range end model of System z processor family (2011)

z196   *zEnterprise 196* - High end model of System z processor family
                (2010)

zAAP   *System z Application Assist Processor* - System z processor to ex-
                ecute Java code. This processor type can only be used by z/OS
                and only for instrumented software like the Java Virtual Machine.
                A special instruction tells the dispatcher when Java execute starts
                and ends.

zFS   *System z File System* - UNIX file system on z/OS

zIIP   *System z Integrated Information Processor* - System z processor
                to execute code which is subject to get offloaded from regular
                processors. The offload capability is described by the middleware
                through an interface to WLM and the z/OS dispatcher. Exploiters
                are middleware like DB2 and TCPIP.D5

B. Trademarks

The following are trademarks of the International Business Machines Corporation in the United States and/or other countries:

AIX®, AS/400®, BatchPipes®, C++/MVS, CICS®, CICS/MVS®, CICSPlex®, COBOL/370, DB2®, DB2 Connect, DB2 Universal Database, DFSMS/MVS®, DFSMSdfp, DFSMSdss, DFSMShsm, DFSORT, e (logo)®, ECKD, ES/3090, ES/9000®, ES/9370, ESCON®, FICON, GDPS, Geographically Dispersed Parallel Sysplex, HACMP/6000, Hiperbatch, Hiperspace, IBM®, IBM (logo)®, IMS, IMS/ESA®, Language Environment®, Lotus®, OpenEdition®, OS/390®, Parallel Sysplex®, PR/SM, pSeries, RACF®, Redbooks, RISC System/6000®, RMF, RS/6000®, S/370, S/390®, S/390 Parallel Enterprise Server, System/360, System/370, System/390®, System z, ThinkPad®, UNIX System Services, VM/ESA®, VSE/ESA, VTAM®, WebSphere®, xSeries, z/Architecture, z/OS, z/VM, zSeries

The following are trademarks or registered trademarks of other companies:

- Java and all Java-related trademarks and logos are trademarks of Sun Microsystems, Inc., in the United States and other countries

- Linux is a registered trademark of Linus Torvalds in the United States, other countries, or both.

- UNIX is a registered trademark of The Open Group in the United States and other countries.

- Microsoft, Windows and Windows NT are registered trademarks of Microsoft Corporation.

- Red Hat, the Red Hat "Shadow Man" logo, and all Red Hat-based trademarks and logos are trademarks or registered trademarks of Red Hat, Inc., in the United States and other countries.

- SET and Secure Electronic Transaction are trademarks owned by SET Secure Electronic Transaction LLC.

Bibliography

[1] *Exploring IBM eServer zSeries and System/390 Servers, Seventh Edition*, Jim Hoskins and Bob Frank, 2001, ISBN 1-855068-70-0

[2] *RAS Strategy for IBM S/390 G5 and G6*, M. Müller et al., IBM Journal of Research and Development VOL. 43 NO. 5/6 Sept./Nov. 1999

[3] *Computer Engineering 30 Years After the IBM Model 91*, Michael J. Flynn, IEEE April 1998

[4] *TSO Time Sharing Option im Betriebssystem z/OS*, Dr. Michael Teuffel, Oldenbourg, 2002, ISBN-13: 978-3486255607

[5] *Das Betriebssystem z/OS und die zSeries: Die Darstellung eines modernen Grorechnersystems*, Dr. Michael Teuffel, Robert Vaupel, Oldenbourg, 2004, ISBN-13: 978-3486275285

[6] *ESA/390 Interpretive-Execution Architecture, foundation for VM/ESA* Osisek, Jackson, and Gum, IBM SYSTEMS JOURNAL, VOL 30, NO 1, 1991

[7] *IBM System /370 Extended Architecture, Interpretive Execution* Publication Number SA22-7095-1

[8] *In Search Of Clusters, The Ongoing Battle in Lowly Parallel Computing*, Gregory F. Pfister, Prentice Hall, 1998, ISBN 0-13-899709-8

[9] *Cluster Architectures and S/390 Parallel Sysplex Scalability*, G.M. King, D.M. Dias, P.S. Yu, IBM Systems Journal, Vol. 36, No. 2, 1997, Seiten 221-241

[10] *S/390 Cluster Technology: Parallel Sysplex*, J.M. Nick, B.B. Moore, J.-Y. Chung, N.S. Bowen, IBM Systems Journal, Vol. 36, No. 2, 1997, Seiten 172-202

[11] *A Locking Facility for Parallel Sysplex*, N.S. Bowen, D.A. Elko, J.F. Isenberg, G.W. Wang, IBM Systems Journal, Vol. 36, No. 2, 1997, Seiten 202-220

[12] *Performances of DS8000 Metro Mirror over Distance* Gausach, et. al,

PSSC Customer Center Montpellier, TotalStorage, 65. GSE z/OS Expert Forum, 2006

[13] *Adaptive Algorithms for Managing A Distributed Data Processing Workload*, J. Aman, C.K. Eilert, D. Emmes, P. Yocom, D. Dillenberger, IBM Systems Journal, Vol. 36, No. 2, 1997, Seiten 242-283

[14] *Validity of the single processor approach in achieving large-scale computer capabilities*, Gene Amdahl, In Proceedings of the AFIPS Conference, Seiten 483-485, 1967

[15] *MVS Performance Management (ESA/390 Edition)*, Steve Samson, J. Ranade IBM Series, Printed and bound by R.R.Donnelley and Sons Company, ISBN 0-07-054529-4, 1992

[16] *Introduction to the New Mainframe: Large Scale Commercial Computing*, IBM Redbook, SG24-7175-xx

[17] *IBM zEnterprise 196 Technical Guide*, IBM Redbook, SG24-7833-xx, July 2011

[18] *The zEnterprise 196 System and Microprocessor*, Curran et al., IEEE 0272-1732/11, March/April 2011

[19] *Design and micro-architecture of the IBM System z10 microprocessor*, Shum et al., IBM Journal of Research and Development, Volume 53, NO. 1, 2009

[20] *IBM zEnterprise 196 microprocessor and cache subsystem* Busaba et al., IBM Journal of Research and Development, Volume 56, NO. 1, 2012

[21] *IBM System z Software Pricing*, http://www-03.ibm.com/systems/z/resources/swprice/reference/

[22] *Large System Performance Reference for IBM System z*, https://www-304.ibm.com/servers/resourcelink/lib03060.nsf/-pages/lsprindex?OpenDocument

[23] *IBM zEnterprise redundant array of independent memory subsystem* Meaney et al., IBM Journal of Research and Development, Volume 56, NO. 1, 2012

[24] *Performance innovation in the IBM zEnterprise 196 processor* Greiner et al., IBM Journal of Research and Development, Volume 56, NO. 1, 2012

[25] *Overview of IBM zEnterprise 196 I/O subsystem with focus on new PCI Express infrastructure* Gregg et al., IBM Journal of Research and Development, Volume 56, NO. 1, 2012

[26] *How Do You Do What You Do When Youre a z196 CPU* Bob Rogers, Share Proceedings, Anaheim 2011 and IBM Systems Magazine, February 2012

[27] *z/OS Workload Manager: How It Works and How To Use It* Robert Vaupel, 2nd Edition, May 2011, http://www-03.ibm.com/systems/z/os/zos/features/wlm/WLM-_Further_Info.html

[28] *z/OS Workload Manager Managing CICS and IMS Workloads* Robert Vaupel, March 2011, http://www-03.ibm.com/systems/z/os/zos/features/wlm/WLM-_Further_Info.html

[29] *ABC of z/OS System Programming*, IBM Redbooks, Volume 11, SG24-6327-xx

[30] *OS/390 MVS Parallel Sysplex Capacity Planning*, IBM Redbook, SG24-4680-01, January 1998

[31] *z/Architecture Principles of Operations*, SA22-7832-xx

[32] *z/OS MVS Planning: Workload Management*, z/OS Literatur, SA22-7602-xx

[33] *System's Programmer Guide to: Workload Management*, IBM Redbook, SG24-6472-xx

[34] *z/OS MVS Programming: Workload Management Services*, z/OS Literatur, SA22-7619-xx

[35] *z/OS Resource Measurement Facility: Performance Management Guide*, z/OS Literatur, SC28-1951-xx

[36] *z/OS Basic Skills Center*, http://publib.boulder.ibm.com/infocenter/zos/basics/index.jsp

Index